Lawrence in Love

Letters to Louie Burrows

Lawrence in Love

Letters to Louie Burrows

✳

Edited with introduction
and notes by
James T. Boulton

NOTTINGHAM
University of Nottingham
1968

First edition December 1968

S.B.N. 900572 00 0

Contents

Preface

The papers of Mrs. Louisa Heath—formerly Miss Burrows—came into the possession of the University of Nottingham in 1966. They were purchased from her executors with the aid of a government grant. Most important among the papers is the collection of 165 letters and postcards written by D. H. Lawrence between 1906 and 1912 to 'Louie' Burrows, to whom he was engaged for fifteen months. She wished them to be published after her death (which occurred in May 1962). They nearly treble the number of published letters by Lawrence for the period 1906-1910; they double the number for his 'sick year' 1911. This collection, then, represents a substantial addition to our knowledge of Lawrence during these years; it finally clarifies his relationship—hitherto obscure in most details—with the girl who was the main prototype for Ursula in *The Rainbow*. Together with the poems to Louie Burrows—'the woman of "Kisses in the Train" and "Hands of the Betrothed"'—the letters written to her significantly contribute to that 'biography of an emotional and inner life' of which Lawrence spoke in the Preface to his *Collected Poems*.

While I remain solely responsible for the opinions expressed, many people have given valuable assistance in the preparation of this volume. I am indebted to Dr. Harry T. Moore, who read the typescript and made a number of helpful suggestions. I am grateful to Professor James Kinsley and the University Librarian, Dr. R. S. Smith, who have been intimately associated at every stage with the production of this book; to Mr. C. Burrows, Miss Helen Corke, Professor J. D. Chambers, Mr. David Garnett, and the late Sir Herbert Read, who willingly put their knowledge of Lawrence and Louie Burrows at my disposal; to Mr. Michael Cane, who designed the volume and saw it through the press; to the present and former

vii

Keepers of the University Manuscripts, the Director of the Nottingham Castle Art Gallery, and Nottingham's City and County Librarians; to the editor of the *Sunday Express*; to Dr. Harold I. Shapiro and several others (some of whom prefer anonymity) for their co-operation in solving editorial problems. Mrs. Susan Butler and Miss Jenny Wootton deserve thanks for their excellent secretarial assistance. And, finally, I wish to acknowledge my wife's help on many occasions, especially when checking the text and preparing the index.

J.T.B.
University of Nottingham
1968

NOTE ON THE TEXT

Addresses and dates at the head of the letters have been standardised; otherwise the spelling, punctuation and paragraphing of the manuscripts are followed exactly. Where Lawrence's own errors might cause confusion minor corrections are made silently; any significant departure from the original is shown. Lacunae due to torn manuscripts are indicated by square brackets. No attempt has been made to reproduce typographically the appearance of Lawrence's letters; where, for example, he wrote a postscript in a convenient space at the head of a letter, it is shown here in its normal position at the end. Wherever evidence of the destination and postmark of a letter or postcard remains, it is provided; the name of the addressee (the same in all cases) has been omitted. In footnotes letters are referred to simply by number. Unless otherwise stated, all manuscripts cited are from Nottingham University Library.

Introduction

The setting for Louisa Burrows' earliest memories proved to be the source of one of Lawrence's most memorable fictional creations: the 'honeymoon house' of Will and Anna Brangwen in *The Rainbow*.

> It was the cottage next the church, with dark yew-trees, very black old trees, along the side of the house and the grassy front garden; a red, squarish cottage with a low slate roof, and low windows. It had a long dairy-scullery, a big flagged kitchen, and a low parlour, that went up one step from the kitchen. There were whitewashed beams across the ceilings, and odd corners with cupboards. Looking out through the windows, there was the grassy garden, the procession of black yew-trees down one side, and along the other sides, a red wall with ivy separating the place from the high road and the churchyard. The old, little church, with its small spire on a square tower, seemed to be looking back at the cottage windows.[1]

Louie was brought to the original of this Church Cottage, in the small Nottinghamshire village of Cossall, before she was two years old. Born in Granby Street, Ilkeston, on 13th February 1888, she was the first child of Alfred and Louisa Ann Burrows. Like the birth of Ursula in *The Rainbow*, Louie's was followed in due succession by those of three girls (Ethelreda, Cecilia and Constance), a boy (Alfred), and another girl (Gertrude); eventually (with William and Nora) the children numbered eight. All were conscious of 'the old, little church' of St. Catherine overlooking their young lives. It was the focus of their father's energies when he was free from his work as a draughtsman in first an Ilkeston, then a Nottingham lace

---

1. *The Rainbow* (1915), chapt. 4. (See Ada Lawrence and G. Stuart Gelder, *The Early Life of D. H. Lawrence* (1932), p. 216, for a photograph of Church Cottage.)

factory. The prototype for Will Brangwen, Alfred found his greatest contentment in his activities as choir-master or in caring for the fabric or furnishings of the church. And though the family left Cossall in 1907, it was almost inevitable that Alfred and Louisa should record their gratitude for 60 years of marriage, in 1947, by installing a window in St. Catherine's; it was equally appropriate that their children should later dedicate a second window to their parents' memory. To this same church Louie herself gave £100 to beautify the building, a short time before her death.

Louie grew up in a tightly-knit family group; it was not without foundation that Lawrence remarked on 'the curious enveloping Brangwen intimacy, so warm, so close, so stifling'.[1] This same intimacy brought the children, especially Louie, under the direct and prevailing influence of their father's cultural interests. His passion for wood-carving, architecture and music remained Louie's throughout her life. Her interest in William Morris probably derived from her father; one suspects, too, that the luxuriance of her descriptive style (criticised by Lawrence) was formed by contact with Victorian mediaevalists. Alfred Burrows' orthodox Christian morality exerted a further influence on Louie, as Lawrence discovered. She was no Clara Dawes. Moreover, the affectionate intimacy of the family screened from her the harsher realities of life in the industrial Midlands to which Lawrence was exposed in his youth. Louie's home was relatively free of the tension, violence and near poverty he associated with family life; the culture it provided was foreign to him. That this culture should emanate primarily from the father of the family was beyond Lawrence's experience: his father could barely read or write.

Scarcely had Louie begun to attend the village school before she was confronted with evidence of her father's devotion to the ideal of the artist as craftsman; this devotion was seconded by his natural teaching ability. Like Will Brangwen, he responded to a growing public recognition that crafts are an educational instrument; at the age of 30 (in 1894) Alfred Burrows gathered together a group of boys, arranged twice-weekly evening classes in the village school, and taught handicrafts. The signal achievement of the master and his pupils was the fine oak reredos still to be seen in St. Catherine's Church. And, not satisfied with his amateur status, Alfred qualified himself as a teacher in 1899 with the City and Guilds Manual Training Certificate.

1. *Rainbow*, chapt. 7.

x

His part-time activity as a teacher unsettled him at the Nottingham factory; 'his work in the lace designing'—like that of his fictional counterpart—'meant little to him personally, he just earned his wage by it'.[1] To become a full-time teacher became his overriding ambition. The opportunity to fulfil it came late in 1907 when he was appointed a peripatetic teacher of handicrafts by the Leicestershire County Council. The family's removal from Church Cottage was essential; the house had, in any case, become too small now that the youngest of the eight children was already two years old. Quorn (Lawrence's 'Beldover'), a village near Loughborough, on the edge of the beautiful area of Charnwood Forest, appeared a convenient centre for the schools which Alfred Burrows was to visit day by day; the family moved to a 'good and substantial'[2] Victorian house there early in 1908. As testimony of the family's affection for the village they left behind, the house was called 'Coteshael', the ancient name of Cossall. Lawrence seems to have considered the name rather pretentious—'quel mot' he wrote on the envelope containing his third letter to Louie at the new address; but it was to 'Coteshael' that he wrote the majority of his letters to Louie over the next four years.

Lawrence and Louie had known each other since about 1900.[3] From 1902 they both attended the Pupil-Teacher Centre at Ilkeston (Lawrence for three years, Louie for four); there they 'earned their education by teaching for two and a half days in the week and being taught for the remainder'.[4] Though, then, they were well acquainted before they became students at the Day Training College of University College, Nottingham, in 1906, their relationship was not more intimate than that prevailing among all members of the Eastwood friends known as the 'Pagans'. This group included several mentioned in Lawrence's letters to Louie: Jessie and Alan Chambers, George Neville, Gertrude and Frances Cooper, and Kitty Holderness. The peculiar intensity of the bond between Lawrence and Jessie is well known; but among the group as a whole there existed the normal camaraderie of young people engaged in common pursuits and sharing a common background. There is scarcely a hint in the early letters of Lawrence to Louie that their attachment would develop beyond a youthful friendship. However, it is perhaps

1. *The Rainbow*, chapt. 14.   2. Ibid.
3. Cf. *The Collected Letters of D. H. Lawrence*, ed. Harry T. Moore (1962), i. 60.
4. *D. H. Lawrence: A Personal Record by E. T.* [Jessie Chambers], ed. J. D. Chambers (1965), p. xxviii.

significant that whereas most members of the 'Pagans' were casually referred to, Lawrence was obviously ready (even in 1906) to compare Louie with Jessie Chambers. Louie's writing was brighter and more readable in his view, Jessie's more 'powerful'; and when he advised Louie on her literary style—'Be your own bright ingenuous self'—he was probably making an implicit comparison with Jessie, who longed to 'wheedle the soul out of things'.[1] Subsequently the ingenuousness became less attractive to him, possibly even a positive irritant.

The records of University College, Nottingham, report Louie Burrows as an outstanding student (specialising in history and English literature). In the list of candidates who had successfully completed their first year (1906–7) her name is asterisked, indicating a student 'Specially Distinguished'; Lawrence was not given this mark (nor were their friends Hilda Shaw and Nina Stewart). At the end of their second and final year, both Lawrence and Louie were placed in the First Class on their performance in the examinations for the Teacher's Certificate. We know from other of his publications that Lawrence had serious misgivings about University College. The letters to Louie rather indicate his enjoyment of his friends' company during College vacations: their parties at Christmas or a country hike on Easter Monday; the pleasure of a 'united gathering' at the Haggs Farm, Jessie's home; discussions of pictures seen at the Art Gallery in Nottingham Castle, philosophical issues like 'Universal Consciousness', or perhaps the Suffragist movement in which Louie was interested; and the exchange of family news.

This last may appear of trivial importance; but it isn't. Lawrence clearly found family activities and relationships of absorbing interest; they were to provide material for imaginative use in the early novels. The intimate knowledge of the Burrows' family life, which is reflected in his account of the Brangwens, points not only to the fineness of Lawrence's observation and his remarkably retentive memory, but also to the depth of his concern. Undoubtedly, too, his feeling of involvement with the families of Jessie and Louie strengthened his emotional attachment to both girls. The intimacy then existing between Jessie and Louie further united the trio and gave a particular poignancy to subsequent events.

In view of these circumstances it is not surprising that, when Lawrence wished to enter three stories for the Christmas competi-

1. *Sons and Lovers* (1913), chapt. 9.

tion in the *Nottinghamshire Guardian*, in 1907, he should ask Jessie and Louie to submit two of them under their own names. (The regulations of the competition allowed each entrant to submit only one story.) The subterfuge was appropriate also on other grounds. Jessie's literary ability has long been recognised; Lawrence's respect for Louie's (long before their engagement) is now evident. For the 1907 competition he was prepared to let her re-write *The White Stocking* in her own style before submitting it. And his interest in her original compositions, as well as requests for her criticisms on his own work, appear intermittently throughout their correspondence. Lawrence encouraged Louie to write short stories; urged her to publish one entitled *The Chimney Sweeper*; willingly read and commented on her manuscripts; and at least on one occasion felt that they were collaborators. He told her that his short story, *Goose Fair*, was 'as much your child as mine';[1] when he was paid for it by the *English Review* (in March 1910), he shared the fee with her as 'the first-fruits of [her] literary tree'.[2] Lawrence had bluntly informed her two months earlier that she had 'a certain quaint little talent . . . but it is superficial'; nevertheless he considered it sufficiently promising to enable her to 'do things very likely as good as W. W. Jacobs'.[3] No short stories published by Louie have been traced; but this cannot deny her talent.

In the summer of 1908 Lawrence was vainly seeking a teaching post. He wrote scores of letters and was interviewed at Stockport as late as 25th September, before he was appointed in October to Davidson Road School in Croydon. Louie was employed before the summer term ended. As soon as she completed her training in Nottingham she secured a post at St. Mary's School, Castle Street, Leicester, at a salary of £75. In August she went on holiday with her family to Scarborough; so does Ursula in *The Rainbow*; and the parallel is reinforced by another piece of evidence. A fragment of an envelope overwritten in French, in Lawrence's hand, was found among the Burrows papers; as if by Louie herself it gives an account of her Scarborough holiday.[4] Part of the text reads:

Nous sommes au bord de la mer [à] Scarborough. . . . Il y a là deux baies magnifiques qui sont séparées par un grand pic couronné d'un vieux château. Là je vais regarder la mer, qui

1. 45.   2. 50.   3. 49.
4. Lawrence was presumably drafting a letter for Louie, describing her holiday for her 'Français' mentioned in 16.

est bien orageuse, et je parle aux vieux pêcheurs. Hier matin un de ces vieillards delicieux m'a dit que j'etais la jeune fille la plus belle (the finest girl) qu'il n'eût jamais vue.[1]

In the novel Ursula likes to go off by herself to look out over the sea; rough seas give her acute pleasure; but 'sometimes she loitered along the harbour, looking at the sea-browned sailors, who ... laughed at her with impudent, communicative eyes'.[2] As Lawrence was drafting the letter for Louie, probably on 14th August in Filey —a convenient meeting-place between Scarborough and Flamborough where he was on holiday—he was completely unaware of the way his creative imagination would subsequently transmute the details then being stored in his memory.

Though Louie had escaped the unemployment which beset Lawrence, she was desperately unhappy in the Leicester school. Consequently—partly responding to Lawrence's advice—she resigned her post at the end of the year, and on 1st January 1909 took up the appointment as headmistress of the village school at Ratcliffe-on-the-Wreake, about four miles from Quorn. She remained there for two years. Meanwhile Lawrence, newly arrived in Croydon, suffered an agony of isolation; he was cut off from 'the few people with whom [his] heart would wish to stay'.[3] He wrote to Jessie in a tone she described as 'like a howl of terror ... how could he live away from us all?'[4] In this situation his correspondence with Louie came to have an extra significance: she was one means by which he could retain his links with the companions and experiences of his youth.

This was not all. Louie offered to Lawrence a relationship free from the torments in his association with Jessie Chambers. She appears to have been unaffected by the tension between Lawrence and 'Miriam'; indeed she may even have been ignorant of its severity. Lawrence's letter of 9th February 1909 suggests this. Louie had obviously urged him to visit her in Quorn, and had proposed that Jessie should join them. 'Do you think J., you, and I make a happy triangle?' Lawrence enquired; 'somebody has a bad time when we three meet. Do you not feel it? It gets between my teeth.'[5] Jessie, on the other hand, had known for no less than eighteen months of his physical attraction to Louie. In her *Personal Record* Jessie claimed that Lawrence offered her the 'writing', the

1. See Appendix, p. 175. 2. *The Rainbow*, chapt. 15. 3. 20.
4. *D. H. Lawrence: a Personal Record*, p. 151. 5. 27.

artistic half of his nature, but would satisfy 'the purely animal side' with Louie. She continued:

In his aggressive moods he pursued the idea of marrying [Louie]—as animal pure and simple, he said. But I could never believe that he would be able to do it. He was too vehement; I felt that he was trying to force himself in that direction. Once when we three were together he said to her cynically: 'When one can't attain to genuine love one has to make shift with the spurious.' [Louie] tittered and agreed, never suspecting its personal application.

On a day in the summer of 1907 Lawrence went to her home to tea, giving me to understand that he meant to find out whether his feeling towards [Louie] was what he thought it was. Some days later he handed me, with a significant glance, the poem *Snapdragon*, in which the lines:

> And there in the darkness I did discover
> Things I was out to find:

is a literal description of the situation.[1]

The poem—one of the most vivid from his early period—conveys a keen sense of physical desire; sexual overtones, associated with powerful emotion, predominate. But other lines than those cited by Jessie should be noted. Following the poet's excited account of his symbolic ravishing of the flower in the presence of the girl, bright-eyed but reserved—

> I pressed the wretched, throttled flower between
> My fingers, till its head gaped back, its fangs
> Poisèd at her: like a weapon my hand was white and keen,
> And I kept the choked, snake flower in its fangs
> Of anguish till she ceased to laugh, till down
> Her soul's flag sank, and her pride put off its crown—

the girl 'murmured between her lips/The low word "Don't!"' And then:

> I bade her eyes
> To mine, I opened her helpless eyes to consult
> Their fear, their shame, their joy that underlies
> Defeat in such a battle.[2]

1. Op. cit., p. 142.
2. *The Complete Poems of D. H. Lawrence*, ed. V. de S. Pinto and Warren Roberts (1964), ii. 936.

XV

Though the poet's 'heart was fierce to make her homage rise', the girl's emotions were an amalgam of fear, shame and a guilty joy—unsophisticated but natural to a girl of Louie's upbringing. Indeed the whole poem supports the view that she was not a person who would delight in exacerbating the tension between Lawrence and Jessie.

During 1909 and a large part of 1910 Louie was by no means the sole focus of Lawrence's attentions. In letters previously published his pleasure in flirtations is manifest. In February 1909 he could write to Quorn: 'Louisa, oh Louisa, my heart aches for the country, and those splendid hours we have had.'[1] One month later he told Blanche Jennings: 'I am having one or two delightful little flirtations—quite little, but piquant';[2] and in the autumn and winter of the same year he was contemplating marriage with Agnes Holt, a Croydon teacher. Letters to Louie from Lawrence during 1909 were regular but not frequent; they spent a day together in London in July; otherwise their meetings occurred during school holidays. One such meeting at Christmas, however, occasioned a sudden upsurge in Lawrence's feelings. 'An old fire burned up afresh', he told Blanche Jennings; Louie was not named but she was undoubtedly the girl 'attached to [him] so long', living 150 miles from Croydon who was in question.

> She knows me through and through, and I know her. . . . We have fine, mad little scenes now and again, she and I—so strange, after 10 years, and I had hardly kissed her all that time. She has black hair, and wonderful eyes, big and very dark, and very vulnerable; she lifts up her face to me and clings to me, and the time goes like a falling star, swallowed up immediately; it is wonderful, that time, long avenues of minutes—hours—should be swept up with one sweep of the hand, and the moment for parting has arrived when the first kiss seems hardly overkissed.[3]

He adds ominously: 'What would my people and hers say?—but what do I care—not a damn!'; but he did care. The very occasion of this ecstatic meeting described to Blanche Jennings was probably the day he planned in a letter to Louie on 11th December: 'I *must* squeeze in a day this time, at Quorn. I will see what mother says.'[4] This needs no comment. However, there was no increase in the

1. 29.   2. *Collected Letters*, i. 52.   3. Ibid. i. 60.   4. 46.

warmth of affection expressed for Louie in Lawrence's letters during the months that followed; nothing to correspond to the rapture of the account quoted above. And their meetings in 1910 were not more frequent than before.

Lawrence's ability to absorb and accommodate himself to new experiences—what he called his 'elastic capacity'[1]—was tested then possibly more than he recognised. He was making his entry into London literary circles, meeting Ford Madox Hueffer, H. G. Wells and Ezra Pound among others; but having to adjust his literary ambitions to a future seemingly confined to the classroom. Also Eastwood and all it represented had to be reconciled with London and all it offered. Earlier associations were disintegrating: 'the old clique [the Pagans] is broken: it will never be restored, I expect'.[2] Relations with Jessie were a source of severe strain. Finally—most traumatic of all—in August 1910 his mother became ill with the cancer that eventually killed her, while staying with her sister Ada in Leicester. His agony during her four-month illness was harrowing, as *Sons and Lovers* vividly testifies. In the early stages of Mrs. Lawrence's illness Louie was, for Lawrence, one means of contact with her. From Quorn Louie could easily visit her in Leicester; she could take the proofs of *The White Peacock* for Mrs. Lawrence to read if she were able; and she could actively show a sympathetic kindliness towards the person Lawrence loved above all others. In retrospect, then, it is relatively easy to understand Lawrence's apparently precipitate action on 3rd December 1910, six days before his mother's death; his relatives and friends, unaware that he had been contemplating the step for about a month, found it much less simple. He described the occasion to Rachel Annand Taylor:

> I have been to Leicester today, I have met a girl who has always been warm for me—like a sunny happy day—and I've gone and asked her to marry me: in the train, quite unpremeditated, between Rothley and Quorn—she lives at Quorn. When I think of her I feel happy with a sort of warm radiation—she is big and dark and handsome.

Jessie, said Lawrence, had made the mistake of demanding his soul, which belonged to his mother; whereas

> Louie,—whom I wish I could marry the day after the funeral— she would never demand to drink me up and have me. She

1. 69. 2. 52.

loves me—but it is a fine, warm, healthy, natural love—not like Jane Eyre, who is Muriel [Jessie], but like—say Rhoda Fleming or a commoner Anna Karenina. She will never plunge her hands through my blood and feel for my soul and make me set my teeth and shiver and fight away.[1]

Faced with the imminent loss of his mother—his 'first, great love'—Lawrence had snatched at happiness. 'This surcharge of grief', he told Louie, 'makes me determine to be happy.'

> I have been very blind, & a fool. But sorrow opens the eyes. When I think of you, it is like thinking of life. You will be the first woman to make the earth glad for me: mother, J—all the rest, have been gates to a very sad world. But you are strong & rosy as the gates of Eden. We do not all of us, not many, perhaps, set out from a sunny paradise of childhood. We are born with our parents in the desert, and yearn for a Canaan. You are like Canaan—you are rich & fruitful & glad, and I love you.[2]

Further—and most importantly—Mrs. Lawrence had given her approval. 'She hated J.—& would have risen from the grave to prevent my marrying her.' But when, in late October or early November, Lawrence had asked whether it 'would be all right for [him] to marry Louie—later' the answer came:

> Immediately she said "No—I don't"—and then, after half a minute "Well—if you think you'd be happy with her—yes."

This assent, not less hesitant than he would expect, was essential; possessing it, Lawrence could act confidently. 'I must feel my mother's hand slip out of mine', he confessed to Louie; but then 'I can really take yours'. He could then also express his love for Louie with the intensity formerly reserved for his mother; he did so in thirteen letters during the last three weeks of December.

They were written against a background of hostility that was quickly revealed. On the day of Mrs. Lawrence's funeral Lawrence assured his fiancée: 'I saw J on Sunday & tried to make it look right to her. I think she does, a bit more.'[3] Jessie's account is different and rings true. In 1933 she wrote to Helen Corke (an intimate friend of Lawrence during this period), in a way that anticipated remarks in her *Personal Record by E.T.* two years later.

> The day before his mother's funeral we went for a walk together, and during that walk I reproached him for having become

1. *Collected Letters*, i. 70.   2. 59.   3. 60.

xviii

engaged to Louie Burrows. I said: "You ought not to have involved Louie in the tangle of our relationships." DHL's reply took my breath away; he said, "With *should* and *ought* I have nothing to do."[1]

This almost arrogant ruthlessness on Lawrence's part lay hidden behind the calm statement to Louie six days later (17th December 1910): 'I think J is taking it quite nicely—I heard from her yesterday.' He wisely added: 'But don't you write to her yet.'[2]

Members of Lawrence's own family were unsympathetic. His Aunt Ada was hostile, though he thought she would 'come round'.[3] His brother George, according to Jessie, was convinced from the outset that Lawrence and Louie would never marry: 'How d'you suppose he let me know about his engagement? ... On a blooming postcard.'[4] Nor were Louie's parents more favourably disposed. Their initial objection was specious: that Lawrence and their daughter were too young. A letter from Lawrence to Louie when their engagement was three weeks old clarifies the real situation:

> Give my regards to your father & mother: say nice things to them on my behalf. When they are bigoted, take no notice. It's no good booing a persistent ox for plodding its bit of track: it would be no good abroad, at large. Some folk are best fitted with a narrow creed, as are docile horses with a bluff: they're not scared & bewildered, & theyre more useful.[5]

Lawrence was too *avant-garde* and unorthodox for Louie's parents; his not attending church would further alienate their sympathy; and there was evidently a mutual intolerance.

In the midst of this encircling hostility Louie seemed to offer security, integrity and the hope of sexual fulfilment. She represented 'abundant life', in sharp contrast to 'the kingdom of death' where Lawrence felt himself to be.

> I have a tiresome character. But don't doubt me—dont. I do love you. When we are together, & quiet, it will be delightful. I do want you to be peaceful with, to grow with, to slowly & sweetly develope with.[6]

Such statements often occur. 'I want you to succour me, my darling—for I am used up';[7] or, as he told his Eastwood friend,

1. MS LaM 20 in the Nottingham University Library (cf. *D. H. Lawrence: a Personal Record*, p. 183).
2. 63.   3. 66.   4. *D. H. Lawrence: a Personal Record*, p. 188.   5. 69.   6. 65.
7. 67.

Mrs. Hopkin, his need was for a girl who was 'fruitful & reposeful in her being...[not] the acid sort'.[1] The Lawrence who wrote these words was spiritually and emotionally exhausted as the result of his mother's death, the growing hostility of his closest relations, his unhappiness in teaching, fears for the reception of *The White Peacock* (to appear in three weeks), and sexual frustration. He passionately desired 'somebody to rest with'; in December 1910, Lawrence knew more than most 'what a deep longing that may be'.[2]

The engagement was doomed from the outset. 1911 was 'the sick year' for Lawrence.[3] There is evidence in the letters to Louie of the irony and bitterness Helen Corke noticed in him.[4] Even before the end of 1910—less than four weeks after the engagement—he warned Louie that he was ' "cured" with the salt and salt-petre of bitterness & sorrow'; that the 'hard, cruel' side of his nature was in the ascendancy; and that it might cause her 'real grief for the first time in [her] life'.[5] Yet in the same letter he proclaims: 'Remember I love you and am your husband.' Between these two extremes of hardness and affection his feelings were destined to ricochet through the remainder of their correspondence.

Insufficient money was another corrosive in their relationship. Lawrence became aware as early as January 1911 that his minimum conditions for marrying—'£100 in cash & £120 a year income'[6]— were going to prove difficult to achieve; as the months passed it was clear that, in any reasonable time, they were unattainable. For her part, Louie never ceased to urge him to economise and save. As his doubts increased about the wisdom of marrying her at all, their financial exigency provided a ready course of friction. In July, for example, Lawrence flared up over Louie's enquiry into how he spent the £10 he had received on the publication of *Odour of Chrysanthemums*. Ironically he informed her of the petty details. One can sense his irritation at the multitudinous demands on his slender resources, combined with guilt at his unwillingness to husband them: 'chuck me if you're going to be sick of my failures.'[7] Teaching offered the only certainty of a steady income and therefore of the security Louie sought; Lawrence himself found the prospect increasingly repugnant. He was ready to take the risk of earning

1. MS letter, 23rd December 1910, from the Hopkin collection in the Nottinghamshire County Library; quoted by permission of the County Librarian.
2. 60.   3. Lawrence's Foreword to *Collected Poems*, in *Complete Poems*, ii. 851.
4. E. Nehls, *D. H. Lawrence: A Composite Biography* (University of Wisconsin Press, 1957–9), i. 142.
5. 69.   6. 72.   7. 107.

a living in the free-lance literary and journalistic world; Edward Garnett was encouraging him in this direction; but it ran contrary to Louie's inclinations. Her parents' reactions may be imagined.

It is noticeable that, within a few months of the engagement, Lawrence's letters get shorter, less intensely personal and more perfunctory. One suspects that he quickly realised he and Louie would never achieve the complete mutuality necessary for marriage; in charity to her, Lawrence probably refused to admit it even to himself. The chief sources of incompatibility appear to have been two: sexual frustration and what Lawrence came to regard as Louie's immaturity of character. Both were doubtless exacerbated by his need imaginatively to re-live experiences of the recent past while writing 'Paul Morel', the novel which was to become *Sons and Lovers*. To be vividly reminded of the moral and sexual conflict with Jessie, the physical liberation of his encounter with 'Clara Dawes', and the hardships suffered by his mother culminating in the agony of her final illness—all would reinforce his growing reluctance to face a permanent union with Louie, possibly with any woman.

None the less, the strength of his feelings for Louie cannot be doubted. Two stanzas from the poem *Kisses in the Train* reflect it:

> ... And still in my nostrils
> The scent of her flesh;
> And still my blind face
> Sought her afresh;
> And still one pulse
> Through the world did thresh.
>
> But firm at the centre
> My heart was found;
> My own to her perfect
> Heartbeat bound,
> Like a magnet's keeper
> Closing the round.[1]

Occasionally his feelings were 'red hot'; they were mutual; but they had to conform with Louie's strict 'code of manners'.[2] The resulting frustration and inner conflict appear in another poem concerning her, *The Hands of the Betrothed*.[3] The eyes of the girl in this poem

1. *Complete Poems*, i. 120–1.   2. 132.   3. *Complete Poems*, i. 127–9.

are hardened 'like gems in time-long prudery'; her heart is 'Hungry
for love'—

> Yet if I lay my hand in her breast
> She puts me away, like a saleswoman whose mart is
> Endangered by the pilferer on his quest.

She feels constrained to repress the desire which naturally erupts:

> And I have seen her stand unaware
> Pressing her spread hands over her breasts, as she
> Would crush their mounds on her heart, to kill in there
> The pain that is her simple ache for me.

The final lines are touched with irony about the restraint to which
the poet must submit and which the girl exerts only by an immense
effort of will:

> to me she's the same
> Betrothed young lady who loves me, and takes good care
> Of her womanly virtue and of my good name.[1]

The girl's attitude is 'wicked' according to the definition of that
word found in one of Lawrence's letters to Louie: 'only that . . .
which is a violation of one's feeling & instinct'.[2] Yet Louie could
make him feel 'ashamed of passion'[3] and, by her code of values,
morally inferior; while his dreams of suppressed sexuality recounted
in the letters tell their own story and make the likelihood of conflict
all too plain. Lawrence became sensitive to the variety of deeds or
circumstances which might violate Louie's code of propriety: the
suggestion that he would stay overnight in Gaddesby (the Leicestershire village where she taught during the first half of 1911); the
possibility that he might do something to excess, whether working
or thinking, eating or drinking; or his readiness to ignore her parents'
anxiety lest Louie and he should be unchaperoned on their Welsh
holiday in the summer of 1911.[4] Consequently, their meetings were
increasingly occasions for intense but 'unaccomplished'[5] and therefore self-defeating passions. 'I've now got to digest a great lot of

1. For 'womanly' (in the text in *Amores*, 1916) Lawrence later substituted 'maidenly'.
2. 85.   3. 76.
4. 90, 97, 111, 112. (Louie assured her mother by postcard (MS LaB 223): 'We have
very nice rooms—quiet and good with relatives of a Methodist parson.' The Prestatyn
landlady subsequently wrote to Louie, 21st August 1911 (MS LaB 200): 'You can tell
Mrs. Burrows from me, for her peace of mind, that her daughter was exceedingly good
whilst here—a credit to herself, to her up-bringing etc. etc.')
5. 121.

dissatisfied love in my veins', he wrote after one such occasion. 'It is very damnable, to have slowly to drink back again into oneself all the lava & fire of a passionate eruption.'[1] When, therefore, Lawrence eventually told Louie, 'I dont think now I have the proper love to marry on',[2] by 'love' he meant not only affection but also patience and self-restraint.

The second source of friction had a history at least equally long. As early as November 1908, in answer to Louie's account of her unhappiness in her first post, Lawrence wrote:

> Your soul is developing its bitter rind of maturity—it must do so, sooner or later, unless you remain forever immature, as most folks do. When you have a good rind you are safe.[3]

He later forced her to become 'safe' through bitter disappointment, but now he clearly considered her immature. Hence his pleasure at the signs of her independence from 'the threatening shadows' of her parents: 'I am glad you are going to walk abroad with no shadow but your own';[4] but he felt in her the disabling absence of harsh experience. She remained at the stage of believing sorrow to be 'beautiful'—'a century or so behind'; whereas he, 'at the tip of the years', found it 'awful' and 'cruel'.[5] Thus, though his remark after his mother's death was perhaps accurate—that Louie had never known 'real grief'[6]—it was not devoid of a kind of arrogance or morbid self-satisfaction: he had been forcibly matured by suffering on behalf of his mother in her lifetime and now on his own behalf by her death; Louie, on the other hand, was immature because of her relatively unscarred youth. It is an attitude which was subsequently reflected in his comment on the fictional character Ella, who became Ursula in *The Rainbow*: that she must 'get some experience before she meets her Mr. Birkin' (the Lawrentian figure in *Women in Love*).[7] Further, compared with his letters to Blanche Jennings and Rachel Annand Taylor, Lawrence's letters to Louie assume in her a much less mature, poised and dynamic personality.

This general estimate of Louie's character lay behind the published letter from Lawrence to his sister, Ada, of 26th April 1911:

> I never want Lou to understand how relentlessly tragic life is— not that. But I want her not to jar on me by gawkishness, and that she must learn. . . . When she is a bit older she'll be more understanding. Remember she's seen nothing whatever of the

1. 132. 2. 155. 3. 24. 4. 27. 5. 31. 6. 69. 7. *Collected Letters*, i. 263.

horror of life, and we've been bred up in its presence: with father. It makes a great difference.¹

Less than a month earlier he had asked Louie: 'Will you, I wonder, get through life without ever seeing through it.'² He will never, he adds, 'try to disturb any of [her] faiths', but there is an ambivalence here: one feels that if, without Lawrence's intervention, Louie were to have confronted 'the tragic issue' he believed life to be,³ he would have considered it beneficial. However, it is certain that, several months before he broke their engagement, Lawrence had decided that he did not regard Louie as sufficiently mature and 'separate' in her self-reliance to marry her. Perhaps he felt that, like Ursula in *Women in Love*, she was 'only too ready to knock her head on the ground before a man . . . when she was so certain of [him] that she could worship him as a woman worships her own infant, with a worship of perfect possession'.⁴

Lawrence suffered an agony of indecision. His love for Louie was deep; yet their relationship was ultimately unsatisfactory. Jessie Chambers reported that after Louie had stayed in Croydon (possibly in March 1911), Lawrence wrote: '[Louie] was here for the week-end, but its no good. Somehow as soon as I am alone with her I want to run away.'⁵ Further evidence of the tension revealed here is contained in an hitherto unpublished letter he wrote to Helen Corke in September 1911:

> The common, everyday, rather superficial man of me really loves Louie. Do you believe that? But do you not think the open-eyed, sad, critical, deep-seeing man of me has not had to humble himself pretty sorely to accept the imposition of the masculine, stupid decree. There is a decree for each of us— thou shalt live alone—and we have to put up with it. We may keep real company once in our lives—after that we touch now and again, but do not repose.⁶

Behind these words lay the bitter frustration of a man seeking an ideal relationship which would provide mutual fulfilment while not denying the individuality, the fundamental integrity of each of the

---

1. Ibid, i. 77.   2. 78.   3. *Collected Letters*, i. 77.
4. *Women in Love* (1920), chapt. 16.
5. *D. H. Lawrence: a Personal Record*, p. 154.
6. Quoted in a letter to the editor from Miss Corke and published with her permission.

two people involved. Birkin expresses this ideal in *Women in Love*, in his vision of

> the new day, when we are beings each of us, fulfilled in differ-
> ence. The man is pure man, the woman pure woman, and they
> are perfectly polarized. But there is no longer any of the horrible
> merging, mingling self-abnegation of love. There is only the
> pure duality of polarization, each one free from any contamina-
> tion of the other. In each, the individual is primal, sex is sub-
> ordinate, but perfectly polarized. Each has a single separate
> being, with its own laws.[1]

Lawrence had come to recognise that such an ideal would not be
achieved with Louie. The resulting conflict between his love for her
and rejection of her produced a feeling of guilt that approached
despair. The evidence is again in the letter to Helen Corke quoted
above:

> Really the one beautiful and generous adventure left seems to be
> death. . . . And this is not because I am inactive altogether.
> My soul has strenuous work to do in intimacies. But then I
> scorn the intimacy when it is formed; it is always a lot short.

A serious illness precipitated events. Lawrence contracted pneumonia—partly due to mental and nervous exhaustion—in November
1911. His sister Ada rushed to Croydon and stayed at his lodgings;
she kept Louie informed of his progress; and, signing herself 'Your
Sister', reassured Louie: 'keep a brave heart for his sake and try
not to worry . . . as soon as he can bear I shall send for you'.[2] Louie
spent Christmas and the week following at Croydon, but the time
was not propitious for what Lawrence had to tell her. He wrote to
Edward Garnett on 30th December: 'My girl is here. She's big, and
swarthy, and passionate as a gipsy—but good, awfully good,
churchy.'[3] Convalescing at Bournemouth during January 1912,
Lawrence again procrastinated. Not until 4th February when he
was staying with Garnett at Edenbridge did he write decisively to
Louie: 'I ask you to dismiss me.'[4] He invoked medical authority—
the doctor advised him not to marry; he adduced Ada's opinion—
she thought it unfair to Louie to prolong the engagement; and he

---

1. *Women in Love*, chapt. 16.   2. MS LaB 203, 28th November 1911.
3. *Collected Letters*, i. 90.   4. 154.

claimed that illness had 'changed [him] a great deal'. Ada corroborated the argument, in a letter to Louie twelve days later:

> It's surprising how very much changed Bert is since his illness, and changed for the worse too I think. I've had a serious talk with him about it too—his flippant and really artificial manner gets on my nerves dreadfully. Perhaps he may get alright by and by but he's very strange now, I can tell you.[1]

As we have seen, Ada was wrong to attribute the change in Lawrence solely to his illness; it had begun months before. Whether or not Louie had been alert to it, Ada's final remark would give her cold comfort: 'You really deserve someone better than Bert Louie, I wouldn't marry a man like him, no, not if he were the only one on earth.'

A few days before Ada's letter, Lawrence and Louie met in Nottingham. Garnett received a vivid description of the occasion:

> I saw Louie yesterday—she was rather ikey (adj.—to be cocky, to put on airs, to be aggressively superior). She had decided beforehand that she had made herself too cheap to me, therefore she thought she would become all at once expensive and desirable. Consequently she offended me at every verse end—thank God. If she'd been wistful, tender, and passionate, I should have been a goner . . .[2]

Shortly afterwards she wrote penitently, but Lawrence ignored the overtures.[3] If he needed evidence to confirm his estimate of her emotional immaturity, the meeting in Nottingham had supplied it. Moreover, he had already decided to visit his aunt Ada's relatives in Germany; his decision was propitious in the light of subsequent events. A few weeks later he met Frieda Weekley; on 3rd May they crossed the Channel to Ostend; and a new phase had begun. Louie received two postcards from Germany; she wrote for Lawrence's birthday (having obtained his address from his sister Ada[4]); but not until mid-November did she hear of Frieda from Lawrence himself:

> I am living here with a lady whom I love, and whom I shall marry when I come to England, if it is possible. We have been together as man and wife for six months, nearly, now, and I hope we shall always remain man and wife.[5]

1. MS LaB 206, 16th February 1912. 2. *Collected Letters*, i. 100.
3. Ibid, i. 101. 4. MS LaB 208, 5th September 1912. 5. 164.

Despite his plea that the correspondence should cease, to avoid pain to each other, Louie wrote again; she received a reply; then there was silence.[1]

The termination of the engagement together with Lawrence's subsequent marriage caused intense bitterness among her closest relatives. From the evidence available, Louie's painful disappointment caused her the 'real grief' Lawrence believed she had never experienced at an earlier date; it may also have accelerated the maturing of her personality. At any rate, those who knew her as head-mistress first of Quorn Church of England School (from September 1911 to September 1924), and then of a new Leicestershire school (till her retirement), remember her as a cultured woman of strong character and great decisiveness. A piece of objective evidence appears to substantiate these impressions. At a teachers' conference in Oxford, in 1925, she vigorously denounced a masculine view (expressed at a meeting of the National Association of Schoolmasters in Nottingham) that manhood was humiliated by the appointment of women as school inspectors. The *Sunday Express* at once commissioned an article from her re-stating her views, and printed it, on 19th April, under the heading: 'Woman-Hating School-Masters'. There is a Lawrentian fire in her remark on the Schoolmasters' Association: 'Sex obsession colours all their pronouncements', and in a passage that follows:

> These Nottingham protestants are obsessed by a perverted eroticism that is the inevitable aftermath of War. In seven years they have not managed to adjust themselves to normal conditions. It was necessary in war time to produce men of extraordinary muscular development, but in these days a balanced mind is equally necessary.

This militant concern for the rights of women teachers was characteristic of Louie throughout her career.

There is incontrovertible proof of her continuing regard for Lawrence. A letter from her College friend, Nina Stewart, just three weeks after his death on 2nd March 1930, obviously commented on Louie's proposal to visit his grave at Vence.[2] Her correspondent advised against the journey, as unwise and 'inopportune'; moreover, since Louie was strongly 'religious', there seemed little point

1. She may have written again in February 1913 (having sought Lawrence's address from Ada—MS LaB 210); if she did so, apparently there was no reply.
2. MS LaB 218.

in going merely to mourn over Lawrence's body: 'Why should you grieve because Bert has gone to sleep?... Wait a bit, Lou, until time has healed the wound: it is wicked not to give it every chance of healing.' The depth of Louie's feeling for Lawrence is unmistakable; the wound received in 1912 had not healed in 1930. She disregarded her friend's advice and twice went to Vence. On the first visit, probably in 1930, she arrived without having arranged accommodation; for a woman used to administrative thoroughness this smacks of an impulsive determination to see Lawrence's grave. Sir Herbert Read met her in Vence. He recalls that Louie 'obviously had never renounced her love and devotion for Lawrence. She was rather a dispirited and sombre kind of person, and I think she felt she had been ill-treated by Lawrence.'[1]

She was still unmarried, living with her parents in Quorn. Her father had retired from teaching in 1929 and devoted much of his energy to his work as a Diocesan Lay Reader. Louie herself, in addition to her responsibilities as a headmistress, developed interests in astrology, spiritualism and archaeology, as well as maintaining those in music and art. She married Mr. Frederick Heath in April 1940; a year later she retired from teaching. But her devotion to Lawrence's memory remained. As late as 1942 she was collecting material probably with the intention of writing a memoir of him; but she never permitted scholars to examine the letters he had intended for her eyes alone. Lawrence could have remarked of her until her death in 1962 (on holiday in Bournemouth)—as he had written in the poem over 50 years earlier—that she 'takes good care ... of my good name'.

---

1. Personal letter to the editor, 20th September 1967. Louie was seen at the cemetery —possibly on the same visit as is recorded here—by Frieda's daughter, Mrs. Barbara Barr. 'One day a tall dark woman came into the cemetery, but, seeing us went away. This was the "Louie" of Lawrence's early days. ... After we had left the cemetery, she came back and left some flowers there. On her return to the Midlands she wrote to Ada: "I went to Vence and saw the poor lad's grave."' (E. Nehls, *D. H. Lawrence*, iii. 448.)

Letters

·❨[1]❩·

[September 1906][1]

Dear Louie,

I am going to quizz your essay, not in the approven school-mistress style, but according to my own whimsical idea, which you may or may not accept. First of all I will find fault.

I do not like the introductory paragraph, it is like an extract from a Catalogue of Pictures for sale at some auctioneers. Nor am I quite sure that you are justified in saying that other artists have failed in depicting eastern colours as well as the painter of 'Homer'.[2] In fact the painting is not, I think, remarkable for its colour scheme, but for its striking personal characters and grace & harmony of form. Those are particulars of this essay. Then as to your style as a whole.

Like most girl writers you are wordy. I have read nearly all your letters to J,[3] so I do not judge only from this composition. Again & again you put in interesting adjectives & little phrases which make the whole piece loose, & sap its vigour. Do be careful of your adjectives—do try & be terse, there is so much more force in a rapid style that will not be hampered by superfluous details. Just look at your piece & see how many three lined sentences could be comfortably expressed in one line.

I know my essay was squeezed down almost to incoherence because I did not want it to be too long. I am very glad you saw how I had compressed it; if I had filled in & merged off my thoughts Miss B[4] would not have accused me so strongly of confusion.

1. Dated by Louie Burrows.
2. Louie may have been describing *Homer singing his Iliad at the Gates of Athens* by Le Thière (1760–1832), owned by the Nottingham Castle Art Gallery.
3. Jessie Chambers (1886–1944), the 'Miriam' of *Sons and Lovers*.
4. Miss Becket, Lecturer in the Department of Education, University College, Nottingham.

Again, don't use hackneyed adjectives. 'Shapely heads—fallen heroes—white beard on aged breast' you know these are in everybody's mouth. If you would write, try to be terse & in some measure original—the world abounds with new similes & metaphors.

I wish you had studied the characters of the picture more than the City—the Greek Art—the magnificent carvings. Things which are obvious are worth no more than a mention. If you cannot tell people of something they have not seen, or have not thought, it is hardly worthwhile to write at all. Try & study people, & the living soul which is the essence of mankind. If you have externals, they must represent something. I write to you as a would-be aspirant after literature, for I know you are such.

I like above all things your enthusiasm, & your delightful fresh, youthful feeling. Don't be didactic; try & make things reveal their mysteries to you, then tell them over simply & swiftly, without exaggerating as I do. I think you will do well. You are brighter than Jessie, more readable, but you are not so powerful. You will doubtless succeed far better than I who am so wilful. Be your own bright ingenuous self, & you are sure to make a delightful impression.

I am going to make my next try now. Let me see what you do— I am all interest

Yrs DHL

·◁[2]▷·
[c. 29th October 1906]

Dear L.,

You see how splendidly Madame[1] has crushed me. She has asked me now to write the essay she wanted—viz the Description of a Picture. I'm not quite sure whether I shall comply—if so I shall merely do it as a written exercise.

She told me some of my phrases are fine, but other ludicrous; that I was not entirely incapable of writing, but mixed up some sense with a great amount of absurdity. Therefore I must restrain myself to writing just what other people think, & are therefore willing to accept.

Bien—I consent—I am merely a pupil, therefore I must work by rule. I only wish Madame were not so ready to laugh at us as silly

1. Possibly Miss Becket (cf. p. 1 n. 4).

infants. Are you still thinking of contributing to the Gong? I saw a number in the Library, & thought it a very mediocre publication. I do not think I shall try to be admitted as a contributor.[1]

Write me your opinions & criticisms—your advice if you like—I shall like it.

J. is not very well—has a very bad cold her brother told me. May is married on Thursday[2]—I shall go if it is fine, & will tell you thereof. Shall I let J. see the essay? I shall look for a note from you this afternoon. I like people to criticise me—even Madame. Also I forgot to say that my thoughts expressed in the essay are in hopeless muddle—most likely it's true, but it is hardly encouraging to be told so many unpleasant things. That essay took me about 4 hrs—the next I do shall not occupy me more than 45 minutes, & it will then be better

I want to see your attempt—do not be afraid, I am not exacting; nor carping; give me your book this afternoon, with the various papers in it, if you have time please

DHL

·◁[3]▷·
[? *November 1906*]

Dear Louie,

I have hardly seen you this week to know how you are progressing —or retrogressing. Things are not very rosy, are they? I feel a bit flat. Miss Beckett surprised me with those marks—both yesterdays & Mondays. How did you go on? I am sick of work, there is no end to it.

Have you developed any new ideas or plans? Let me know if you do. When I saw J on Sunday she seemed much better—she had written you she said. When she has anything interesting to tell you that is not private show me the letter will you? She & I do not know much of each other nowadays. It is my fault—my temper is so variable—yet I do not like to lose her intimate acquaintance & she never writes me letters.

1. In his 'Foreword' to *Collected Poems* Lawrence confessed: 'I had offered the little poem *Study* to the Nottingham University magazine [*Gong*], but they returned it' (*Complete Poems*, ed. V. de S. Pinto and W. Roberts, 1964, ii. 851).
2. May Chambers (1883–1955), Jessie's sister, married William Holbrook on 1st November 1906.

3

Did I tell you Birdie[1] gave me 9/10 for my essay, & did not vouchsafe a single remark or correction, but let me severely alone. I was surprised—I should have liked her opinion—generously expressed—better than her silence. Do you know anymore about the Gong—have you sat down yet to adorn it. For goodness sake send me some news either of yourself or someone else, for everything is as dull as the day. I am slogging Latin—how I suffer. Would I had a little leisure to employ myself congenially. How many had you for yesterdays history—I was surprised not to see your name on the board. But don't worry, satisfactory work here only means gratification of a sum of individual fads—most teasing

DHL

·◁[4]▷·

Lynn Croft, Eastwood, Notts
24th December 1906

My dear Louie,

I saw Jessie's card from you before I saw my own. Is not that remarkable? You see I had just run up to get some holly, when their post came. I want to know if you will come over on Wednesday to take tea with us. Ada & mother would be so glad to see you, and Jessie is coming down.[2]

Come in the morning, about half past ten if possible, so that we may have a long & jolly time. Now don't refuse. Let us know what train you will come by and we will meet you at Shipley Gate.[3] I think 10.30 or 11.0 would be a nice time. At any rate, suit yourself on the score of time.

Wishing you all a very [?happy] Christmas—I am,

Yours D. H. Lawrence

1. Miss Bird, Lecturer in Education, University College, Nottingham.
2. Lawrence's younger sister (1887–1948); his mother Mrs. Lydia Lawrence (1852–1910); and Jessie Chambers, respectively.
3. Louie would be travelling from Ilkeston Junction-with-Cossall.

I shall be pleased to come on Monday by the train arriving in the Junction[1] at 2.36 or thereabouts. Ada cannot come, as you will remember she was already claimed for that time, but I expect Jessie will gladly acquiesce, tho. I have not yet seen her.

DHL

Addressed: Cossal Notts   Postmarked: Eastwood DE 29 06

·◁[6]▷·

Lynn Croft, Eastwood, Notts
Good Friday 1907

Dear Louie,

If this wonderful weather holds we shall have a delightful day on Monday. The train we have decided on leaves the Junction at 10.33 —the Town at 10.42—arrives in Langley Mill at 10.52, and in *Alfreton* 11.8. So if you take the train at the Junction we shall join you at Langley Mill and we will skip off for Alfreton. Thence we go across the Park & about four miles on to Wingfield. There I suppose we shall eat dinner, and after a time proceed on to Crich. We shall arrive there—D.V.—about teatime, and if you would care to we could buy tea, though before we carried all the tuck we had—a good quantity—except sixpennyworth of bread & butter. Jessie & Alan are going—Gertie, Frances Ada[2] & I. We shall be delighted to have Ethel[3] if she would care to go with us. Let us hope for a nice time. I should think we shall leave Ambergate by the 7.45 which arrives in the Junction at 8.52. So Ethel would be home quite early. You will come home with us for the night, and after dinner on Tuesday it is proposed we all proceed to the Haggs[4] for a united gathering. That night you will spend with Jessie, and Wednesday afternoon is set aside for a picnic up at the New House farm, near Annesley. If we should be late from the picnic you will stay with us again till Thursday.

---

1. Ilkeston Junction station.
2. Respectively: Jessie Chambers and her brother Alan (1882–1946)—the original of George Saxton in *The White Peacock*; Gertrude and Frances Cooper, daughters of Thomas Cooper, a neighbour of the Lawrences at Lynn Croft. All were members of the group known as the 'Pagans'.
3. Louie's 16-year-old sister, Ethelreda Helen.
4. The farmhouse occupied by the Chambers family.

How elaborate it all sounds—but if it may come to pass how jolly it will be! I trust everything will meet with your approval. Remember me to your father & mother,[1] & the little ones.

I am Yrs Sincerely D. H. Lawrence

Addressed: Cossal Notts   Postmarked: Eastwood MR 29 07

·◁[7]▷·
Lynn Croft, Eastwood, Notts
20th October 1907

Dear Louie,

I have a request to make. Perhaps you know that the 'Nottm. Guardian' asks for three Christmas stories, & offers a prize of £3 for each. I have written two just for fun, & because Alan & J asked me why I didn't, & so put me upon doing it to show I could. I may write a third.

They ask for an Amusing Adventure, a Legend, and an Enjoyable Christmas.[2] But one person may not send in more than one story. So will you send in the Amusing in your name? They say 'In sending a story each person undertakes it is his or her original work & property which has never been published.' That is rather a sneezer, but I don't see that it matters, for I make the story your property, & you will write it out again according to your taste—will you?

It is the Amusing I want you to send, because it is the only one that is cast in its final form. I want you to write it out again in your style, because mine would be recognised. Indeed you may treat it just as you like. I am sorry to take up your time—but would you mind? If not I will bring you the story & give full instructions. The

---

1. Alfred (1864–1948) and Louisa Ann (1865–1954) Burrows.
2. Louie Burrows submitted *The White Stocking*, on Lawrence's behalf, as an 'Amusing Adventure'; it was later re-written (cf. 85) and included in *The Prussian Officer and Other Stories* (1914). Lawrence himself submitted the 'Legend' which later became *A Fragment of Stained Glass*, and was also published in *The Prussian Officer*. The 'Enjoyable Christmas' story, apparently written last, was *A Prelude to a Happy Christmas*; it was sent in by Jessie Chambers, under the nom-de-plume 'Rosalind'; it won a prize and was printed in the *Nottinghamshire Guardian*, 7th December 1907.

legend you shall read when you come & see us, which will be next Saturday if you please, or the foll. Sat if you prefer.

If you have scruples do not hesitate to say so. The story, if published, bears a nom-de-plume, & I am pretty nearly certain that the Amusing will *not* be accepted, though the Legend may. So you would be fairly safe in sending it, & I see no wrong. However, that you must decide.

I have not seen J this week end owing to the atrocity of the weather. But I will post your note to her.

I await your reply

                                         & am Yrs. DHL

Miss Louie Burrows

·◁[8]▷·
Lynn Croft, Eastwood, Notts
23rd December 1907

My dear Louie,

You will not mind accepting these few words of Tolstoï in memory of 'The White Stocking'? You, who love to romance, look at the blue binding & think of it, years hence, catching your eye in your study as you sit writing your newest novel. Then give a sigh for our abortive effort—or better, give a smile. I am sure Tolstoï will be interesting to you—& see how good I am to choose thus for you.

If you accept Jessie's invitation for Christmas day I expect you will stay a few days & come down to us for one of them. But I expect you will stay at home until the 30th. In that case I shall wait to hear from you concerning our visit to you. Thursday will be an excellent day for us all except Ada—she is then engaged. Friday also is good—then everybody is at liberty. If you prefer that we should come Thursday Ada bids you say so—she would be very loth to put you to any inconvenience.

While you are over here we propose having a discussion among ourselves on the ultimate questions of philosophy raised in the education class—a discussion of a 'Universal Consciousness' for instance—the matter with which we left off last Wednesday.

You do not mind accepting Tolstoï do you? Be good, Sweet maid, & acquiescent. That is the only way a maid may be good from a

7

man's point of view. 'Take from my mouth the wish of—increasing fulness of life & thought'

I am—Yrs D. H. Lawrence

Addressed: Cossal   Postmark: None (letter sent by hand)

·◦[9]◦·

Lynn Croft, Eastwood, Notts
21st April 1908

My dear Louie,

It is dull and gloomy; the paper says 'rain or snow later'; the way is long and lonely; I am rather tired; I have the inevitable cold. Shall I pile up and continue to pile up? At seven I got up—give me one morsel of credit for that, pray—and cleaned my boots—the sum of your disfavour is decreasing like wrath in the eyes of a girl melting into pity—and I shaved. But as I shaved and looked at myself, and asked my reflection how myself fared, I fell out with myself, and saw that that same estimable person would not make good company today. Therefore, out of magnanimous consideration, I sat down after shaving and poked the fire, and as the dust and ashes drizzled over the bar, I made up my mind to spare you. By this time you are on your knees in gratitude to me for staying away. I am an expert, am I not, at making excuses? I have had many friends.

I am truly sorry not to come today—but it is better not. Why have you gone so far—why couldn't you stay within unwearying distance?[1] You will not be vexed, will you?

Last week I did not go to Leicester. My aunt[2] is very ill—this morning we hear that she can hardly last another day. How *can* I go and see her—how can I? It is enough to suffer my mother's sighs, and to feel the current of her thoughts like an uneasy quivering note of sad music. Oh for some blessed Nirvána!

> 'Om, Mani Padme, Om! the Dewdrop slips
>   Into the shining sea.'
> 'Unto Nirvána—he is one with Life yet lives not.'
> '—Nirvána—where the Silence lives'[3]

1. The Burrows family had recently moved to Quorn, Leics. (See Introduction, p. xi.)
2. Ada Rose Krenkow, Lawrence's maternal aunt, married to a distinguished Orientalist Fritz J. H. Krenkow. They lived at Leicester.
3. Edwin Arnold, *The Light of Asia* (1879). viii. 289–92, 591. (I am indebted to Mr. Anthony W. Shipps, Indiana University Library, for this information.)

8

Still, it would be frightfully slow after a bit, would it not? I have done with my crude philosophising, my thin-air metaphysical rant. I don't care a rap for the beginning of things—it is too far away, and I'm short-sighted—I don't care a button for the end of things—I cannot be sure of Certif. result.[1] Amen! I have sung the Requiem of my Soulfulness—aren't you glad? I'm taking Horace's advice

> 'Dona praesentis cape laetus horae et
> Linque severa.'[2]

which is quite trite, merely:
'Take with a glad heart what the day gives, and stop bothering.'
Au revoir,—jusqu'à jeudi. I trust you and J.[3] are having a good time—have you yet fallen on each other's necks and poured out your hearts in girlish sympathy?

> 'Est et fideli tuta silentio
> Merces.'[4]

which is 'There is a safe reward awaits faithful silence.' I shall go empty away—shall I not? Et vous?

Goodbye Yrs DHL

Addressed: Coteshael Cheveney Rd., Quorn Leicestershire
Postmarked: Eastwood AP 21 08

·◁[10]▷·
Lynn Croft, Eastwood, Notts
10th July 1908

My dear Louie,
I have been conjuring up pictures of you dictating in most sweetly pronounced college terms to your flock of admiring and revering youngsters.[5] How has it been? Have you yet lost that precious jewel, that Holy Grail of teachers, your precious perfect good temper? Have you yet summoned a trembling little mortal in

---

1. Teacher's Certificate.   2. Horace, *Odes*, III, 8, 27–8 ['...horae, Linque...'].
3. Jessie Chambers.   4. Horace, *Odes*, III, 2, 25–6.
5. Louie was teaching at St. Mary's School, Castle Street, Leicester; she remained there till the end of the year.

9

thunder tones to the terrors of the strap? Have you yet flung yourself down in the railway carriage reciting in soul-sick tones:

'Tomorrow, and tomorrow, and tomorrow
Creeps in this petty pace from day to day;
And all our yesterdays have lighted fools
The way to dusty death.'[1]—'And I wish one of 'em
had lighted me.'? Have you?—then you have my heart-felt
sympathy. Have you not?—Then accept my hearty congrats—but
wait till next week before you crow.

Hasn't this been a —— week? I have several times been black in
the face. 'The hay is cut, the clover's shut'—but I cannot go
wielding the fork—I have stewed indoors till I am sick in— Little
Mary. - - -.

Next week, if it is fine, I hope to be in the hay. Should the Sat. be
a blazer, I must remain in the hay, since, as usual, I am an indispensable factor in the well-being of things. 'He that putteth his hand to
the hay-fork'[2]—you know the rest;—I suppose one farming imple-
ment is as good as another. So I don't know quite when I can come
to Quorn. How would it be to leave it till the holiday? You know
we don't go away till the 8th[3]—and I guess you will not depart
earlier. Command me, however, I am as submissive as Puck.

I have no word of a holiday—I mean, fool that I am, of a
job.

I want to read some Verlaine to you[4]—fun!—I shall see your eyes
swing round.

I remember Saturday—it is as good as Alice in Wonderland.

I expect to hear from you—give me your school address.

Yours, DHL

Addressed: Coteshael (quel mot!) Cheveney Rd. Quorn Leicestershire
Postmarked: Eastwood JY 10 08

---

1. *Macbeth*, V, v, 19–20, 22–3.   2. Cf. *Luke*, ix. 62.
3. In fact they were both away by 1st August. Cf. p. 12 n. 1.
4. Verlaine had seized Lawrence's attention at this time (cf. *Collected Letters*, ed. Harry
T. Moore, 1962, i. 21, 25).

Lynn Croft, Eastwood, Notts
29th July 1908

My dear Châtieuse,

On my stream of consciousness has often sailed a cockle boat carrying your tawny image, but the fragile idea of a letter to you which your boat had in tow got wrecked before it came to harbour and set up motor responses. Cependant—now I write, you are not cross, hein?

This I hear from J. of your coming to the Haggs is very jolly. 'Swiftly walk over the Western Wave, Daughter of Night.'[1] You will come?—you must come. Surely nothing will happen to prevent you—if it does I shall jerk my thumbs off—à la mode italienne. Come for Bank Holiday—we are arranging some simple little jaunt; stay till the week end—I want to read to you Verlaine—I want to laugh like a fiend with you at some behaviours of our friends over here.[2]

All last week, and all this, I have been in the hay. Hardly do I know myself; I have cast my tender skin-of-college culture (don't dare to say it never grew)—my hands are pachydermatous (Hurray!) —and still jolly sore; my manners are—dear me, dear me, Mrs Grundy!—my exquisite accent, beloved of Billy,[3] is gone; as the corns rose on my hands so grew gruffness in my speech. You will like me, you hussy. Alas, I forget, I have been to the dentist; I have two teeth out in front; steel yourself against the sight of me. On Sunday we worked in the fields till nearly three o'clock; the righteous went by to church; the bells did ring; we worked and sweated. Monday night we camped out—under the haystack; a tramp came to join us; he mistook us for fellow tramps; it took all Neville's[4] (he was there—with Alan & I) virtuous and indignant 'side' to convince the poor devil of our immeasurable superiority.[5] I have one or two tales to tell you—they will not go onto paper, for I want tones of voice. Do come.

1. Shelley, *To Night* ['. . . Spirit of Night'].
2. Lawrence wrote to Blanche Jennings, 30th July 1908: 'Today, Bank Holiday, we are having a picnic at Beauvale Abbey—not far away.' Among the party (including his Mother, Jessie and Alan Chambers) would be 'Louie—a girl I am very fond of—a big, dark, laughing girl' whose 'nut-brown eyes' will 'laugh and scold' him as he reads Verlaine (*Collected Letters*, i. 24-5).
3. Possibly a reference to William ('Billy') H. Newton, a Lecturer in Education at Nottingham University College.
4. George H. Neville (b. 1886), a schoolfriend and member of the 'Pagans'.
5. For a more vivid account of this incident see *Collected Letters*, i. 24.

I have no news of a job yet—don't care many—jerks of the thumb.

Au revoir—ma chère bohémienne

Yrs DHL

Addressed: Coteshael Cheveney Rd. Quorn Leicestershire
Postmarked: Eastwood JY 31 08

·◅[12]▻·

Thanks for your note—I think Thursday will suit us nicely. I cannot yet make arrangements—will write you tomorrow. We are having a ripping time—do you think you could get down here[1]—it is so delightful? Till tomorrow then—Love from all

DHL

Addressed: 39, Moorland Rd. North Bay Scarborough
Postmarked: Bridlington AU 1 08

·◅[13]▻·

Dear Louie,

We will come on Thurs. if it is quite fine. We propose to walk—start about 8.0 or 8.30 & arrive at Filey about 12.0, or thereabouts. Meet us at the station—we will try to get there by 12.0. You will come in by the 10.25 perhaps, & have a look round. You might come out to meet us a very little way on the Flam. (Brid)[2] Rd.

DHL

(Our train returns at 8.50 p.m. hope this will suit you)—we may get a later.)

Addressed: 39, Moorland Rd. North Bay Scarborough
Postmarked: Flamborough AU 11 08

1. While the Burrows were on holiday in Scarborough (like the Brangwens in *The Rainbow*, chapt. 15), Lawrence was at Flamborough with his mother and other friends. (Cf. *Collected Letters*, i. 24.)

2. i.e. Bridlington.

Good old Filey!—did it improve your cold? Make haste to be well & come to Flamboro. Will you come Tuesday, Wednesday or Thursday? Any day will suit us. We have Alan to despatch on Monday, after that we are prepared to enjoy a day with you, and Ethel. Write & say times etc. Shall we have another day at Filey?

Yrs DHL

Addressed: 39, Moorland Rd. North Bay Scarborough
Postmarked: Flamborough AU 15 08

Ma chère Louise,

Your card comes too late for me to reply as you ask. Our posts go out at 6.0 a.m. and 5.0 p.m.—is it not ridiculous. I have just received your card; it is seven o'clock & drizzling with rain. I am afraid tomorrow may be wet. If it is, come Wednesday; if Wed. is wet, come Thursday. Is the earlier train too early? Tide is high now about 9.0, you know, so we want you to come quite early. Mother is anxious for you to come—and why do you not mention Ethel—is she not coming?—if so, why not? We wanted you both. Alan is gone—Tim desolate.[1] You *must* be well—I hope for a jolly day

DHL

Addressed: 39, Moorland Rd. North Bay Scarborough
Postmarked: Bridlington AU 18 08

1. Lawrence's cousin Alvina Lawrence, nicknamed 'Tim'; she later married Alan Chambers.

Lynn Croft, Eastwood, Notts
2nd September 1908

Ma chère Louise,

So you command me to write you something lively! Divessa, (fem. of Dives, not some young person out of the Faery Queene), flourishing on seventy-five quid a year commands poor Lazarus whose soul is covered with sores to whistle her a comic song. My days are spent in uttering that mournful lament 'Meine Ruh is hin, mein Herz ist schwer'—'My peace is gone, my heart is sore' (Do you know 'Gretchen at the Spinning Wheel'?)[1] Truly I am in a sad state, although I am getting fatter. I have used pounds of paper in applications; when I am not singing 'Meine Ruh' I am repeating to myself the verses of my testimonials "Mr D H Lawrence has just completed a two years' course of training at this College. We have never had a student—" I can recite two long testimonials by heart—Post time is a period of painful suspense—about 8.30 a.m. & 7.0 p.m.—when the postman should come. He brings me a letter —the house holds its breath—'We beg to inform you that your application was not successful'—the devils! And you ask *me* to write something lively. The most amusing thing I can do is to console myself that I am not in your shoes. Ah, would it were holidays for ever! I don't want to begin work in school, oh dear no; I only want the filthy lucre. I hate school, I love an eternal holiday —Hurray!

Another lugubrious tale! We began to cut the corn on Monday. The crop is thin & wretched; the knife cottered and clogged vilely; it rained; I am sure Hell is a cold wet place; they invented the fiery business somewhere in Arabia, by the bright Saharas sunny strand; my hell has a N.E. wind & rain varying from drizzle to pelting sleet. On Monday I expiated all the sins I ever committed, & all that I ever inherited. Two of us raked out after the damned machine; plodded over the sticky field with its thin dragged stubble, to the corner where we must wait for the machine; there we squatted by a little hedge, and got wetter and more like 'Canterbury' lamb. Such is harvesting, harvesting the oats.

'The little god works wonders in Alan'![2] Lord, Lord, the poor lad's tipsy with a foolish gibbering intoxication. He has not enough

---

1. Schubert set to music the words ('Gretchen am Spinnrade') by Goethe.
2. Alan Chambers was paying court to Lawrence's cousin Alvina.

of the choleric element to give his passion colour, so he trots off like a fussy spaniel to pay his court. Lord, Lord! When the oats will be gathered I do not know. The rain, oh the rain!

Me, with sores on my soul (most of 'em painted on); me, on my doorstep; me, the unemployed, I lift up my hands to heaven and thank a beneficent deity that I am not as that opulent girl reaping another harvest in Leicester. Mais felicitez Ethel de ma part. (I won't trust myself in English)

Keep up your courage, I implore you; think what an expense a funeral would be, and how like a wretched Sansjoy I should look in a black tie & a crape band round my arm. When J. told me of your expectations for the end of last week I said 'I should think she won't be such a brute. Think how it would knock some poor body about "laying her out".' Be of good cheer, and get those chapters ship-shape; I know it will be harder work for you to make them tidy than it was to originate them, but screw your courage to the sticking point—in other words 'Hold on tight, Eliza'. I shall look soon for that bit of dainty literature from you, don't be lazy.

I am highly interested in your cricket score; I am contemplating writing a Lay in its honor—after the manner of Horatius.

> 'But the Captains brow was sad
> And the Captain cursèd low
> And darkly looked she at score
> And darkly at the beaux'
>
> ———
> ———
> ———
>
> ——— —
>
> Then forth strode bold Louisa
> The mistress of the field
> Her chin was high, her arm was strong
> The trusty bat to wield
>
> ———
> ———
>
> ———
>
> Louisa struck out wildly
> And high the dust did rise
> Then as she bolted down the pitch
> Caught the fieldsman in her eyes.
> ! ! !

The Kaleïdoscope[1] I find a bit too kaleïdoscopic; it is too confused for my poor English sense; I can't make out the pattern, and the suggestion is only such as makes me feel puzzled. Let's translate it.

'In a street in the heart of a dream city comes a moment that seems a fragment repeated from a life before this, an instant at once vague & clear – – – Ah, that sun through the rising mist!

Oh, that cry away on the sea, that voice in the forest!—like when one knew nothing about the causes of things—A slow awakening after the soul has inhabited many bodies—things will be more the same than they were before (what the last line means I don't know) In this street in the heart of a magic town where street organs grind out jigs in the evenings, where there are cats on the side-boards of the cafés, and where bands go playing down the streets—It will be so fatal for one to believe there is any death for it.'

It recalls moments such as one has felt—but it is all so intangible —I don't know what death has to do with it. Give your Français[2] an English translation of the thing and ask him where you are wrong, & to kindly explain; he had better explain in French.

I cannot say when I shall come to Leicester; think of the weather. I like to play; I like to feel childish & irresponsible, it is possible to be so much more gay. This morning when the post-man had brought me that kind 'not successful' I bethought myself of my old dodge for peeping into the future, one I borrowed from 'La Jeune Sibérienne',[3] that is, sticking a pin in the bible on a certain verse (at hazard), & reading one's fate. I stuck Zachariah—I did not know that old boy had a book to himself—& it said 'And on the 4th day of the 9th month news came unto Somebody or other'[4] I have therefore high expectations from Friday's post.

Hope I'll see you soon. I'm glad you can write to me as a last (and, I'm afraid, rather unsuccessful) escape from boredom.

Vous me flattez. Au revoir DHL

Addressed: Waeshael, Quorn Leicestershire
Postmarked: Eastwood SP 2 08

1. Verlaine's poem 'Kaléidoscope' in *Jadis et Naguère* (1885).
2. Most likely a 'pen-friend'. A letter from Jessie Chambers to Louie, 28th June 1908, refers to a correspondent named 'Marcy', a 'lad of 18' (MS LaB 190).
3. By Xavier de Maistre (1825). 4. *Zechariah*, vii. 1.

Lynn Croft, Eastwood, Notts
12th September 1908

Louisa Carissima,

Your good memory surprises and flatters me; I offer you a thousand thanks for your congrats.[1] You, also, why do not you write me cheerfully, me, a poor hungry unemployed, still employed busily transcribing my testimonials. I shall soon mark myself as 'unsaleable goods', and withdraw from the market.

How wicked you are to rebuke me for the tone of my last letter; not only am I called upon to make you smile, but to make you smile on the right side when everything wears a wrong face because school is a bit purgatorial. I am much interested in the matrimonial adventures of your Sandowian[2] assistant—I have never heard of him before, by the way; tell me when the new meek assistant embarks on similar adventures. Mr. Mott[3] must have derived his name from the fool's attire in which his ancestors were clad; he himself seems eligible for the motley. The only thing to do with a fool is to treat him as such—an object to laugh at.

After much nibbling of bad cake you come to the almond paste at last: I'm coming to Leicester on Wednesday, to stay for a week or two.[4] Damn it, no, the corn is n't in, but I'm sick of it! One Sat. I'll come to Quorn, shall I? What is the name of your school—and where is it?[5] I'll come to look for you on Thursday—at 4.30 eh? My aunt's address is 20 Dulverton Rd—somewhere near the Foss.[6] Is it a hundred miles from you? We'll have a few trips round town —hurray! I am biking in on Wednesday. On the way I hope to be able to have the model for my teeth taken. Alas, the poor hiatus in my upper jaw!

Do you want me to bring you any book or anything? I shall expect at least a card from you before Wed.

A jeudi, donc DHL

Addressed: Coteshael Quorn Leicestershire
Postmarked: Eastwood SP 12 08

1. Lawrence's 23rd birthday fell on 11th September 1908.
2. i.e. muscular, after 'strong-man' Eugen Sandow (fl. 1900).
3. Herbert H. Mott (b. 1864) had been on the staff of St. Mary's School for 16 years.
4. With his Aunt Ada.   5. Cf. p. 9 n. 5.
6. The Fosseway, originally one of the great Roman military roads.

Unsuccessful here—tomorrow must go to Croydon after another. I am writing on a Manchester car.[1] Stockport is a dirty ugly place— I'm rather glad I've not got it. Hope I get Croydon[2]   DHL

Addressed: Coteshael Quorn Leicestershire
Postmarked: Manchester SEP 25 08

Dear Louie,

You see I am now at home. I had a pleasant ride on Sat. evening, and another yesterday. My bike behaved like a gentleman, & the paints did not rattle off, & the flowers did not die. I spent all Sunday painting those nasturtiums; they look rather pretty; ask Auntie to show you the thing when you call for the paints. I don't suppose it matters when you go, but I would just drop my Aunt a card if I were you. She will be glad to see you again, I know, for she was quite taken. I have not yet heard from Croydon, but expect a letter tomorrow. Bristowe[3] has just written to say he can find me employment very shortly, but I have written & refused, with thanks. No more Notts. C.C.[4] for me. I wish Saturday were coming over again. Regards to all.

Adieu. DHL

Je vous enverrai une lettre et votre conte en deux ou trois jours.

DHL

Addressed: Coteshael Quorn Leicestershire
Postmarked: Eastwood OC 6 08

---

1. i.e. tramcar.   2. He was interviewed at Croydon on 26th or 27th September.   3. Charles John Bristowe, Director of Education for Nottinghamshire.   4. Nottinghamshire County Council.

Lynn Croft, Eastwood, Notts
7th October 1908

Liebeste Ludwigin,

I have read your tale; it is very jolly; I'm sure it will take if you write it out again once or twice. The great thing to do in a short story is to select the salient details—a few striking details to make a sudden swift impression. Try to use words vivid and emotion-quickening; give as little explanation as possible (e.g.—the facts about the keepers being in certain parts of the wood at certain times); make some parts swifter, (e.g.—the girl's adventure in the night—that is not a rush enough); avoid bits of romantic sentimentality like Crewsaders & too much Wishing Well; select some young fellow of your acquaintance as a type for your lover, & think what he probably would do—Bonnie & the girl are good, but the young keeper is not well defined; be *very careful* of slang; a little is as much as most folks can stand. Send it me again when you have re-written it; I am interested.

I have to begin work at Croydon on Monday;[1] I go down on Sunday. My school is the Davidson Rd; my salary £95. That's all I know.

In certif—I called in Coll. & Pa[2] seized me & took me upstairs—I have distinction in French, Botany, Maths. & Hist. & Geog:[3] Never anything in English—is it not a joke? I could not see anything but Education against your name, but only had a slight glance at the list. I don't know any results besides mine—Miss Domleo[4] has French & English—I did not see anyone with four—but my glance at the list as Pa turned it over was most cursory.

Soon I shall be far away in Croydon; alas, unhappy fate which sends me from the few people with whom my heart would wish to stay. But Christmas! that is the magic word I conjure with.

I am immensely busy rushing round to see everybody. Oh the lamentations heard abroad!

---

1. Lawrence took up his post on 12th October 1908.
2. Professor Amos Henderson, Normal Master (i.e. Head of the Day Training College) and Professor of Education at University College, Nottingham.
3. Jessie Chambers claimed that Lawrence achieved also a distinction in Education (*D. H. Lawrence: a Personal Record*, p. 82).
4. Mary B. Domleo: a prizewinner at the end of her first training year, she obtained a First Class Teacher's Certificate (with Lawrence and Louie) in 1908.

I've bought one of those round cloth hats, and look so comical therein. I would like to see you laugh at me. Oh, I must close. Adieu, adieu—one kiss?

DHL

Am coming into Nottm on Saturday—must be at the Dentist at 4.0. Shall I see you—where? I shall bike in if fine. DHL

Addressed: St. Mary's School Castle St. Leicester
Postmarked: Eastwood OC 7 08

·◁[21]▷·

12 Colworth Road, Addiscombe, Croydon
23rd October 1908

Dear Louisa,

I cry peccavi to your unuttered reproach. The fact of the matter is I'm sick to death of telling the same thing to different folk. I've spent 4/- in stamps since I've been here, & written an unholy host of letters. It is so amusing—they all sound breathless—my letters, I mean.

Here goes. I have excellent digs. Mrs Jones was a schoolmistress in Manchester—Jones[1] is superintendent of school attendance officers here. They are both delightful people—he has rather a lot of his own sayings which he considers savoury, & which he must repeat to me—otherwise—. But I like his missis best. Then there is Winnie, a jolly quaint little maiden of five—she is 'infatuated with me', Mr Jones says, manipulating the syllables of the big word cautiously; then there is a baby which is sometimes good. But I'm ever so much at home here—I am really lucky. I have a room to myself—when Win or her Dad are not in—& good and copious (save the word) food for 18/- per wk. Digs are not half bad.

School—a great big new red-brick imposing handsome place, with a fair amount of open space—looking across in front over great stacks of timber, over two railways to Norwood where the musichall folk live in big houses among the trees, & to Sydenham, where the round blue curves of the Crystal Palace swell out into view on fairly

1. John William ('Super') Jones.

20

clear days. Inside all is up to date, solid & good. Class rooms open off a big hall—like Gladstone Street[1]—but classrooms here on one side only. There is plenty of accommodation—floors are block wood— thirty dual desks for forty five boys—all very nice. But the head[2] is a weak kneed windy fool—he shifts every grain of responsibility off his own shoulders—he will not punish anybody; yourself, when you punish, you must send for the regulation cane and enter the minutest details of the punishment in the Pun. book—if you do. Discipline is consequently very slack & teaching is a struggle; but it's not so bad—we shall soon be comfy. At any rate one is not killed by work. I have Std. IV—45 lads—there is much pretence of high flown work —not much done.

I am rapidly getting over my loneliness & despair; soon I'll settle down & be quite happy here. But there don't seem to be many nice folk here. They are all glib, but not frank; polite, but not warm. Lord, Lord,—I went to a literary society conversazione[3] & nearly discovered the North Pole—such poor fools.

I am making a vain attempt to study—I never get anything done. Somehow I cannot bring my nose down to a good swot. I feel the lack of somebody to be lively with—somebody to swear at & fall out with & enjoy. Pray translate yourself here. Your letter was 'killing'. I shall preserve it.

Au revoir—soyez sage.

DHL

·⟨[22]⟩·

Dear Lou,

Now I've seen sweeter country than Quorn & Woodhouse. Down here it is wonderful. The masses of gorgeous foliage, the sharp hills whose scarps are blazing with Autumn, the round valleys where the

---

1. An Ilkeston school very close to the Pupil-Teacher Centre; probably used for teaching practice.
2. Philip F. T. Smith.
3. Possibly a meeting of the English Association (see E. Nehls, *D. H. Lawrence: A Composite Biography*, Madison, Wisconsin, 1957–9, i. 88, 93).

vivid dregs of Summer have collected—they have almost intoxi-
cated me. Your letter was exceedingly interesting. I'm sure Mr
Smith[1] is quite a ravishing person. Come, come, Louise!

DHL

I've come thro Epsom to Dorking—am going on to Reigate

Addressed: Coteshael Quorn Leicester
Postmarked: Dorking NO 7 08

·◁[23]▷·
12 Colworth Road, Addiscombe, Croydon
16th November 1908

My dear Louie,

Your letter—rather your p.c.—somewhat alarms me. Is school so
bad that you think of chucking up before you get another job?
From my heart, I am sorry. I thought you had got over the most
devilish time; I thought you were comparatively comfortable; I
thought Mr Smith was a great consolation. Are you knocked up?
Why don't you write me a letter? What has put a coldness in your
heart 'envers moi'? Can I guess?

I am so sorry the fight of school is too long, too painful for you.
My God, it is bitter enough at the best; it is the cruellest and most
humiliating sport, this of teaching and trying to tame some fifty or
sixty malicious young human animals. I have some days of despair
myself—this has been one. We are not allowed to punish, you know,
unless we send to the boss' desk for the regulation cane, and enter
up full particulars of the punishment in the cane-book. The boss is
nice, but very flabby; the kids are rough and insolent as the devil. I
had rather endure anything than this continual, petty, debasing
struggle. Shortly I shall be good for very little myself. But this is
one of my black days: it is not really so bad: not so bad. I shall get
on a level some time. Now I am off balance; my life will not go; the
machinery of my soul is all deranged by these shocks of conflict.
It is not broken—I shall recover soon—I may even be happy.

Write and tell me how you are. Why will you be funny half out
of spite—why will you be trivial? Well, well, we must make belief

1. Not identified.

22

we are whole, but most of us are being ground down under one millstone or another.

Forgive me if I am a wet blanket. You make me feel a bit downy, with your news. Tell me how all the world is—tell me you are better

DHL

Dont you think my seriousness rather comical—I do?

Addressed: Coteshael Quorn Leicester
Postmarked: Croydon NO 16 08

·◁[24]▷·
12 Colworth Road, Addiscombe, Croydon
24th November 1908

My dear Louise,

What desolating little letters for my Louise to write—Louise with her arch insouciance, and sportful frivolity. Never mind, my dear; there is a bladder of indigo hanging over every poor young devil's head, and it must squash sooner or later and paint things a black purple. It'll all wash off again—won't it—this damned indigo?— when you have altered your circumstances. It is a cruel position to put you in, in full fight with all that is barbarous and devilish in youthful mankind on the one hand, and with all that is supercilious, and snobbish, and mean, and fault pecking—inspectors, know your-selves—on the other. I'm glad you're chucking up. I would do it straight away, before I got another school, if I were you. Why should you sell—not yourself, because you keep your suffering— but all the sunshine out of yourself for £75 dirty quid. I feel myself swelling with bad language.

As for me—it only needs that I gird up my loins, and take to arm me for the fight the panoply of a good stinging cane—and me voilà! I am making things hum this week: you can guess what things.

Don't be naughty and reserved with me. You know the wells of my sympathy are really profound—the surface just winks a little bit wickedly. I understand your position now too perfectly to treat your confessions with levity. I swear I am a sweet Father Confessor. But seriously, my dear girl, my blood runs hot when I think of the

23

suffering and indignity you are exposed to for the sake of a dirty pittance. If—if—.

What about your writing?[1] Are you too used up to do any now? It is a shame. As for me I have not much time, and not enough tranquillity of soul. My amusements are painting; (go to Aunties & see the three sketches I have sent her) and playing chess with Mr Jones, and larking with Hilda Mary, our eight month, jolly baby. It comforts me inexpressibly if I am a bit downy (that is not often)— to see her bright hazel eyes laughing into mine, and to feel her fat little hands spreading over my face and trying to grasp it. She is such a jolly little beggar—you should hear her laugh when I dance her round the room, or play hide and seek with her.[2]

I hope you will soon be settled—but don't be desperate—it does n't really matter—and don't take anything (I don't mean arsenic—but any job that offers). Your soul is developing its bitter rind of maturity—it must do so, sooner or later, unless you remain forever immature, as most folks do. When you have a good rind you are safe.

Au revoir—soyez encore gai   Yrs DHL

Addressed: Coteshael Quorn Leicestershire
Postmarked: Croydon NO 24 08

·◄[25]►·

Are you going to have your photograph taken this term? I am dubious whether I shall confer a benefit on mankind by having mine taken & thus transmitting my charms through the ages.[3]

---

1. Cf. postscript to 19; and 20.
2. Lawrence's delight in this child led to his two poems *Baby Movements* published in the *English Review*, November 1909 (*Complete Poems*, ii. 912–13).
3. This note (undated) was placed at this point in the correspondence by Louie herself. Cf. Lawrence's letter to Blanche Jennings, 15th December 1908, announcing that he has been photographed (*Collected Letters*, i. 41).

12 Colworth Road, Addiscombe, Croydon
12th January 190[9]

My dear Louise,

How is the mistress of the thirty?—how are the thirty?—how is the kingdom?—who killed the mouse?—was it killed, or merely frightened to death by the shrieks?—or did you get a little boy to do the deed?—do your subjects tremble at the sway of your sceptre? —are you a grand personage in Ratcliffe[1] (it should be Mousecliffe)? —do you prepare your biceps in preparation for the irate mothers?— do you sneak down the byways, avoiding the highways?—does your landlady think you will stand more fattening, or has she decided to reduce your flesh by regulated diet?—do you love the parson?—or is he a curate?—is there anything or anyone to relieve the deadly monotony?—except the thirty?—and the mouse?—and the occasional inspector? do you want any instructions regarding your work in school?—such as how to model mice in clay and cardboard?— or make petticoats—if so you know where to apply. I do not know the Mistress of Mousehole cum Squeake—how shall I address this majesty? Princesses and Persons of Authority must be rather lonely; but power will jam much stale bread. Besides, one is lonelier in a crowd than in a 'cum squeake' with thirty. Here, where one can only herd a few of the shaking multitudes, the herdsman is mucky and insignificant and heavy with indignity. But when the whole flock baa's after one's petticoats, it must be different; it must gladden the heart. Is it not so?

What do you propose to do with your nights, Louise? Read the Life of Charlotte Brontë[2] and weep?—Let it bide a bit, don't let bitterness for poor Carlotta blind your eyes to the young merits of your flock. Will you write—don't begin too soon? Will you draw?— do, it will soothe you, and make yourself a companion to yourself.

We had a devilish jolly time at Christmas; Lord, we were imps; I know three or four folk who would love to shake me. Do you?

I wish I were your assistant in your Kingdom—prime minister, so to speak. Lord, what larks we'd have. I do detest the hundred

1. Ratcliffe-on-the-Wreake, a Leicestershire village where Louie took up the post of headmistress of the Church of England school on 1st January 1909.
2. Probably the biography (1857) by Mrs. Gaskell. (Cf. Lawrence's letter to Blanche Jennings, 4th November 1908: '. . . *Shirley* and *Jane Eyre*, two of my favourite English books', *Collected Letters*, i. 34.)

miles which push you so far off. I should love to visit you in Cum Squeake.

It is you who must write & tell me things. You are a new person to me.

Don't get puffed up   DHL

12 Colworth Road, Addiscombe, Croydon
9th February 1909

My dear Louise,

You do not want me to come so urgently, do you, ma mie? For you know;— out of a host of difficulties, I will give you two:

I am short of money and worse than that: do you think J.,[1] you, and I make a happy triangle? I have a large spicing of devilry and perversity in me; it is more flagrant since I left home; somebody has a bad time when we three meet. Do you not feel it? It gets between my teeth. You understand, do you not? I am sorry I have said it—but—but – – –.

I am glad you are so heavenly. No—I do not know you when there is a murmur of content in your throat like the cooing of doves. Who ever did know you destitute of a grumble and an animosity; not that they were predominant; oh no, they only gave a flavor to the whole, like my devilry does me. But when the days get warmer; when the wild flowers are out, then I will come to you. I promise you. I am impatient for the day.

It is nice to attain one's majority.[2] It is nice to walk, to learn to toddle; there is a great satisfaction in it; there are also, generally, many nasty bumps and much trepidation and anguish of spirit. I am glad you are going to be major. One has always felt behind you the threatening (!!) shadows of Mr & Mrs Burrows. I am glad you are going to walk abroad with no shadow but your own. Damn the hundred miles that push between us; I damn them through my clinched teeth.

I send you a volume of Ibsen; I send it before your birthday; there is generally a blank before a long awaited day. I have a second volume that I will send you on Saturday. Read, in these plays, the

---

1. Jessie Chambers.
2. Louie's 21st birthday was on 13th February 1909.

26

Pretenders first, the Vikings second, and Lady Inger last, so that the first may be best. The Pretenders is by far the best of the three—I will say no more that you may form your own judgments.

I went up to the Academy on Saturday. The winter collection is magnificent.[1] They have some sad, wonderful pictures of the French peasant Bastien Lepage; how sad they are too; grey, with not one gleam of light; that is literal. Then there is our Sargent, a man of startling vigor and brilliance O and cold heart. Leighton has a magnificent piece—the Garden of Hesperides; Millais is only so-so; Waterlow is exquisite; so is Adrian Stokes. There is a Norwegian— Fritz Thaulow—original—striking—very much like Ibsen.

There—I'll send you the other vol soon. Write and tell me if you are not satisfied with me. With all good wishes, I am

Yrs DHL

Addressed: The Lodge, Ratcliffe on Wreake Leicester
(*Postmark torn off*)

·❧[28]❧·
12 Colworth Road, Addiscombe, Croydon
12th February 1909

My dear Louise,

This is the eve of your majority, and I guess you are wildly excited. People send you presents; I wonder why; to comfort you for the loss of your youthful insouciance;? to congratulate you that you have come into your inheritance? Well, you at any rate are to be

1. The artists named by Lawrence (together with their pictures exhibited in the winter collection) are as follows: Jules Bastien-Lepage (1848–84): 'The Potato-Gatherers', 'Pauvre Fauvette', '"Pas Mèche"'. John S. Sargent (1856–1925): 'On his Holiday: Salmon-fishing in Norway', 'Salmon', two portraits of George McCulloch and one of Master Alec McCulloch. Lord Leighton (1830–96): 'The Garden of the Hesperides', 'The Daphnephoria'. Sir John E. Millais (1829–96): 'Sir Isumbras at the Ford', 'In Perfect Bliss', 'Lingering Autumn'. Sir Ernest Waterlow (1850–1919): 'The Orphan', 'Autumn Glory'. Adrian Stokes (1854–1935): 'The Setting Sun', 'The Edge of the River'. Fritz Thaulow (1846–1906): 'A River in an Autumn Sunset', 'A River in Winter with Trees', 'A Factory in Norway' and 'An Old Factory in Norway'. (Thaulow's snow scenes impressed Lawrence: see the poem *A Snowy Day at School*, in *Complete Poems*, ii. 865.) For other accounts of his visit to the winter exhibition, see *Collected Letters*, i. 49, 51–2.

27

congratulated on the last score. You have a good fortune of vigour, and lusty Atalantan strength; there is a treasure of good blood & good health come down to you from countless generations; when your wild ancestors frisked about in meagre wolf-skins, Lord, what wild eyed, shaggy, massive blunderbusses they were; you have plenty of fresh savage blood—Hurray! Can't you just frisk! You have inherited no old sorrow, no dim uneasy culture; you lucky young Amazon. Why do I send you Rosmersholm and Hedda Gabler?[1] But really, my dear, you must be on bowing acquaintance with these people. You, in happy thoughtless—in your comparative jolly savagery of leopard skins and ox-hide buskins—well, I sent you The Vikings; —you will only stare in young, tawny wonder at the pale spectre of Rosmersholm, and the new-fangled madness of Hedda Gabler.

You will like 'The Lady from the Sea'—all English people do; you will say it is the best. Hedda Gabler is subtlest, profoundest— and, I think, truest; least imaginary. Never mind, what have you to do with truths, you, you Atalanta; you would make a good Bacchante, but for your training. You are all right bossing a little show and flinging your big arms about. You would be better on horseback, riding like the devil. Well, well, the world won't let us be young, if it can help it—damn it. I salute you, you breezy Atalanta. You are a woman, remember, so you may run with Hippomenes, or you may enter for contest in Corydon; you might, but for your training. Be jolly, and tell Ibsen's people they are fools; you'll be right.

Why do you ask me about great men, naughty. You know it is a question of the books you have to get 'em from, rather than the choice you may make for yourself. What books have you?

I would select a few typical people: Julius Caesar, Hannibal, Attila, Julian the Apostate, Constantine; one or two of the great saints: Jerome, Anthony, St Francis of Assisi, Catherine of Siena, Thomas à Becket; then Charlemagne, Bayard, Roland, Cœur de Lion, Christopher Columbus; then Hy VIII, William the Silent, Peter the Great; Oliver Cromwell, Chas IX of Sweeden, Kosciusko, Garibaldi; Napoleon; you might have stuck in Robespierre or Danton after Cromwell; you please yourself about Nelson, & Washington, and Abraham Lincoln and so on. Will this do.

---

1. In the second volume of Ibsen's plays referred to in the preceding letter.

Mr Jones[1] is waiting for the letter. Give my regards to all; to J.[2]—is she with you. Tell her I'll write her soon; & I'll write Hilda.[3]

Be jolly—be a woman

Yrs DHL

·◁[29]▷·
12 Colworth Road, Addiscombe, Croydon
28th February 1909

Ma chère Louise,

I have been reviling myself these last ten days for my ingratitude in not replying and thanking you for the snowdrops. They were so beautiful—alas, they are dead. At first I could not reply to you, because the flowers made me long so much for the country, for Ratcliffe on Wreake, and the mill bank covered with snowdrops. Flowers are scarce here. Mrs Jones buys a bunch of box-leaves and laurel—funereal evergreen, enough for one vase—it is two pence. In the town the flower sellers are gay and brilliant; but in the daytime the flowers are dear, and one is not there to buy late at night. Besides, the mimosa, the vivid scarlet anemones, and the flaccid narcissi from the flower-trays in the street are not snowdrops gathered in the mill garden, on the banks of the Wreake. The snowdrops one buys in bunches, with their poor little noses packed tight together, turned upwards to the winter sky, like white beans stuck in a green cup—these are not snowdrops gathered in the mill garden on the banks of the Wreake—these are not snowdrops from under the hazel brake in the steep dell in the woods of Strelley.[4] Louisa, oh Louisa, my heart aches for the country, and those splendid hours we have had. The town too is good; it has books, and people; it is not so desolating; one cannot there be lonely enough to feel the wistful misery of the country; above all, the town is valuable for the discipline it gives one's nature; but, in the end, for congenial sympathy, for poetry, for work, for original feeling and expression, for perfect companionship with one's friends—give me the country.

1. Lawrence's landlord. 2. Jessie Chambers.
3. Hilda Shaw, a contemporary of Lawrence and Louie at University College where she too gained a First Class Teacher's Certificate. She corresponded with Louie until at least 1911.
4. A small village 3 miles east of Ilkeston.

29

In the end—after a while—a year or two—I shall come back into the country. If I can, I too shall take a headship in the country—not quite so small as yours, oh Louisa, school-mistress Louisa—but I too shall not be very exacting.

School is really very pleasant here. I have tamed my wild beasts—I have conquered my turbulent subjects, and can teach in ease and comfort. But still I long for the country and for my own folks. I think one never forms friendships like those one forms at home, before twenty. I have no need, I have no desire, to fold these new people into my heart. But the old folks—!

To cure me of my madness for the country I took a trip last week to Wimbledon, through Kingston Vale, over to Richmond Park, and back over Wimbledon Common. Kingston Vale is lovely—beautiful groves of silver birch more silvery than any I have seen. Richmond Park is glorious; it is history, it is romance, it is allegory, it is myth. The oaks are great and twisted like Norwegian tales, like the Vikings; the beeches are tremendous, black like steel—Robin Hood, and Sir Galahad have travelled through the bracken up the steep little hills, the nymphs and satyrs have sported round the ponds, where surely there are naiads. You would love Richmond, Louisa; together, we should spend a perfect day there. Some time in the summer, do come here for a week end. Have you any relatives in London? But do come down here some time. Wimbledon Common, too, is fascinating: ladies, gentlemen, grooms, girls, galloping on horseback over the heath and down hill through the birch-woods; Territorials playing at war all over the great Common; scarlet coated golfers moving like vivid flowers; the old windmill—the great view of Surrey—come with me to Wimbledon too sometime.

What do I write. I continue that old work of mine.[1] Sometime, I hope, it will be finished. I have to do it over and over again, to make it decent. Some time, surely, it will be of some value—and then you shall read it too.

We are only six weeks from Easter. What are your plans, if any? The time will soon be upon us. What are your plans?

I wrote Hilda[2] a long letter—and she has replied with a longer. I must write her again. I do not love writing letters, though.

---

1. He had begun *The White Peacock* about Whitsuntide 1906; he re-wrote it in its final form during his first year in Croydon, 1908–9.
2. Cf. p. 29 n. 3.

What books do you read now. I have read much modern work since I came here Joseph Conrad, & Björnsterne Björnsterne,[1] Wells,[2] Tolstoi. I love modern work. You have more time than I to write—Write long letters

Au revoir DHL

Addressed: The Lodge, Ratcliffe on Wreake   Leicester
Postmarked: Croydon MR 1 09

·◁[30]▷·
12 Colworth Road, Addiscombe, Croydon
11th March 1909

My dear Louise,

Now that the flowers are almost dead I write to thank you for them. They have looked lovely on the table. I have had them in a low dish. Now only a few snowdrops and primroses remain, so they are in a little vase. Snowdrops are exquisite little things; poor little mites!—long into the night—we don't go to bed with the sun—they have poised with spread wings over the piano, widespread wings that are pathetically lifted in a hopeless flight. It was better in the day when the canary sang—but after eleven o'clock—near midnight —when Dick sat secure in his false night—immune in the dark blue wrapping of an old apron—poor little things—they were still wide spread. I enjoyed the winter aconites immensely—they are very delicate and pure in their colouring. They are found wild a few miles out from here; the boss brought some to school. Do these grow wild round Mousehole?

We have had some despicable weather—I can hardly say vile enough things about it. How have you found it? Of course, in town, it is not quite so bad as in the country. But I have to cross a piece of wild waste land on my way to School—land where the grass is wild and trodden into mud—where the brick-layer's hammer chinks, chinks the funeral bell of my piece of waste land—and there the mud is inexpressible.

1. Björnson (1832–1910), Norwegian poet, novelist and dramatist.
2. Lawrence had just read *Tono-Bungay*, Wells's latest novel serialised in *The English Review* (see *Collected Letters*, i. 51, 55).

I am just going down town to a lecture by some pot or other on Arithmetic—I guess I shall be bored—We had a lecture on geography last week by Dr Herbertson[1]—a very great gun from Oxford —and he bored me excruciatingly. I liked Margaret von Wyss[2] on Nature Study—very much. I am sick of meetings & one thing & another.

In a month today I shall be home. Great Scott—Christmas is yesterday—Easter tomorrow. Tempus fugit. We are grown up.

What are you going to do at Easter? Are you coming over? I hope the weather will pick up before then—the brute! I must have a day with you somehow. Perhaps when we take our Easter Monday jaunt we may meet.

You have soon established a circle of friends—and they make much of you, do they? Oh lucky girl—the world has always a cosy corner for thee if thou turn thy face to look for it.

I am very sorry to hear of your father's accident. I hope he is better now. Remember yours was only such a little note.

Au revoir—Miss Country Mouse

DHL

Addressed: The Lodge Ratcliffe on Wreake Leicester
Postmarked: Croydon MR 11 09

·◁[31]▷·
12 Colworth Road, Addiscombe, Croydon
28th March 1909

My dear Louise,

You shocking girl—fancy talking about 'Coals to Newcastle' as a figure for Snowdrops to me digging in the City! And I make verses to those same 'Coals'![3] Louisa—you are the same wild barbarian— do not ever pretend to be cultivated.

I am sorry you have been knocked up. The Roots[4] will cure you. At any rate your life is very comfy. Why do you tell me *about* the

---

1. A. J. Herbertson, Oxford Professor of Geography.
2. Perhaps Clothilde von Wyss, author of *Gardens in their Seasons, a Nature Book for Boys and Girls* (1912) and *The Teaching of Nature Study* (1927).
3. No poem survives written specifically *to* snowdrops.
4. Mrs. Pearl Root was Louie's landlady at The Hall Lodge, Ratcliffe-on-the-Wreake.

funniness of your world in general, & never give me the fun. It is not fair. I don't like '*abouts*'—I want some of the real stuff of the fun.

Here fun is fast and furious, as you will see if you take a London paper. It is election—voting day on Monday.[1] There are great crowds surging through the streets—there is a searchlight wandering overhead through the darkness—there are cinematographs at upper-storey windows, there are Suffragettes in thousands & tens of thousands processing and crying in the wilderness—the place is strident with voices & placards—rustling with leaflets & pamphlets.

I was in the fun the other night; I was in the mad grip of the crowd before the Suffragettes. If you had felt the surge, the vicious rush of one solid mass of men towards the car where the two women were alone, one standing crying scorn on the brutes, the other sitting with dark, sad eyes!

'If men cannot control themselves' said Miss Cameron 'it is time women had some power to control them.' We in front heard, and the fellows yelled. Then the whole mob howled and like one shoulder, the hundred men in the mob pressed onto the car, threatening to overturn it. The women gave way—inch by inch the car retreated—amid howls & yells of derision. The search-light splashed down the street on the close pack white faces and dark mouths—Louisa, have you seen such, you barbarian?—it would have frightened your fresh, barbarian heart.

I went to the radical van. A handsome, sensitive man with a face of extraordinary pallor was trying to speak, & the mob was enjoying itself. Chant to yourself, to the tune of the Bow chimes, which had just rung out from the Town Hall clock 'Sit down, Sit down— sit down, sit down'—& so on—varying it with 'Shut up, Shut up—Shut up Shut up.' Think of fifty fools chanting together, while the words of hot, painful conviction were crushed on your lips. Yap to yourself 'Hodge, Hodge, Hodge, Hodge' some thousand times,[2] and imagine fifty throats yapping in unison whilst you uttered the cry of your heart. Speak your deep convictions to somebody, and let them insult you and heckle you and call you a liar. Louisa, tell me about your farmers who fall out. I tell you about the town, where

1. The bye-election at Croydon on 29th March was the scene of keen activity by the suffragettes. The National Union of Women's Suffrage Societies campaigned vigorously and particularly harassed the Conservative candidate Sir Robert Hermon-Hodge; he had declared his opposition to their cause. (See *The Times* account on 29th March 1909.)
2. Conservative supporters voiced their opposition to the suffragettes by chanting the name of their own candidate.

a sensitive, handsome man of culture is tortured for three long hours. When at last his voice breaks, & a word becomes a screech—the crowd jeers to shake the little red stars high up. There was a big, splendid woman in the wagon, a woman with full, oval face—great swinging ear-rings, and gold ornaments along her arms. See her put her hand on the arm of the speaker, and look up pleading that he should not let it hurt him—that he shall not answer in wrath; he looks down at her with his pale drawn face and does not see her. He goes on with his speech—he lifts his hat, and the dark hair falls on his forehead—he is overwhelemed in the din, and his eyes glitter from side to side. The woman stands behind knitting her brows, and opening her mouth pitifully with bewilderment & despair. She too is a barbarian, big and splendid—but smoothed and shapely through the grooming of great world. She mounts the side of the cart boldly—and aloft there, laughs out a splendid laugh to the mob, & lifts her arm to them for respite—in vain. Their souls are lusted with cruelty. Louisa, is the twang of the Roots quaint—and is there nothing more in life? Louisa, do any of your youngsters limp to school; through the snow or the fine weather, limp to school because they are crippled with broken boots. Have you seen wounds on the feet of your boys, from great mens boots they wear which are split across. My dear old button boots—they are barely recognisable under the front desk. Have you seen the children gathered to free breakfasts at your school—half a pint of milk & a lump of bread— eighty boys and girls sitting down the bare boards? Louisa, my dear, life is not gentle, and amusing, and pleasant, I am afraid.

I went to the Dulwich Art Gallery yesterday—took the car to the high level of the Crystal Palace, and looked out over the great glade, to Westminster far in the distance, and the mist of all London between. I felt a long way from home and the quaint, amusing country. I went down the long College hill to the gallery. It is a lovely & lovable little place, full of old, fascinating pictures— Colonel Lovelace looking with full, womanly glance; the saddening face of Chas II—pale Chas I[1]—all the old people in one dear nook. There is a fine collection of Dutch picturs—Cuyp, Teniers, Wouverman, Jordaens, Hobbemas, Van der [Velde],[2] & the rest. I love the

---

1. The three portraits mentioned by Lawrence are of Richard Lovelace (catalogue No. 363), artist unknown; (No. 424) Charles II, ascribed to John Greenhill; (No. 414) Charles I 'a copy after Van Dyck'.
2. Lawrence wrote 'Helder'. Dulwich possesses works by both Adriaen and Willem Van der Velde.

human, sturdy, noble Dutchies. There are one or two charming Watteaus, some splendid Guido Renis, three or four great Murillos, & Velasquez, & Titian, & Reynolds & the rest. Many quaint interesting Poussins—such a splendid little gallery—so little, so rich. I should like to take you—& then to the Academy, to see the moderns. In the old pictures sorrow is beautiful; in the new it is awful—Bastien Lepage; the old is the divine sorrow of fruitfulness, the new is the cruel sorrow of destruction. Louisa, my dear, thou art a century or so behind—and I am at the tip of the years. So thou art very comfortable & charming, & I am uncomfortable & a nuisance.

I should like to come to see you—I should like you to come & see me.

Addio DHL

Addressed: The Lodge Ratcliffe on Wreake Leicester
Postmarked: Croydon MR 28 09

◄[32]►
Croydon   4 Mai 1909

Ma chère Louise,

Mille mercis du livre—il est arrivé aujourd'hui, et je le trouve charmant. Je vais copier quelques-uns des tableaux—vous me permettrez de le retenir pendant quelque temps, n'est ce pas?

Ne m'avez vous pas écrit un billet pour accompagner le livre ou pour m'en prévenir?—je n'en ai pas reçu. Vous n'êtes pas fachée contre moi, assurément. J'attends avec impatience quelque chose de votre part, car il est étrange que le livre soit venu sans aucun mot. Une bonne poignée

DHL

Addressed: The Lodge Ratcliffe on Wreake Leicester
Postmarked: Croydon MY 4 09

I have not written that letter—I am *so* lazy. Today I've had a ripping time out on the North Downs. You *would* have enjoyed it had you been with me. Your flowers lasted such a long time—you would hardly believe the great admiration they received.

I *will* cycle to Quorn for a day. I want to go to Leicester too.[1] Perhaps I may stay there the night. It will be towards the week-end. I must see how I can arrange it. Auntie told me you had been to see her—you are a favourite of hers.

When will you come to London? Will you stay the night at Croydon, like J.[2]—or is it too improper?

When I see you at Whit—will you tell me the news that you are going to tell me sometime. I am looking forward to seeing you. The weather is glorious & I revel in it. We have a holiday next Wednesday—I think I may go to the Derby at Epsom.

Au revoir DHL

Addressed: The Lodge Ratcliffe on Wreake Leicester
Postmarked: Caterham Valley MY 22 09

Addiscombe   22nd June 1909

Time is barren, and my wits are sterile in these grey days—so I am not productive enough for a letter. It *is* a fraud you can't come to Shanklin.[3] Are you really going to wait till the 10th of July—a fortnight on Saturday?—it seems a long time. Things are going rather slowly here—how is the Mousehole?[4] Has the Cat of Fate committed many depredations yet?—she was on the warpath when last you wrote, and the mice were scuttling about pit-a-pat with grief and

---

1. To the home of his Aunt Ada.   2. Jessie Chambers.
3. In the Isle of Wight, where Lawrence had arranged to take a holiday in August. (See 36, 38, 39.)
4. Cf. 26.

woe. Those drawings, alas—I got them ready, and some malicious fiend made off with them; I must wait till I get some more. I'm very sorry. How are you?

Addio. DHL

Addressed: The Lodge Ratcliffe on Wreake Leicester Postmarked: Croydon JU 22 09

·◁[35]▷·
12 Colworth Road, Addiscombe, Croydon
30th June 1909

My dear Louie,

What am I to write to you about? There is only one thing to confess, and that is that I have been cross this last week or so; I think it must be the weather.

I wish you were coming on Saturday, instead of the following. I just feel like a fuddle. I vote we don't go to the Tower—that we go straight down to St. Pauls—then down the Strand to Trafalgar Square. You can choose for yourself there. Either you can have a glance through the National Gallery, to look at the Corot and the Velasquezs & the Rembrandts, or you can go straight down to the Embankment, to Westminster & the Tate Gallery. You will do as J. did, I presume, bring lunch, and eat it by the River, then we will get tea in Town. After tea we will go into Hyde Park for a little time, and then we can go east again to the theatre—we *will* go to the theatre—we'll go to Drury Lane, where there is an Italian Opera company: no we won't we'll go to Covent Garden Opera, and I hope Tetrazzini will be singing.[1] Since you are not going to have a holiday, I don't see why you shouldn't have a real downright fuddle on that memorable day. To be sure I am not very well off—I wish I were not so handicapped for cash—so that I cannot pay the heavy ex's, but I want a giddy time with you. I am always so disappointed that I am so poor and that I cannot stand the treat altogether.

Life is flowing very slowly just now. Why *aren't* you coming on Saturday—I think it will be fine. Why will it be more convenient to come on the 10th?

1. She was to sing in *Lucia di Lammermoor* at the Royal Opera, Covent Garden, on Saturday, 10th July 1910.

I have got your book of pictures yet.[1] Shall I send it, or let you take it? What time do you come—there is not the slightest fear of my missing you. By the way, you will come to Marylebone—G.C.[2] —wont you? I want some particulars. If you come G.C. we shall be fairly well west to start with, and you could go to Marble Arch straight off & walk down Oxford St to see the great shops, if it so likes you, & we could move East, finishing at St Pauls before the theatre.

I am glad you are writing stories. I can't do 'em myself. Send me them, please, & I'll see if I can put a bit of surface on them & publish them for you. We'll collaborate, shall we?—I'm sure we should do well. At any rate send me the tales at once, and I'll send em to the publisher some time or other in your name.

Be good, now, and keep a good stock of energy & spirits for your coming to London.

'Till I see you, farewell   DHL

Neville[3] wants your address—I am giving it him. He wishes—wistfully—you were going with us to Shanklin. I am sure he would be gone on you if you'd let him—and for all you say you dont I know you rather like him.

·◁[36]▷·

Vous devriez me penser longtemps à vous écrire. J'ai envoyé le cinq schellings—cela était la somme, n'est ce pas—5/-?—Je l'ai mise à la poste aujourd'hui.[4] Bientôt, avant la fin de la semaine, je vous enverrai l'autre histoire—je ne l'ai pas encore préparée tout à fait. Je suis heureux à apprendre que vous allez à Barrow. Certainement, donnez beaucoup de choses de ma part à notre petite Nina.[5] Je vous y écrirai. Mon addresse à Shanklin, c'est

c/o Mrs Holbrooks, Fern Villa, Carters Rd, Shanklin, I.o.W.

1. Cf. 32.   2. Great Central Railway.   3. Cf. p. 11 n. 4.
4. Lawrence had sent his short story *Goose Fair* to the London and Provincial Press Agency, to be placed with a publisher. The Agency wrote (on 20th July 1909) requesting 5s. as the registration fee.
5. Nina Stewart—a contemporary of Louie and Lawrence at College—lived at Barrow-in-Furness; Lawrence's letters 38 and 39 were addressed to her home. She remained a correspondent of Louie for many years.

Nous y allons le Samedi—et vous partez pour Barrow le même jour, n'est ce pas? J'espère que vous continuez d'être de bon coeur—les vacances commencent le jeudi, heureusement

Addio. DHL

Addressed: Schoolmistress Ratcliffe on Wreake Leicester
Postmarked: Croydon JY 26 09

·◁[37]▷·
12 Colworth Road, Addiscombe, Croydon
27th July 1909

My dear Louise,

Here is your tale—you will not like it. But tell me what you think of it. After Thursday, till Saturday, my address is

c/o Mrs Berry, Low Hill, Roxburgh Park, Harrow on the Hill.

—then, after Saturday, Shanklin.—Fern Villa, Carters Rd. I told you, did I not, that I had sent the five bob to the Press Agency. I had forgotten all they said in the letter, so don't know whether they wanted anything else.[1] You may go whacks with me in that, if you like, and then we will go whacks in the profits[2]—when they come: 'Ah, woful when!'

We are in a bit of a muddle. Did I tell you that father went and had an accident last week, and that they are not sure whether he and mother will be able to come down on Saturday? I shall be raving mad if they can't, but I'm hoping for the best. We are having about five hours in London before proceeding to Portsmouth—it is very giddy to contemplate. I am beginning to get excited, although the weather is so damnable that if the most milky saint in heaven had to endure it he'd curdle your blood with wicked language.

I assure you, by the way, that my stories are most freezingly polite. The nom de guerre, as you will see, is a happy mixture of you and me: you are the body, I the head. Qu'en dites vous! I believe you are utterly unrecognisable under my figurehead.

---

1. Cf. p. 38 n. 4. Lawrence had sent the Agency's letter to Louie; it is preserved among the Burrows papers (MS LaB 186).
    2. i.e. share the 5s. fee and share the proceeds. Cf. 50.

My cold is somewhat better—I have not done any more tales. I shall be glad to see your other buds—when we get back from the holiday—Shanklin & Barrow. I will send you a line there & I'll greet Nina by the way. Don't let my tone in 'Cupid & the Puppy'[1] influence you—you write in your best sentimental vein. I send it to school to occupy your dinner hour

Au revoir, love DHL

·◖ 38 ◗·
Fern Villa, Carter Road, Shanklin

Here we are, in a most lovely place. We are sitting on the cliffs among the bracken looking down through the ash-trees at the sea. The sea is shimmering pale green and purple (do you remember the pictures in the Tate?) There are eight men-of war in the offing, and the guns are muttering in salutes as the King's ship passes.[2] We are on the way to Ventnor—walking over the cliffs. Give my regards to Nina[3]—I hope she is well. Why do you want to copy out the 'Cupid'?[4]—what for?

Addio DHL

Addressed: c/o Mrs Stewart   44 Nelson St   Barrow-in-Furness
Postmarked: Ventnor 2 AU 09

·◖ 39 ◗·

Thanks for your card: are not we having ripping weather? We spent the day at Cowes on Friday—at the regatta—& we went over Osborne House:[5] it was very nice, but Queens have poor taste— German & vulgar. Yesterday we sailed round the Island—it was

1. Presumably the title of Louie's short story mentioned in the opening sentence, and re-written by Lawrence. Cf. 38, 40, 41, 42.
2. The Fleet was reviewed by Edward VII and the Czar of Russia. (This and other experiences during the holiday were later adapted for use in Lawrence's second novel, *The Trespasser*.)
3. Cf. p. 38 n. 5.   4. Cf. n. 1 above
5. The favourite home of Queen Victoria. A Royal Naval College was opened there in 1903.

40

ripping—steamed a long way between the iniquitous ironclads—the Dreadnought[1] was in the harbour. Give my regards to Nina—what day shall I ride over to Quorn?   DHL

Addressed: c/o Mrs Stewart 44 Nelson St Barrow in Furness
Postmarked: Shanklin AU 10 09

·◁[40]▷·

I am writing at my brother's,[2] in Nottingham. It is he who is the holy man[3]—not I. He is ill, and mother & I are come to see him. I am so sorry I could not come today: last night I went for Alan's[4] bike, to be ready for the morning. When I was at the top of Underwood hill the rain came on & I was drenched. The bike was not ridable this morning, & I have a cold. Mater does not want me to come while the weather is unsettled, she was so upset about my state yesterday—poor ma, she takes trifles so seriously. I will write you a letter tomorrow or so—j'ai une petite nouvelle, mais elle n'est pas bonne. Envoyez moi, s'il vous plait, le conte de Cupide.[5] Je l'enverrai à un 'Mag'. Je me fâche beaucoup de n'avoir pu venir. J'écrirai une lettre demain.

                                        Yrs DHL

Addressed: Coteshael Quorn Leicester
Postmarked: Nottingham AU 18 09

·◁[41]▷·
Lynn Croft, Eastwood, Notts
19th August 1909

My dear Louie,
    I am very sorry if you have been disappointed again—don't expect me any more, the devil holds the whip hand of affairs. I had

1. The famous battleship, launched in 1906; its name provided a synonym for an 'ironclad'.
                    2. George Lawrence.
3. A reference to the printed heading on the postcard: 'St. Ann's Well Road and Edwin Street Baptist Mission.'
            4. Alan Chambers. 5. Cf. p. 40 n. 1.

41

engaged myself out today, tomorrow, Saturday, and four or five times next week. When there is only left one day, odd, here & there, & there is the weather to contend with, & somebody else's old bike, and ma's, and my own temper—Oh Lordy Lordy, it's enough to make you swear.

Then my little news—damn it! When I was at Shanklin the agency people wrote me to say that they had received my letter, but no p.o.[1]—that they would have written before, but that they awaited my word, thinking I had made a mistake. I believe it is a palpable lie—I will not send them any more money. I shall ask them for the 'Goose Fair' back, if they don't write me soon. There is a new Magazine coming out—should be out now—The Tramp.[2] I'm going to send my tales direct to the mags now: so let me have the Puppy,[3] & I'll go through it & revise it & send it; send me any more of yours you want to see 'slaughtered'—& send me those you wish to preserve as they are, so that I may crit them. I am beastly disappointed about one thing & another, but it's no use letting on. When does your mother come back—where has she gone?—are the children with her?—how do you like housekeeping? For the Lord's sake, send me that draft of a novel, I bet it would amuse me. You know, your forte would be short stories—it will take you at least three years to write a novel—at school.

Are you cross?—well, so I am also. Devil take everything!

Valete DHL

Addressed: 'Coteshael' Quorn Leicester
Postmarked: Eastwood AU 19 09

·◄[42]►·
12 Colworth Road, Addiscombe, Croydon
11th September 1909
My dear Louise,

It is so nice of you to remember me—how did you know the date? I am very fond of Jefferies, and the pieces in the Open Air are so

1. i.e. postal (money) order. Cf. p. 38 n. 4.
2. The first number appeared in March 1910; the magazine ran for one year.
3. Cf. p. 40 n. 1.

many of them down here.[1] There is always a tiny pain in receiving—I suppose it comes from a lurking sense that we get more kindness than we deserve.

I have been very busy this week, or I would have written to you. I have never even written for the story from those people. Is the address: London & Provincial Press Agency, 26 Shaftesbury Avenue W. If not, write & correct me, then will I demand back your, my, story.[2]

The truth is, I am very much occupied with some work of my own. It is supposed to be a secret, but I guess I shall have to tell you. The editor of the English Review has accepted some of my verses, and wants to put them into the English Review, the November issue.[3] But you see they are all in the rough, and want revising, so this week & so on I am very hard at work, slogging verse into form. I shall be glad when I have finished: then I may get on with the prose work. The editor, Ford Madox Hueffer, says he will be glad to read any of the work I like to send him—which is a great relief, is it not? No more thieving agencies for us. Before I do anything with the Puppy tale,[4] I want to write it out again, and I don't know when I shall have time to do that. I never thought of myself blossoming out as a poet—I had planted my beliefs in my prose.

I am glad to hear you managed your inspectors so well—you are a dab. I wish I were in Nottingham at this moment—it is two o'clock —to be going with you to the theatre. I should very much like to see 'Strife'.[5] Last week I went to the Lyceum, to see Justin McCarthy's[6] 'Proud Prince'—never saw such rot in my life.

Mary[7] is responsible for this shocking page—she is larking with me as I write on my knee—another onslaught!

What devilish weather we're having! Can you keep happy?

Addio DHL

Addressed: 'Coteshael' Quorn Leicester
Postmarked: Croydon SP 11 09

1. Louie had sent for Lawrence's birthday on 11th September a copy of Richard Jefferies' *The Open Air* (1885).
2. Cf. p. 38 n. 4.
3. It is well known that Jessie Chambers sent some of Lawrence's poems—possibly without his consent—to Ford Madox Hueffer, editor of the *English Review* (see E. Nehls, *D. H. Lawrence*, i. 102–6). The sequence entitled *A Still Afternoon* appeared in the November issue.
4. Cf. p. 40 n. 1. 5. John Galsworthy's latest play (1909).
6. The Irish playwright (1830–1912).
7. The eighteen-month-old daughter of his landlord.

43

12 Colworth Road, Addiscombe, Croydon
17th October 1909

Dear Louisa,

Here I am at last, & I have got 'Goose Fair'.[1] See what you think of it. I am sorry I have kept the pictures so long.

You ask me first of all what kind of a 'paper' is the English Review: It is a half-crown magazine, which has only been out some twelve months. It is very fine, and very 'new'. There you will meet the new spirit at its best: and, if you belong to the N.U.T.,[2] you can get the Review at much reduced rates. It is the best possible way to get into touch with the new young school of realism, to take the English Review. In this month's issue, there is a particularly fine story 'The Nest'—such a one as you would find nowhere but in the English, and a magnificent story.[3] My four pieces of verse come out next month:[4] I am not taking a nom de plume: I feel rather daft when I think of appearing, if only in so trivial a way, before the public.

You ask me also how you will get your stories typed. You must send them to a professional typist: look in any newspaper among the Authors, Agencies list in the adverts, and you will see men wanting to type M.S.S. for about 8d. per 1000 words. Since a short story is only about 3 or 4 thousand words, it would not ruin you to have one done, when you got a really good one. I return you the 'Goose Fair' —you may as well keep it entirely.[5] If I had it I should write it all out again, & vivify in places: but you will use your own discretion. When you have got your story from J.,[6] let me see it. I am always interested. But pray, do not write *too* romantically: write as near to life as possible. You needn't be pessimistic or cynical, but it is always best to be true. The English Review is finely truthful, on the whole.

I went to Wagners Tristan & Isolde last night, and was very disappointed. I would much rather have seen 'Strife'. Tristan is long, feeble, a bit hysterical, without grip or force. I was frankly sick of it.

I am glad your school thrives so well. For myself, I am sick of things: I shall go to France as soon as I can. Forgive me for being so long writing.

Yours DHL

1. Presumably Lawrence had recovered his manuscript from the Agency. (Cf. 36, 41.)
2. National Union of Teachers.
3. A story by Anne Douglas Sedgwick, *English Review*, October 1909, pp. 392–425.
4. Cf. p. 43 n. 3.   5. Louie kept it to the end of her life.   6. Jessie Chambers.

44

[early November 1909]

Dear Lou,

Many thanks for your suggestion. If there is anything else, you alter it.

What I want you to do is to send in the story[1] for the Christmas prize competition: get a Guardian & see what it says. The prize per story is £3, & they keep the copyright. They would print your name: are you satisfied? You will also have to swear that the story is yours—but what does it matter! If we win we go whacks, according to agreement. Do you recognise the people?—a glorified Lois Mee (is she glorified) & a glorified (?) Taylor?[2]

Tom Smith is just the same:[3] no worse, I think. We had a very good time—went to the Haymarket to see 'Don'[4]—jolly good! We enjoyed ourselves. I saw Machen:[5] he is the same blithering cocky fool.

You will have seen the Review by now: they sent me a complimentary copy.[6] Yes, tell me what you think, I am really anxious to know. Have you done any more at the story of yours?

I have not been up to much just lately: forgive me if I do not write any more, I am tired tonight. School is all right, but the weather! Floods—and the fog has blown down thick from London today.

Addio DHL

---

1. *Goose Fair*. (Cf. 45.)
2. Lois Mee was a fellow student at University College, Nottingham, and presumably is the 'Lois' in the story. 'Taylor' was probably Lewis Taylor, another College contemporary; he was most likely the original of Will Selby.
3. Probably another fellow student at Nottingham, T. A. Smith.
4. A comedy by Rudolf Besier. Lawrence saw the play on 30th October 1909 (see *Collected Letters*, i. 57); hence the conjectural date of this letter. (*Don* was taken off on 29th November.)
     5. Perhaps John S. Machin, a fellow student at College.
6. Cf. p. 43 n. 3.

12 Colworth Road, Addiscombe, Croydon
20th November 1909

My dear Louie,

If I don't write you, don't be cross. I am so busy.[1]

Concerning 'Goose Fair'.[2] You will have got the rules, & you will have found, I think, that I could not send in the tale for the competition. If you think I might, I am quite willing to have the thing under my own name: only you can legally claim that the tale is as much your child as mine.

Last Sunday I went up to lunch with Ford Madox Hueffer,[3] & with Violet Hunt,[4] who is rich, & a fairly well-known novelist. They were both delightful. Hueffer took me to tea at Ernest Rhy's:[5] he edits heaps of classics—Dents Everyman's, for instance. He is very nice indeed, and so is his wife, Grace Rhys, who writes stories. After tea we went on to call on H. G. Wells who also lives up at Hampstead. He is a funny little chap: his conversation is a continual squirting of thin little jets of weak acid: amusing, but not expansive. There is no glow about him. His two boys, in pale blue dressing gowns, came in and kissed us goodnight.

Hueffer is reading my novel.[6] He says it's good, & is going to get it published for me. He also says I ought to get out a volume of verse, so you see how busy I am.

I went on Tuesday to Violet Hunts 'at home' at the Reform Club in Adelphi Terrace, on the Embankment. It was very jolly. Elizabeth Martindale[7] & Ellaline Terriss[8] and Mary Cholmondeley[9] were there—and Ezra Pound.[10] He is a well-known American poet—a good one. He is 24, like me,—but his god is beauty, mine, life. He is jolly nice: took me to supper at Pagnani's, and afterwards we went

---

1. A contributory factor to his busy life was his friendship with Agnes Holt, a colleague on the Davidson Road School staff.
2. Cf. 44.
3. Hueffer, later Ford Madox Ford (1873–1939), novelist and critic; editor of the *English Review*.
4. Hueffer was hoping to divorce his wife in order to marry Violet Hunt.
5. Rhys (1859–1946) had edited Dekker's plays (1888), and *The Lyric Poets* (1894–99), as well as the Everyman's Library.
6. *The White Peacock*. 7. Mrs. Hueffer's sister.
8. A well-known variety actress; later Lady (Seymour) Hicks.
9. A minor novelist (1859–1925); her satirical novel *Red Pottage* created a stir in 1899.
10. The 24-year-old poet had been dismissed from his post at Wabash College, Indiana, travelled in Europe, and now settled in London. His *Personae and Exultations* appeared in 1909.

down to his room at Kensington. He lives in an attic, like a tradi-
tional poet—but the attic is a comfortable well furnished one. He is
an American Master of Arts & a professor of the Provençal group of
languages, & he lectures once a week on the minstrels [at] the London polytechnic. He is rather remarkable—a good bit of a genius, &
with not the least self consciousness.

This afternoon I am going up to tea with him & we are going out
after to some friends who will not demand evening dress of us. He
knows W B Yeats & all the Swells. Aren't the folks kind to me: it is
really wonderful. Hueffer is splendid: I have met a gentleman
indeed in him, & an artist.

There, I have no time. Write and tell me your news, I like to
receive letters.

Forgive me this rude haste, will you

Yours DHL

·◦[46]◦·

[12 Col]worth Road, Addiscombe, Croydon
11th December 1909

My dear Louie,

What a wretch I am to neglect you so long! In truth, I am
become a shocking correspondent. I have not any news to tell.

I sent the story, with another I have written,[1] up to Ford Madox
Hueffer on Thursday. He will tell me what to do with them.

I am going up to dine with Ezra Pound tonight. We shall meet a
crowd of other literary folk. I will tell you about it later. Next week
I am going up to Grace Rhys to meet various poetry people. I am
to take some of my unpublished verses to read.[2] I do not look forward to these things much. I shall feel such a fool. I shall be able to
tell you all about things at Christmas.

I hear Ada has asked you over for a few days.[3] That is all right!
And she is going to see you? I *must* squeeze in a day this time, at
Quorn. I will see what mother says. I hope the weather will be fine,
& we can have a giddy time. I am anxiously awaiting Christmas—
are not you? I am sick of this term.

1. Probably *Goose Fair* and *Odour of Chrysanthemums*.
2. For an account of this (or another similar) occasion by Ernest Rhys, see E. Nehls,
D. H. Lawrence, i. 129–32.
3. Lawrence's sister Ada had invited Louie to Eastwood. (Cf. 48.)

Have you heard the B Sc. results—everybody failed except one second year man: T A Smith, Preston, Morrison, everybody. Sad, is it not? I am very sorry for T.A.S.[1]

Don't be cross with me for not writing. You write to me instead. There is only a fortnight

A Noël DHL

Addressed: 'Coteshael' Quorn Leicester
Postmarked: Croydon DE 11 09

·⊲[47]⊳·
12 Colworth Road
23rd December 1909

Dear Lou,

I am so tired. It is nearly midnight. I have just finished packing —I go home tomorrow. I hope you'll like Benson.[2]

When are you coming to us? Oh, I have been so busy—such a rush! I feel as if I had not had a rest for years. But will make everything straight in the holiday.

A jolly, jolly Christmas to you. I shall see you before the New Year

Vale DHL

·⊲[48]⊳·
Eastwood 30.12.1909

Chère Louise,

Pourquoi ne vous avez pas écrit? Nous attendons de vos nouvelles. Vous allez venir le Samedi, n'est ce pas—le jour de l'An? Dites nous l'heure, et nous allons vous rencontrer au station. Empressez de me répondre

DHL

Addressed: 'Coteshael' Quorn Leicestershire
Postmarked: Eastwood DE 30 09

1. A T. A. Smith graduated B.Sc. in Chemistry in 1910. (Cf. p. 45 n. 3.)
2. Not identified.

12 Colworth Road, Addiscombe, Croydon
23rd January 1910

My dear Louise,

Do not be cross with me if I do not write letters. I scribble so much, I can only set to a letter with greatest difficulty

Thanks for the enclosures. I have re-written the White Stocking.[1] The Chimney Sweeper[2] is much improved, I think. You need, I think, to elaborate a bit: do a bit of character drawing, & give your locality: you want to give more setting: the figures are all right, but examine the scene *pictorially*—it is not there. Gather the picture— get the essentials for *description*—present to the eye. The conversation is very amusing. I should offer it to the guardian.[3] You have a certain quaint little talent of your own, but it is superficial. Accept it as such—& make the best of it—then you'll do things very likely as good as W. W. Jacobs.[4]

My novel is practically accepted.[5] I went up to Wm Heinnemann on Friday: he read me his readers crits: mostly good. I am to alter a bit in parts, then the thing will come out, & I shall have royalties.

Fordy has given up the English. Austin Harrison[6] wrote me that he would be glad if I would continue to submit my work to him. Is he the man that wrote the 'Puntilla?' I think so.

You must study the presentation—be a little more accurate—for instance would they see the white & blue of the eyes of a man lifted up against the sky, therefore in shadow?—would the creeper in the chimney see 'white flesh'? Why did the kid do it? Where is the place? Describe the seen 'particularly', & the butcher, & Siah—put a paragraph or two in front to show *why* the sweep should behave so—don't tell us, show him in the situation which leads up to it. Then send the tale to the 'Strand'[7]—they would very probably have it.

Mrs Jones[8] likes the tale very much. Get W W Jacobs out of the sevenpenny Nelsons,[9] & read his amusing tales, & study their development. You should do as well.

Farewell now—DHL

1. Cf. p. 6 n. 2. 2. A short story by Louie. 3. *Nottinghamshire Guardian.*
4. Popular writer of short stories (1863–1943).
5. *The White Peacock*, which Heinemann published on 20th January 1911.
6. Harrison (1873–1928) succeeded 'Fordy' Hueffer as editor of the *English Review.*
7. The *Strand Magazine*, founded in 1891. 8. His landlady.
9. The famous library of small red cloth-covered volumes which exercised considerable influence on contemporary taste.

Davidson Road Boys School, South Norwood SE
9th March 1910

My dear Louie,

I have got the cheque at last for Goose Fair,[1] & I hasten to remit you. It is not a vast sum that I send you, but it is worth having, & being the first-fruits of your literary tree, you ought to make much of it. I think I told you I could not do anything with the other story.

Austin Harrison has just sent me the proofs of some verses which he is putting in next month,[2] & as they are just the verses I dont want him to put in, I am rather mad. However, we may not as yet have our own way over these things.

Are you really getting sick of your little school? I am tired myself of being here, but I cannot think of moving till the autumn. I must grin & abide till then. I have nearly finished the novel ready for the publisher.[3] You will also see another story of mine in the May Review.[4]

Could you send me a box of hazel catkins. If you could, I should be very much obliged, but don't put yourself to any trouble over them. The spring is also very beautiful here—in Hampton Court and in Richmond it has arrived with a wonderful silken bravery of green and crocus flowers. I could write you prose poems, if I had time.

Tomorrow night I am going up to the Rhyses to meet some celebrities, & to read some of my own verses.[5] I am not very keen, and not very much interested. I am no society man—it bores me. I like private people who will not talk current clippings. What do you want to do? What have you in mind?—Anything? Pray tell me all the interesting things that are happening inside you—I know they are happening.

When you see Tom Smith[6] give him a kiss from me & tell him I am much too bashful to tell him all about myself that he asks. You may tell him if you like.

I'm in a devilish hurry as usual, but I like to get your letters & hear your news.

Forgive me DHL

---

1. Published in the *English Review*, February 1910.
2. A group of poems under the title *Night Songs* appeared in the *Review* in April.
3. *The White Peacock.*
4. There was nothing by Lawrence in the May *Review*. *Odour of Chrysanthemums*, the next to appear, was published in June 1911.
5. Cf. p. 47 n. 2.   6. Cf. p. 45 n. 3.

·◁[51]▷·
Eastwood   Thursday

Ma chère Louise,

It is ↓ ↓ , this weather. Pouring all morning, & every morning.
I am afraid we shall not get to Leicester at this rate. When are
you coming to Cossall? Is there any chance of our seeing you?
Wish you could come over tomorrow—Friday—to tea.—Things do
criss-cross disgustingly

Vale D. H. Lawrence

Addressed: 'Coteshael' Cheveney Lane Quorn
Postmarked: Eastwood MY 19 10

·◁[52]▷·
12 Colworth Road, Addiscombe, Croydon
24th July 1910

My dear Lou,

Thanks for your letter. I am shockingly remiss.

I'm sorry life is so dead-level with you. Coteshael I always
thought a very craggy place—what has happened to it?

So you're going to Scarboro for three weeks! I am swearing
because the holiday this year is so muddled. But I am determined to
go away. I am going with Neville[1] to Blackpool, I think, for the
second week in the holiday. To tell the truth, I rather look forward
to escaping the annual feminine party this year. The old clique[2] is
broken: it will never be restored I expect.

We break up on Thursday—I shall get home the same day I
think. I think I shall go Midland:[3] have not quite decided. School
is very decent just now: I've only about 20 kids, & they are very
amenable.

I was thinking that, if I went to Blackpool I would like to run up
to Barrow & see Nina.[4] Do you think it would be proper for two
young men to call there? But I think I'll write her a note. Her
address is 44 Nelson St, is it not? I hope we may have a good
time.

---

1. Cf. p. 11 n. 4.   2. The group of friends known as the 'Pagans'.
3. i.e London Midland Scottish railway.   4. Cf. p. 38 n. 5.

Fancy Tom Smith's stopping in Loughboro to swot.[1] I had said I would spend a day or so with him, at Lincoln or somewhere. Tell me what his Loughboro address is, will you, & I'll write him. Perhaps he'd come to me for a day or two. I'll ask him.

I do not know what J.[2] is thinking of doing this holiday, not having heard from her to that effect. Do you know?

As for the literary affairs, they are tiresome. They are worrying me for another title for the first book[3]—let them go to blazes. They have sent me back a rather nice story from the English[4]—asking me to cut it 5 pages: a devilish business. I have finished another book[5] —nearly—but what the world will say to it I do not know. However, things will, I think, begin to develop now. How slow literature is. As to 'Matilda'[6]—when I looked at her I found her rather foolish: I'll write her again when I've a bit of time.

Those Red Mag.[7] fatheads—are you doing them anything? Do you ever see the Tramp?[8] Thats not a bad mag. I don't know what books to recommend. Go to Nelsons Sevenpenny, & get 'Odd Women'—'White Fang'—'The Pit'—'The Octopus'—'The Farm of the Dagger'—'The House with the Green Shutters'[9]—all good.

Let me hear from you. Good luck for the holiday.

D. H. Lawrence

1. Cf. p. 45 n. 3.   2. Jessie Chambers.
3. *The White Peacock* was originally submitted to Heinemann as 'Nethermere'.
4. Possibly *Odour of Chrysanthemums* which was already in proof; the first proofs, dated 10th March 1910, are among Louie's papers.
5. *The Trespasser* (published May 1912), at this time entitled 'The Saga of Siegmund'.
6. Perhaps a short story which has not survived.
7. The first number of the magazine appeared in July 1910.
8. Cf. p. 42 n. 2.
9. Novels respectively by George Gissing (1893); Jack London (1906); two by Frank Norris—*The Pit* (1903) and *The Octopus* (1901); Eden Phillpotts (1904); and George D. Brown (1901).

Have you heard from Auntie.[1] I am going into Leicester, with Page,[2] on Monday morning, & expect to see you there. I at least will come to Quorn as you suggest on Tuesday morning, & we'll have a full day.

Regards DHL

Addressed: Coteshale Cheveney Lane Quorn Leicester
Postmarked: Eastwood AU 19 10

Croydon   Friday

My dear Louie,

Many thanks for your letter: you are very good. I understand mother is worse.[3] I am going to Leicester on Sunday by the half-day trip.

I sent mother some of the first batch of proofs of the novel.[4] She will not be able to read them. Ask Auntie to let you have them when you go again, & you shall have the rest.

There is no need to worry about me—I'm all right. Regards to everybody

D H Lawrence

Addressed: 'Coteshael' Cheveney Lane Quorn Leicester
Postmarked: Croydon SP 2 10

1. His Aunt Ada Krenkow.
2. Possibly George H. Page, a fellow student at Nottingham.
3. Mrs. Lawrence was seriously ill at the home of her sister Ada in Leicester.
4. *The White Peacock.*

12 Colworth Road, Addiscombe, Croydon
9th September 1910

My dear Lou,

Here are some more proofs.[1] Mother may not read them, may she? If she wants them, take them her. They are duplicates, thanks, so I needn't bother really about the mistakes. I go through the other set twice.

Hueffer wrote me this morning concerning the second novel.[2] He says it's a rotten work of genius, one fourth of which is the stuff of masterpiece. He belongs to the opposite school of novelists to me: he says prose *must* be impersonal, like Turguenev or Flaubert. I say no.

I'm glad mater is fairly. I am looking after myself this week, having a cold.

I'm so glad you like the proofs: it is comforting.

Now I'm sleepy—been so busy.

Goodnight Yours D. H. Lawrence

12 Colworth Road, Addiscombe, Croydon
18th September 1910

My dear Lou,

Here are the last of the proofs:[3] I am devoutly thankful to be done with them. You will not, I am afraid, care for the third part: tell me whether you do, as I am rather anxious concerning it. It is hard to represent in so short a space a fifteen year's development. I'm glad you like the title.

I was very sorry to hear of your uncle Will's accident.[4] It makes me shiver to think of. I tore my hand a tiny bit on the fence on Friday. When I looked at that, & thought what your Uncle's accident must be, it made me feel quite sick.

I am glad your father is getting on. Yesterday I had a little note from mother herself, & she says she is better again this week end

---

1. Cf. p. 53 n. 4.   2. Cf. p. 52 n. 5.   3. Cf. p. 53 n. 4.
4. William Burrows, an art-master; he taught first at Chaucer Street, Ilkeston, later at Loughborough and Leicester.

than she was on Monday & Tuesday. But she would never let me know how bad she was.

I propose to go home for the week-end at the Fair:[1] I should come on Thursday night & stay till Sunday night. I hope mother will keep pretty well.

There will be three poems in the October English, but Austin Harrison is still full up of prose, so the story must wait.[2] However, it can wait. The novel may be out in a month.[3] I did not know sheet 59 was missing. I cannot find it anywhere, so I must have sent it off with the original proofs. However, I'll look again.

It is very warm now, & I'm sleepy. I'll spend this Sunday afternoon as I did last: in bed, dozing. I go out all Saturday—walk 15 or 20 miles. I work all Sunday morning—then I don't feel ashamed to sleep all Sunday afternoon. You will laugh, I know.

It would be jolly to go blackberrying with you at Quorn just now.

Regards to everybody. Addio DHL

I've got Baudelaire's 'Fleurs du Mal'—got them for 9d. in Charing Cross Rd on Friday: it was a fine capture. I'll read some to you when there is an opportunity. They are better than Verlaine.

DHL

·◁[57]▷·

Your news is very interesting. Do come on Saturday I go home tonight. Shall expect to see you then

DHL

Addressed: 'Coteshael' Cheveney Lane Quorn Leicester
Postmarked: Croydon OC 6 10

---

1. Nottingham's annual three-day Goose Fair beginning the first Thursday in October.
2. 'Three Poems' appeared in the October issue of the *English Review*; *The Odour of Chrysanthemums* was delayed until June 1911.
3. Cf. p. 49 n. 5.

55

·◁[58]▷·
Eastwood   Tuesday

Les fleurs sont arrivées fraîches et exquises; ma mère en est charmée.
Vous êtes gentille; et nous vous remercions de bon cœur.
Je crois aller à Leicester Mercredi ou Jeudi.

DHL

Addressed : Ratcliffe on Wreake   Leicester
Postmarked : Eastwood NO 29 10

·◁[59]▷·
Lynn Croft, Eastwood, Notts
6th December 1910

It is morning again, & she is still here.[1] She has had the 'thrush'[2]
rather badly: they say one must have it, either on coming or going.
Many have it when they are little babies: and others when they're
dying. Mother's is nearly better. But she looks so grievous, pitiful
this morning, still & grey & deathly, like a hieroglyph of woe. One
mustn't be bathetic: but there one is vitiated by sitting up. Ada[3] & I
share the night.

I look at my mother & think 'Oh Heaven—is this what life brings
us to?' You see mother has had a devilish married life, for nearly
forty years—and this is the conclusion—no relief. What ever I
wrote, it could not be so awful as to write a biography of my mother.
But after this—which is enough—I am going to write romance—
when I have finished Paul Morel,[4] which belongs to this.

This anxiety divides me from you.[5] My heart winces to the echo
of my mothers pulse. There is only one drop of life to be squeezed
from her, and that hangs trembling, so you'd think it must fall & be
gone, but it never will—it will evaporate away, slowly. And while
she dies, we seem not to be able to live.

So if I do not seem happy with the thought of you—you will

---

1. Mrs. Lawrence died (of cancer) three days later.   2. An infection of the throat.
3. His sister.   4. Later entitled *Sons and Lovers*.
5. Three days before this letter, Lawrence had asked Louie to marry him (see Introduction, p. xvii).

understand. I must feel my mother's hand slip out of mine before I can really take yours. She is my first, great love. She was a wonderful, rare woman—you do not know; as strong, & steadfast, & generous as the sun. She could be as swift as a white whip-lash, and as kind and gentle as warm rain, and as steadfast as the irreducible earth beneath us.

But I think of you a great deal—of how happy we shall be. This surcharge of grief makes me determine to be happy. The more I think of you, the more I am glad that I have discovered the right thing to do. I have been very blind, & a fool. But sorrow opens the eyes. When I think of you, it is like thinking of life. You will be the first woman to make the earth glad for me: mother, J[1]—all the rest, have been gates to a very sad world. But you are strong & rosy as the gates of Eden. We do not all of us, not many, perhaps, set out from a sunny paradise of childhood. We are born with our parents in the desert, and yearn for a Canaan. You are like Canaan—you are rich & fruitful & glad, and I love you.

I have been translating some of those Fellah songs which are done into German.[2] Here is one, called

SELF-CONTEMPT

A laborer speaks

I, the man with the red scarf, I
Will give thee what I have left of my week's wages
　　　　　　it　　　　　　　　it
So thou wilt take ~~them~~ and be mine: ~~they~~ will buy
Thee a silver ring to prove thyself by.

More I have nothing, yea, I will wear
~~And besides this I have~~
A cap of sweat day-in, day-out, and thou
Shalt see me come home with steaming hair,
Shalt know then the worth of that money there

---

1. Jessie Chambers.
2. Lawrence's uncle (by marriage), Dr. Fritz Krenkow, translated some Egyptian folk-songs from Arabic into German; Lawrence then translated them into English. (Cf. *Complete Poems*, 2nd edition, 1967, ii. 1039.)

Come hither, cousin, cousin my dear!
I think my cousin cannot hear,
So I'll wave my sleeve for a sign 'Come here!'
Come here, my cousin, cousin my dear,
I am here, and God is near
The gladsome God is very near
I am smiling towards thee for good cheer.
Oh cousin, my cousin, oh very dear
Kiss me, for God is standing near.

They are ingenuous and touching, I think. But I am a bad translator.

I am also copying a picture of Frank Brangwyn's[1] for Ada: it is called the Orange Market—an impressionist, decorative thing, rather fine. Ada says I shall have to begin to paint for myself. That seems very strange. I have no acquisitive faculty. To possess property worries me—I give everything away that I can. Ada has got all the books I have bought—dozens—& various people the pictures I have done, & so on. I cannot accumulate things. Possessions all go under the heading 'Impedimenta'—for me. I must mend my ways.

Perhaps you could come here to dinner on Saturday—if you would. It is funny. I said—but you know, my mother has been passionately fond of me, and fiercely jealous. She hated J.—& would have risen from the grave to prevent my marrying her. So I said carefully, about a month or six weeks ago 'Mother, do you think it would be all right for me to marry Louie—later?'

Immediately she said 'No—I don't'—and then, after half a minute 'Well—if you think you'd be happy with her—yes.'

So you see, I know she approves, & she always liked you.

Your father has not answered my letter. But he won't be exactly anxious to do so. I'm glad they're not hostile, very glad. I like their talking about our being young—what about themselves?[2] I am 25—you 23: very good ages—in fact, the best, I think.

That new way of doing your hair makes you look like your mothers family. I don't know whether I like it better than the old way or not—I must see it again.

1. Augustus John the other Brangwyn (1867–1956) was one of the two romanticists who dominated English art c. 1900–10. 'To copy a Frank Brangwyn is a joy, so refreshing' (*Collected Letters*, i. 171).
2. Lawrence's astonishment was well founded: Alfred and Louisa Burrows were 23 and 22 respectively when they married.

When I think of you, I can always see your mouth, because I should like to kiss you.

I told you you would get £90. Isn't it funny to think of you going to a new school.[1] Oh, I wish I could get some money. There was a money-spider on my hair this morning, dangling in front of my nose. I thought to myself 'Oh, if only that meant £100—we might be married after Christmas.' Because all you want, if we had money, you could buy.

Don't love me too much. I have a fear of being ticketed too high, & having to be bated down at purchase. I am rather showy—don't price me too high.

You are not showy: you are full-fruited & rash and open as a sunflower.—we shall be shy for all that—because we can't help it. I shall laugh at you—& I shall be most timid. When a man & a woman are together—the man is always the younger. I wonder if you'll come. If only I could twirl the time round quick, & make it be gone. Well—pomegranate—that's your symbol[2]—I won't for shame begin another page. My love—I must mend the fire.—

Which—being done—having wiped my fingers on my trousers— I must tell you I've got a cold with going to sleep on the floor in the midst of my watch.—And is your cold better?—but I think you hadn't one, had you? Mine is nothing.

I think that's the doctor—now I think it isn't.

The fire is black & red—thou art like a fire, & I sit by thee. It would conclude with 'I kiss you a thousand kisses', if it weren't such a flagrant lie.

I don't see why I should end. What shall I call you, my dear? But your name is enough.

Addio—Louie DHL

·◁[60]▷·
Lynn Croft, Eastwood, Notts
12th December 1910

My dear Louise,

I am so tired. The funeral is over. I have been generalissimo. Now, I feel as if I have scarcely energy to hold the pen. Everybody

---

1. Louie was to become headmistress of Gaddesby village school on 9th January 1911.
2. Miriam in *Sons and Lovers* (chapt. 8) 'was coloured like a pomegranate for richness'.

has gone. Tomorrow I go to Croydon: Ada[1] goes to school on Wednesday. I too begin to hate trains—loathe them.

I have a peculiar wretched feeling of being old. That comes when your energy's gone—it comes again in the morning.

We want to go to Brighton for the first week of the holiday: Ada, Frances Cooper,[2] & I. You come—yes do come. Come to Brighton the first week of the holiday with me. How should I think you a forward hussy: you make me laugh. I understood you perfectly on Saturday—& that's the best way. I hate clinging to, & sympathy poured out like oil: your way is best. Don't find fault with yourself —there's no need.

Oh yes. Now don't feel like a snail in salt.[3] But why did you cut your 'soupçon de moustache'?—I liked it.—Why did you do it? Don't do it any more. I wish thou wert here. Somebody to rest with —you perhaps don't know what a deep longing that may be—perhaps you do know. I saw J[4] on Sunday & tried to make it look right to her. I think she does, a bit more.

I think this is finally the bitter river crossed. It certainly feels like one of the Kingdoms of death, where I am. It is true, I have died, a bit of me—but there's plenty left for you.

It is thee in the flesh I want

D. H. Lawrence

·≪[61]≫·
Davidson Road Boys, South Norwood SE
14th December 1910

My dear Louie,

Here I am back at school. It is exam., so there's not much to do. For some reason or other—physical, I suppose—I feel most doughily wretched. It is the late afternoon & early evening always that drives me cranky. I've got a devilish little nerve in the middle of my forehead, just under the hair, that clicks away like a ticking spider. I'm not going to write or read till January—not much, at any rate—just paint, which is soothing.

The boys this morning began for exam. a ginger-jar with the straw handles, & 3 reddish oranges: it looks so pretty.

1. Lawrence's sister. 2. One of the Eastwood 'Pagans'. 3. i.e. mortified.
4. Jessie Chambers (see Introduction, p. xviii).

Do you think you'll come to Brighton?—I'm going to write to the Inspector here about a country school. If we can do no other, perhaps they'd have me at Gadsby[1] in your stead, with you as assistant—how'd you like that. I feel as if I can't stand a long spell of lodgings.

Your wreath did not come till late. Ada & I took it down on Tuesday. It was very pretty, all maiden hair, & cold chrysanthemums, & a bunch of Neapolitan violets. I wore one or two of the violets, & I kept catching their scent all the way down to London, in the warm carriage.[2]

No translation today, because I am in school.

I'm so miserable about my 'matouchka'.[3] When I am not in good health my mind repeatedly presents me a picture: no matter what my thoughts are, or what I am doing, the image of a memory floats up. This afternoon, it is just the winsome, wavy grey hair at my mother's temple, and her hand under her cheek as she lay.—Sometimes life ceases to carry us forward unknown, like creatures moving in a great river: then we have to struggle like water-beetles stranded & toiling in mud. Ugh—indigos!

Don't take any notice of such effulgence. You are sane & strong & healthy. Praise be to Jehovah. But you are nearly as unattainable as the insouciante moon. I can hardly believe in you, you are so far away. And this twilight is yellow grey, & sterile. There seems a feeling of sterility over the world.

So I've had the gas lighted. I wish I might light myself at your abundant life.

My dear, in short, I ought not to write just now, when, as the Japs say, silence is a poetic and graceful thing, holy & desirable.

But thou art a long way off, & if I say anything, I shall be forced, like the turtle dove of old renown, to make my moan of solitude.

Farewell—Lèle. I wish you'd tell me whether you approve of my translations.

It is 4.0 o'clock: 25 more minutes—and then 'The desert of Sahara'. No—I shall go out to tea. I want you, not to write to you. Oh damn!

DHL

1. Cf. p. 59 n. 1.
2. The memory of this may have contributed to the poem *Violets* (*Complete Poems*, ii. 910-11).
3. Lettie uses this term of her mother in *The White Peacock*, Pt. II, chapt. 3.

61

12 Colworth Road, Addiscombe, Croydon
15th December 1910

My Louie,

I will write just six lines, because if I get to seven I shall be Jeremiahish. And now I feel I don't know what to say. I'd better take 'Nouvelle Heloïse' down & copy.[1] But I hate love letters—as such.

Oh—tonight I have told Aunt Ada.[2] I don't care in the least how she takes it.

We go to Brighton on the 24th & return on the 31st—I to Leicester, Ada to Eastwood. I wouldn't go to Brighton, but that I shouldn't be any nearer you if I didn't: Aunt Ada is going to Hampstead.

I want you so much I daren't say anything.

I know—I have just got your note—that we are very poor. My poverty at this time is nearly absolute: but for the hope of you. I'm glad you will never understand.

The translation *was* translation. Should I have been so pathetic? I rather like Mrs Root.[3] Give her my kind regards. I have great hopes of her cake.

I always remember the snowdrops and aconite you sent me,[4] when I think of Mrs Root.

It's taken me half an hour to write this, so I'll stop.

I remind myself of Gissing staring forth fierce eyeballs in a pie-shop—& going away more famished.[5]

This is the seventh line.

Goodbye—what a brood of little eternities in Life's belly: Like Faery Queene dragonettes.

Goodbye love D. H. Lawrence

THE WIND, THE RASCAL

The wind knocked at the door, and I said
'It is my coy love come to me!'

1. Rousseau's epistolary novel (1761) telling of the love of Julie and Saint-Preux.
  2. Cf. p. 8 n. 2.   3. Cf. p. 32 n. 4.   4. Cf. 30.
  5. See *The Private Papers of Henry Ryecroft* (1903), Spring, chapt. 10.

But oh wind, thou knave that thou art
To make merry over my sorrowful heart.[1]

* * * * * *

a pure translation.
And another

THE PHYSICIAN

I am hurt, I am very much hurt
Oh bring me my physician!
I am hurt in my heart, in my heart!
Sir, fetch my full-bosomed magician

* * * * * *

and again:

Dusk-flower, look hither
Thou dusk, thou voluptuous dusk flower,
look hither
Over the land at me.
                              dusk
Then looked she out from her ~~moon~~ gold eyes
            so
Shining ~~most~~ wondrously
Like the humming of ~~of~~ two dusk-gold bees
—And longing tortures me.
'Have pity, look hither at my miseries!'

·◦[63]◦·
[*17th December 1910*]

Having come to a concert[2] all by myself, I am bored to death in the
interval, for there is no 'foyer' & no 'bar'. I have been thinking a
lot of things. Tonight I called to see our Inspector: he's very sweet

1. An early version of the poem published in *Poetry*, January 1914 (see *Complete Poems*,
ii. 731, 1018).
2. The letter was written over the programme of a concert given in the Public Hall,
Croydon, on 17th December 1910.

with me, & says he thinks I'm wise to want a country school.[1] He will do anything for me he can—& he's very nice. So henceforward I shall study the Schoolmaster[2] weekly, & try to get a decent shop. I may succeed—I hope so.

I wondered why you didn't send me a letter this morning. Truth to tell, I was disappointed. When I don't write to you it is because I am afraid I shall be lachrymose & disgusting. I will not write lamentations to you—if I write nothing at all.

It is funny. I have had a tooth filled today—& I hardly thought about it. It is reminding me just now with a sore little aching. But this morning I lay in the chair & let the dentist drill away, hardly minding the pain though it's always pretty bad. That's how sorrow acts as an anaesthetic. I am sure I am half stupid just now. So I can't write nice letters. Just wait a bit.

There—they've begun. I wish I could get a drink.—I love Debussy.

I'll continue in the Cafe. I think J[3] is taking it quite nicely—I heard from her yesterday. But don't you write to her yet.

I am wondering how long it will be before I shall have enough money to furnish a house. It seems what grains of happiness we get are to be condensed most painfully from our breath of labour & suffering.

There—I'm beginning.—Have you ever read 'Jude the Obscure?'

As for those translations[4]—when I have written a letter I hastily seize the book & rattle them off. They never take me ten minutes: so don't talk about my working at them. At present I am merely painting.

I have wondered whether you want any 'Confessions' from me. I suppose you have a right to claim such. But you are welcome to a brief résumé of my life—if you want it. There's nothing very striking, I think: nothing, to my mind, very bad.

There's a fat old woman drinking sherry who will not stop staring at me. I don't know why I'm interesting. To be sure—I am alone—& am not eating. The waiter in this place seems so familiar to me, as if I'd known him since childhood. I'm sure his name is Fritz.

Oh, I forgot to say that I appreciated the manager's choice of books. What a damn farce! I have begun to buy old books for our library—God help us. I've got Religio Medici to begin with. I'll

---

1. Cf. 61. H.M. Inspector of Schools at Croydon was Stewart A. Robertson (1866-1933).
2. An educational journal carrying advertisements of teaching posts.
3. Jessie Chambers (see Introduction, p. xix).   4. Cf. 62.

send it you. It is adulterated with 'Paul et Virginia'[1] & some Early Spanish Ballads—job lot, 1/2.

I daren't ask you if you are coming to Brighton—are you?[2] Are you writing to Ada? Do.

I am not living, I swear. You will get no translation tonight—& I should think this won't reach you till Monday.

Tonight, my mood is dark red: like a very black night at home with the blood-red blotch of Benally[3] burning. C'est a dire—une passion. I wonder if you'll be afraid of me—ever. I wonder if love will turn out, to you, not what it seems. I wonder. 'Garçon, un bock!'—that's a very ugly tale of Maupassants. Louisa, my love, I could kiss the very marble of the table top, so do I ache to kiss you.

I like very much the taste of vermouth.

Oh dear—do say you love me—& don't be so restrained. Some savage in me would like to taste your blood. Oh dear, you'll have to burn this.—No, I never bother to make a copy of the beloved translations.

A week tonight I shall be in Brighton. What do I care where I shall be—I'd as lief be in Hell. But there's you. 'Sole star of my life' etc etc.

Well, I've nearly come to the end of my paper—and it's nearly eleven o clock—when Fritz will tell me 'It iss eleven, Sir.' Shall I ever have any money to marry you. Ach, Louisa! I wish Fritz would sing me a most melancholy love song—I'm sure, by his phiz, he's quite capable.

It's a muggy, mucky night. Do you love me? There's a silly girl having a slice of cake & smiling at me. I look at her, & say to myself 'What a fool you are!—as if *you* were Louise.'

Oh, you'll have to burn this paper. How I chuckle, seeing you doing it. Hell—or here—or you. Dear dear—if I could put my arms round you.—I'm not tipsy, only writing without bar.

Goodnight—I'm going home. A kiss—good God—not one.

Goodbye DHL

---

1. Romance (1786) by Bernardin de St. Pierre. 2. Cf. 60.
3. The reference (with its phonetic spelling) is to Bennerley Iron Works which Lawrence would pass between Eastwood and Cossall. The vivid glare from the works especially at times of 'casting-off', was locally famous.

12 Colworth Road, Addiscombe, Croydon
19th December 1910

My dear Lou,

It is horrid of me (the ink is thick, & there ain't no more, so I've put a drop of beer in to thin it)—not to write to you. But how long did I miss—two days or one? Now look here about my health: always abuse me if I say I'm sick; I'm never ill unless I want to luxuriate in a little bath of sympathy. I shall never die unless I fling wide my arms & say, Hamlettian—'Come death etc'; or unless some stilettoed sickness steal behind me & stick me unaware: which is very unlikely, being well trained as I am in the habits of these bravados. I have a pallid & Cassius aspect, but I'm like a birch tree, tenacious in the extreme. As for thee, thou beech—eh, beware a frost.

I have written to Truro, Cornwall, tonight, for application forms for a Small place on the North Coast[1]—salary £115 per annum. Think of us, by the brawling ocean in a land of Cornish foreigners blowing out our lonely candle as the clock quavers ten.—Oh, there's plenty to think about.—But it'll take me months & months to get a school.

I am not coming to stay at your house: I'm too shy. And I get rather reserved, which would never do at your house. I shrink from so much boisterousness. A day or two if you like—but not a full week.—Now you are blushing with small mortification—dont.

I dreamed of you, that I was asleep and you were awake with me. It was lovely.

I am always saying 'Hush' to the next thing I am going to say to you—or else 'Shut up, Fool!'

I have been interrupted to give Pa Jones[2] a lesson in oil painting. He paints like a bird pecking crumbs off the doorstep—it is funny.

Look here, I promise you I will be in electric health when I come north to you. I will not be flaccid: oh dear no. It is a promise.

I think your mother is very nice.

For my life, I don't know what to say next. What a joke! I always think you have a nice mouth.

I hate ending letters.

Vale D. H. Lawrence

I believe you'd like letters 'à la Nouvelle Heloïse'[3]—oh dear, how disappointing these must be.   I'm sorry—Thine DHL

1. Cf. p. 64 n. 2.   2. Cf. p. 20 n. 1.   3. Cf. p. 62 n. 1.

12 Colworth Road, Addiscombe, Croydon
20th December 1910

My dear —

It is ten minutes to post time—been to the kiddies party at school. Don't let me sadden you—I could not bear to do so.

I told J.[1] she could marry me if she'd ask me. Unawares I had let our affair run on: what could I do! But she wouldn't have me so—thank God. I don't want to marry her—though she is my very dear friend. She has not any very intrinsic part of me, now—no, not at all.

As for the other 3—you were one, & J another: well, I lied. They only liked me & flattered me. I am a fool. One is a jolly nice girl who is engaged now, & whom I hope you will know. She's a schoolmistress in Yorkshire.[2] One is a little bitch, & I hate her: and she plucked me, like Potiphar's wife: and one is nothing. I'll tell you verbatim when you ask me.

I am wild & sudden by nature—but I shall be true & try to make you happy—I am as sure of myself as I can be sure of anything. I have a tiresome character. But don't doubt me—dont. I do love you. When we are together, & quiet, it will be beautiful. I do want you to be peaceful with, to grow with, to slowly & sweetly develope with—it's only now & then passionate. Oh dear—I wonder if you'll ever wish you'd had Court.[3] I wish I were just like ordinary men. I *am* a bit different—& god knows, I regret it.

Nay, my love, don't doubt me. I love you truly.

D. H. Lawrence

Davidson Road Boys School, South Norwood SE
22nd December 1910

My dear Lou,

I did not write you yesterday, because I spent all the evening shopping. You see I've six kiddies to buy for: four nephews & nieces & the Colworth's[4]—besides hosts of grown-ups—so I've got

---

1. Jessie Chambers.
2. Agnes Holt, schoolmistress friend at Croydon; she married in August 1911.
3. Not identified.   4. His landlord's children Mary and Winnie, at Colworth Road.

a couple of night's work cut out. You should see me in a great store, being wafted hither & thither by shopwalkers & bewildered young ladies, buying a little umbrella, some little handkerchiefs, a little silver & enamel brooch. Finally I discover myself in the Bedlam of the great Bazaar, spotting out Books, and little tea-parties, as Mary calls them, and boxes of bricks and beads. Finally, I can hardly get into the tram. It's such a joke: but an awful fag. When I get home, it's nearly eleven: and, in respect to my Father Christmassy appearance, my tower of parcels, everybody is very benign and sweet. It would amuse you to see how tenderly the shop-ladies handle me. They seem to be mutely asking themselves: 'Is the poor young fellow a widower?—and at his age! I wonder how many he's got—perhaps they're twins. Poor dear—we must be sweet to him.'

I am now terrified lest I should not have enough cash to see me through the holiday. I shall have to keep my weather eye open, for there's no one I can borrow from: I'd scorn to go to Aunt Ada.[1] And I'm so disappointed: I wanted to buy you a lovely silver & enamel brooch—only 4/6—that I've had my eye on—and I can't. I'm sure you do not know the multitudes of claims there are on me. I hate to seem paltry. And all I can give you is this volume of Gorki:[2] which I spotted for you on Saturday, & which is a fine volume, but don't let your father read it: put it in your bottom drawer. Poor Gorki: I'm very much of an English equivalent of his. I have not read all the tales, so I'll have a look at them when I'm over. Are you disappointed in me?

I shall come up to Leicester, either on Saturday evening, New Year's Eve, or on Sunday, New Year's morning—because then I could get a trip: though I might manage one on Saturday evening. If you like, I'll come straight to you, & stay with you till Monday. Do you like? I know they run half day excursions to London from Loughboro—perhaps they do from Quorn. You could get me a ticket & send it on—then come & meet me on Saturday evening. That's nine days hence—not long. What do you say? Then I won't go to Leicester till the Monday or Tuesday, if your mother can put up with me for so long.

I shall like to go to Ratcliffe party with you: it will be jolly. As a matter of fact, I'm looking forward to it more than to the Brighton week. I don't want to go there, save for Ada's[3] sake. It will be very

1. Cf. p. 8 n. 2.   2. Perhaps *Tales from Gorky*, translated by R. Nisbet Bain, 1902.
3. His sister.

fine to be at Quorn. And Auntie is quite nice, really: a bit huffy, perhaps—but she'll come round.[1] When you go to see her, Lou, be colder. She doesn't matter a damn: think so, & let her see it. It's not good to give Ada Krenkow too long a rope. Don't let her make you feel like a trespasser: be cool.

I shall have to go down to the class.

I am wondering when I shall manage to get a school. You see so many places now are filled up, as are those in Leicestershire, by the local people. There are very few remain open for foreigners. Literature is disgustingly slow. Heinemann won't bring out the Peacock till March,[2] I suppose—& even then it wont do much for me. I shall not be any nearer having money—unless, indeed, the notices bring me in a fair amount of magazine work. I wish we could have been married right away—but not in Croydon. I did not fill in the Cornwall forms—since you didn't want it.[3] It is altogether very riling.

We do not break up till tomorrow—Friday morning. I meet Ada on Saturday, 1.25 at Kings Cross. I suppose we shall go straight to Brighton. Although I have done nothing all day, I am despicably tired. At present I have eleven boys—& they've been reading all afternoon—'not a sound breaks the stillness, as . . .' etc etc. It is four oclock. At playtime there was an immense gold sunset pouring on everything in a flamy stream. The boys looked beautiful with red faces shining like lamps as they came up the lobby. (ugly word, lobby.) {If I were an artist I should say 'porch'}

They've just sent me a slab of Christmas pudding in from Std[4] I. It represents Std I's Nature Study lessons for the last fortnight. It now takes the form of a lesson on mastication. Happy Std. I. I have eaten a scrap—it's not bad,—& given Manser the rest. He's a dwarf with red hair and a Sunny Jim grin: he always sits on the seat with his legs crossed & feet under him, so as to appear Normal size: he's going to be a tailor.

The days go drearily & the nights are very heavy. Fessissimus sum.

Well, Cara mia—I wish three things: to be with you; to be very drunk; to be—I don't know.

No translations, since I'm at school—& since they are shocking. Do you wish I would write in the 'Be Good, sweet maid & let who will be clever'[5]—style? I will try, to please you, one day.

1. Cf. 62.   2. It appeared on 20th January 1911.
3. Cf. 64.   4. i.e. Standard, or class.
5. Charles Kingsley, *A Farewell* ['. . . let who can . . .'].

I do not run to endearments—don't feel light hearted enough, to tell the truth. But if there is one thing on earth that I wish, it is to be with you altogether—that we were married securely.

My love—goodbye DHL

·◦[67]◦·
12 Colworth Road, Addiscombe, Croydon
23rd Decenber 1910

Geliebte,

This has been one of the days when I have not known what to do with myself: that's why I have not written earlier. Now the 11.0 p.m. post has gone. I am very sorry.

You do not want to leave Ratcliffe—you shrink from the thought of Gaddesby[1]—you are miserable for an evening—& then you understand why I do not write when I am worried. Very good. Then you understand why I have not written today

My dear—sometimes I feel as if I shout—crêver. My temper is damnably serious & melancholic. If I had not a few grains of reason I should be a maudlin idiot. But oh, my love, you do not know what these days cost me. I want you to succour me, my darling—for I am used up.

But enough. This is my Christmas letter. And how will you be jolly at this rate. Pa Jones[2] has just come in: he's rather tipsy, but is very clever at hiding it. Ma Jones can't twig it. But I, through long experience, can tell to a shade how far gone in drink is any man I know at all. It is rather amusing—& rather ennuyeux, to watch this comedy.

This is my Christmas letter. I like to think of you being jolly all the time. I hate to think of you crying your eyes up. Don't cry.

But Oh, my darling, my darling—Pa Jones has had a bottle of whiskey for a Christmas box, & we're just going to have a drop. Forgive me if I'm horrid.

If I but had any hope of being with you, near you—I would dislike whiskey—but what am I to do.

Tomorrow I am going to Brighton. It seems horrid,—but the thought of next week wearies me. I shall have to be nice & bright

1. Cf. p. 59 n. 1.   2. Cf. p. 20 n. 1.

70

and strong, & support & comfort Ada,[1] & keep her, or make her, cheerful. And I want comforting myself, like a kid, and cheering, like a tearful girl. But it is rather despicable—and I shall be ever so glad to see Ada. She & I are very near to one another. I would give a very great deal to make her even a bit happy. But I feel nearly bankrupt—no I don't—at least I shan't tomorrow. You, my love, are my capital. You are my funds. I wish I could but draw on you a little. But it is all so mixed with passion & complicated.

This is my Christmas letter: I want it to be Christmas for you. I want you to forget me—for I'm sure I must fret you—and be gay, gay, gai. If you say you're not jolly I shall curse. Dear, my darling, I shall make you a good husband. I am very faithful to my own.

I wait for you. As [I] hope for salvation, I hope for you, and a home with you. But I dream of my mother. You do not know. If I told you all, it would make you old, & I don't want you to be old.

This is my christmas letter. Is it better to play with jests, & say nothing? Nay, my love, I want you to clasp me soul to soul, as much as we can. I feel as if I could not go another stride away from you. But it is bedtime.

This time next week I shall be coming—next week. But the tracts of days between. Never mind.—next week—my love.

DHL

·◁[68]▷·
c/o Mr Richards, Davigdor Road, Hove, Sussex
25th December 1910
My dear Lou,

I have just finished 'Undine'—de la Motte-Fouqué's old romance.[2] Do you know it?—it is often a bit absurd & German, but contains spots of real beauty. It makes me think of you: of love—and some sad things.

It is a beautiful day. We went out about 10.0. The mild fresh wind was blowing more & more blue into the sky, till soon it was clear as a blue bowl, & the sun shone on the sea, & the wind was sparkling. It is a lovely day. Now a few clouds are orangey over the west.

All morning Ada & I have walked up & down the esplanade, talking, and laughing at the people. They are very dressy; the throng

---

1. His sister. 2. Published 1811.

71

is salted strong with Jewesses & their attendants. It is rather amusing to watch folk. You would like it because it's rather swelly (sic)—and a swell has an immense appeal for you. Don't you pray nightly —'May I live to be a lady, and die in the cream of fashion?' I know you do.

But I'm only laughing at you. I never dare say to you the things I am going to say. Which makes my letters jerky & pattering. You see 'I am daring on paper'.—but I've a few grains of discretion. No, I don't mean anything shocking.

It rather often seems to me as if we were—if not married, then on the brink of marriage. My chest seems lifting in expectation towards you, & I feel as if the banns had been uttered. I wish I were gifted with second sight, & could believe myself.

I tore up that Cornwall application form.[1] Then I saw the same school, with another like it, advertised again, and I wrote for two forms—today. That first I tore up because you didn't want to go to Cornwall. But if I should get the school to Cornwall you shall go, or to the Devil.

There—I don't mean it. I'm on paper, you see.

I meant to go & call on the boss:[2] he's at a boarding house here. I thought I'd have tea with him. But it's getting too late. Those clouds have gone heliotrope.

I wish you were here. We are jolly comfortable—lovely—Brighton would suit you down to the ground—big and 'swelly'. You are a 'jeune fille', you know. Well, I like you so

Court[3] would have called you the darling of his heart: Do you regret him? You don't seem particularly far off from here—why?—I can manage you better in person than through the post. So I await next week to be serious.

DHL

See about that ticket for me, will you—and trains   DHL

---

1. Cf. 64.
2. Philip F. T. Smith, headmaster of Lawrence's school at Croydon. By his account, Lawrence and Ada visited him on Christmas Day (E. Nehls, *D. H. Lawrence*, i. 141).
3. Cf. p. 67 n. 3.

Davigdor Road, Hove, Sussex
27th December 1910

My dear Lou,

I wondered when your letter was going to come. It seemed as if Christmas were specially designed to put a silence between me & everybody. But I received your 'envoi' just now: it is noon, Tuesday, & the letter was not the Croydon one—but the Hove direct letter. The former is not yet arrived.

Do you know, things have rubbed a lot of the elastic capacity for pure happiness out of me: and it is my nature. I am rather 'cured' with the salt and salt-petre of bitterness & sorrow. I have a certain hardness of texture now, the knowledge of which grieves me rather when I think that I have not the beautiful pristine fervour of a young Feverel[1] to meet you with. I am very much afraid indeed of disappointing you & causing you real grief for the first time in your life. It is the second me, the hard, cruel if need be, me that is the writer which troubles the pleasanter me, the human who belongs to you. Try, will you, when I disappoint you and may grieve you, to think that it is the impersonal part of me—which belongs to nobody, not even to myself—the writer in me, which is for the moment ruling. When you see it in my eyes, take no notice, chatter as if it were not so. Remember I love you and am your husband: but that a part of me is exempt from these things, from everything: the impersonal, artistic side. Do you understand?—and does it trouble you? But you don't believe me. It is just as well. I love you sincerely, and when I was thinking that now it would be easy for me to fulfil my old desire & go to France, I was amused, France seems to have grown so distasteful. We'll go some time together.

Here I am very gay—all the time gay. I live in my impersonal self. Nothing matters in the least, and most things amuse me, and very little touches me. I dance, at a boarding house where the boss is staying,[2] and am quite a bright spark. But nobody has any personality to me, so you needn't be jealous. It's a rather pleasant shadow-theatre kind of existence: I am really jolly.

At the boss', there is a young Frenchman, Monsieur Didier, who has been in the army four years & has now come here to acquire the

1. Allusion to Meredith's *Ordeal of Richard Feverel* (1859). (Lawrence's interest in Meredith is also reflected in his description of Louie as a 'Rhoda Fleming'; see Introduction, p. xviii.)

2. Cf. p. 72 n. 2.

73

language. We go out together everyday, & talk French all the time. It's good fun.

At the petite danse last night there were three Asiatics from India. They are extraordinarily interesting to watch—like little beasts from the jungle: but one cannot help feeling how alien they are. You talk about 'brother men': but a terrier dog is much nearer kin to us than those men with their wild laughter and rolling eyes. Either I am disagreeable or a bit barbaric myself: but I felt the race instinct of aversion and slight antagonism to those blacks, rather strongly. It is strange.

I shall have plenty of time to chatter chatter at Coteshael,[1] & then you shall hear, along with the rest, all about everything. But these people are rather sanctimonious, & oh, the mental atmosphere is so stale.

I had just as lief you were a Christian: I have my own religion, which is to me the truth: you have what suits you: I will go to Church with you—frequently.

Of course, tell everybody about our engagement: I do. They all know, at home & elsewhere.

I must run to meet my Frenchman. We shall walk to Rottingdean over the downs. It is very sunny, but *so* rough. The girls[2] will rest this afternoon after their morning blow.

Give my regards to your mother & father: say nice things to them on my behalf. When they are bigoted, take no notice. It's no good booing a persistent ox for plodding its bit of a track: it would be no good abroad, at large. Some folk are best fitted with a narrow creed, as are docile horses with a bluff:[3] they're not scared & bewildered, & theyre more useful.

I'm not sarky—oh, no, not a bit.

Well my dear—I am running away down to Brighton. The day *will* come when I have you—

Vale D. H. Lawrence

---

1. The Burrows' home at Quorn.
2. His sister Ada and Frances Cooper. Cf. p. 5 n. 2.   3. i.e. blinkers.

74

Davigdor Road, Hove, Sussex
28th December 1910

Carissima,

It has been a very sunny morning, with a mist like grey silk veils, and the sun-walk on the sea narrowing and darkening to orange and burnished copper and vanishing ruddily on the horizon into a closed door of fog. 'Varrry prreety', as my Frenchman[1] would say. A morning framed for me and thee, but thou wert out of the picture, and I missed thee from it. Comment by the Frenchman 'What peety!'

Ada, Frances & I have walked the miles of esplanade looking at curio shops, ladies, riders, the sea, fog, the sun, shops, books, people, pet-dogs of all descriptions: 'and so ad infinitum', as Swift would say.[2]

I am glad you are so happy in anticipation. It pleases me immensely to hear it. Ada is always saying 'Oh I shall be miserable to go back: shan't you?'—But then she's had Eddie[3] for three long years, & the savour of expectation is gone. In three years time—in three years time—what?—That's the best of life, it's such a bran-tub. And though we've only fished out tin trumpets & tear-bottles so far, yet we're quite sure that among the bran there are treasures for us, if we rummage. Philosophy,

I want to come up on Saturday by the 6.20, I think. If you take a day trip, I can come by that train, which is a fine one. You see I must dispatch Ada & Frances safely from Kings Cross on the G.N.R. at 5.30, then return to Marylebone.[4]

Why isn't Cornwall wise? I think it is. Do not think me rash: I am rarely that, except in trifles. But let us appreciate promptitude in action. I detest vacillation and waiting.

I've been to have a 'Sticky-Back' taken this morning. They are tiny photos with gummed backs, 3d. a dozen if you've got a coupon. I had a coupon. Ada went first and paid her three'd to a woman at the shop counter. A little man waved her into a box. Before a minute was over she emerged, saying 'Well!' Immediately I found myself in the box. The little man murmured, like a worn out gramophone 'Take a chair, please.' I sat on a pew. He gave me a card, & suddenly

1. M. Didier. (Cf. 69.) 2. Swift, *On Poetry; a Rhapsody*, l. 340.
3. William Edward Clarke whom Ada married in 1913.
4. Great Northern Railway ran from King's Cross Station; Lawrence would use Marylebone Station for Quorn.

turned on a bright light. 'Lord', I said to myself 'I'd better look amused.' At the same instant he was mechanically murmuring 'keep still a moment.' I rushed, (mentally), to find a suitable expression, when the light vanished, & the little man murmured like the last utterings of a phonograph 'Any time tomorrow after six'— then I found myself in the shop exclaiming 'Well!'—while Frances hovered in fear near the opening. If it's a good caricature—the stickyback—Ill give you one for your amusement.

This will reach you on Thursday (-Friday-Saturday). If I were but Lovelace[1]—which I nearly was,—if the potter hadn't bungled & made a beer-pot of my fine china, should have been—I would say 'How can this fair earth please me, or the seductive ocean allure me, when I consider thee'. I wish you'd tell me which of my epistolary styles you prefer: the gay, the mocking, the ironic, the sad, the despairing, the elevated, the high romantic, the didactic, the emphatic, the bullying, the passionate, the disgraceful or the naïve, so that I can be consistent.

Didier is so serious—he nearly makes me burst with laughter. He is *always* serious. He's a poor little devotee of Corneille: has lent me four vols.: and I've got to begin with Cinna:[2] then he's going to expound to me the passages 'plus nobles, plus élevés.' Oh Lordy! The noble and the lofty—how tedious! The farcical, the comic, the ironical—they're amusing.

If I miss writing to you tomorrow it'll be because we're out all day. It depends upon the weather.

Well golubchick (pretty word!)—little pigeon—oh black swan. Farewell.

I wish to goodness you were here—I've captured an afternoon for myself. I shall think of you.

D. H. Lawrence

·◦[71]◦·
Davigdor Road, Hove, Sussex
Thursday 3.0 p.m. [29th December 1910]

Dear Little Ousel,

I have received today your book, two letters, the ticket & the bill: all of which is very sweet. And I laugh at you again: do you not see

1. In Richardson's *Clarissa Harlowe* (1748).   2. Corneille's tragedy (1640).

that I can return by any train after 6.20: and do you not know that, unless it be altered, there is a slow old crawler which leaves M. le Bone at 6.25, & gets in Quorn about 10.0 p.m. (look it up): and of course that is the train I shall come by: and we'll go to the watch-night[1] if you like, & I'm in in time: and all shall be respectable & comme-il-faut: and they shall not laugh at you: Ooray.

Let me see—what do you say? Oh—church—all right, I am plastic in your hands—but treat me gently. Cornwall! I haven't yet received the application forms.[2] When I do, I shall fill them in: and if I get the job, 'to Cornwall we will go great boys, to Cornwall we will go—we'll catch a little—.' And if you won't follow me, you'll have to: a little later, peut-être. It is £115 a year. Also I'll go and help you find digs in ridiculous Gaddesby.[3] You always go to places with daft names.—What else? Oh whiskey. I've just had a glass of Irish: Mrs Richards[4] was so good: but I prefer Scotch. That is true. But I'm always squibbing you, & you're always jumping, because every red spark you see you imagine to be a fearsome cracker that will explode and do God-knows-not-what damage. You won't begin your reforming by insisting on my signing the total abstinence pledge, I hope. Good Lord, what a mill I've got to go through. Sometimes when I have horrors—the ashy sort—I drink a little—to mend the fire of my faith & hope, you see: I can't stand cold ashes of horrors. But, Good Lord, I don't drink. Think of the paternal example. The Good God made whiskey, as I have rather lately discovered. And, as we all know, too much of any divine thing is destruction. Even then, too much whiskey is better than too much melancholies: and a drinking bout better than a bout of ferocious blues. Remember, I am not an imbecile, & I don't know that I want to turn my brains into beery mud. Don't be alarmed, I have no vicious habits, & no vicious tendencies, I believe: save an inclination to blundering forwardness.

We have had a lovely morning. At 10.0 we met the Smiths'—my boss,[5] his young second wife, & his daughter of 15; we walked over the cliffs & downs to Rottingdean. A warm, dimmish day, sunny, with the waves low down & small washing back & forward at the foot of the white cliffs, gulls flashing and daws gleaming, a great wide wake of sunlight slightly dimmed, oxidised with mist: a little

---

1. The service held at or near midnight on 31st December, the day of Lawrence's arrival.
2. Cf. 68. 3. Cf. p. 59 n. 1.
4. The proprietress of the boarding-house where Lawrence was staying.
5. Cf. p. 72 n. 2.

wind. Rottingdean is a delicious village in a fold of the downs, gold with lichens. We walked back over the downs. I did wish very heartily that you were there—except that I've got into that rather comfortable & grown-up habit of not wishing keenly for what I can*not* have.

Next week! This is like driving slowly towards a destination, to a place where I have never been: as I might be driving to Cornwall, wondering what it is like. For I can't *imagine* next week. That's a trick my imagination plays me. I can imagine everything else: but next week eludes me.

Don't be alarmed, I shall be as good as gold, that is, I intend to be: and I am fairly amenable.

I'm going out to see the sunset. I do wish you could come. I take care not to allow any blank spaces in these days. Tonight we are going to a Tchaïkowsky concert in the Dome.[1] If I have a blank space, I begin to shut my teeth & want you there & then—or whiskey—or—Gott in Himmel! The nights are rather bad. But I am very jolly, you know.

Well, dark dove—little pigeon of my breast—I wish I'd got Renan's 'Canticle' (Song of Solomon) to send you.[2]

I'll go & see the sunset & feel sentimental. In 56 hours or so. I wish we could turn into storks or swans, like Fairy tale folk.

Good evening D. H. Lawrence

·◁[72]▷·
12 Colworth Road, Addiscombe, Croydon
27th January 1911

My dear Lou,

So you did not get my letter in the evening after all. I am sorry. You would see it was posted before school in the morning: but of course, you have no night delivery. I knew you would worry: how naughty of you.

My cold is getting better quite rapidly. I shall soon be able to sing like a lark, and shall have forgotten the croaking crow of this week.

---

1. Brighton Pavilion.
2. *The Song of Songs. Translated from the Hebrew by Ernest Renan . . . Done into English by W. R. Thomson, 1895.*

You will be disappointed not to have seen any reviews.[1] I am myself a wee bit disappointed. But I know it's not often a novel gets critted before a fortnight or so, therefore next week is the time. You must not think, my dear, that a work walks up to a man, a public man, and, nipping him by the nose, says 'Behold and proclaim my merit!'. It's this way: The publisher sends a copy of the book to the office of the newspaper or magazine, together with a slip saying when the book is to be issued. If the publisher has puffed the book behind scenes, at his club, where he meets the big newspaper men—or if the writer has friends among the literary circles & clubs—or influence—then the book has been talked about, so the editor pounces upon it & writes it up in reviews. If the book has no friends, & the publisher, knowing there is no chance of 'Scarlet Pimpernel' sales, does not trouble much, then the best book in the world might fall dead. It gets handed to the hack-man for a twelve line review We must take things as they come. I shall be very sorry if I get no success—that is to say, not even a little individual name in the literary world—from the White Peacock: chiefly, because it will leave me miles further off from marrying you; also, because I want a measure of success, and the book deserves it. But no amount of lamentation will stop tomorrow's rain from falling, so it's best to take the weather as it comes, without caring much. One has to have the essential life indoors, quite inside oneself, independent of whatsoever may happen outside. Voilà.

I have not got the least tiny scrap of news, and at night one does not want to chatter. I wish you were here, to be still with. What else is there to say?

Look, Louie: I—we both have agreed that we cannot marry unless I have £100 in cash & £120 a year income. Father is working very little—will soon have done. I shall have to continue to help, as you will. I cannot save £5 a year without descending to petty carefulness. When shall we marry then? We trust to luck & literature. I have worked hard enough at that damned mill to obtain a reward so insignificant in cash. We hope much, but expect very little. Isn't that so, my dear? I am very much afraid of disappointing you. It's such a beastly mill to go through, disappointment. Well—we can have infinite patience if need be—eh? Goodnight, my dear

D. H. Lawrence

---

1. Of *The White Peacock* published a week before.

12 Colworth Road, Addiscombe, Croydon
30th January 1911

My dear Lou,

So you are smitten! Now don't have influenza, don't. Tomorrow is your third day: I shall be ever so mad if you continue to be knocked up. I shall be telling 'whatever Gods there be'[1] that they are a parcel of fools: which would never do.

Did I call somebody's coat old?—Dear me! With a great struggle I have recalled a coat—an astrachan coat—a caracul coat, that is it—a double-breasted caracul coat that used to make my dear aunt look like a bison with a skirt on. She sent it to Emily[2]—the caracul coat—along with a suit of clothes—and I wrote to Mrs Smithard[3]—'received the jacket suit today, together with the old coat my Aunt has sent'. The *old* coat! Did I say old?—Well, I believe it *is* just a trifle passé. That caracul coat seems like a bit of history to me. I connect it with the callow days when, poor reverent youth, I would close my eyes against its loathsome treatment of my aunt. For I believed in her slimness and her grace as dearly as in my own. 'Would you, you brute', I'd address the caracul coat 'would you make my Aunt Ada look like my Aunt Lettie[4] (in a tightish skirt) who's been fifteen stone this last ten years?—*Would* you, you blasphemous obscenity!' I have shaken that caracul coat in my teeth like any waxy little dog with a rabbit skin. And now, it visits its wrath upon me!

'Raro antecedentem scelestum
       Deseruit pede poena claudo'[5]
'Rarely does lame foot retribution
       relinquish the trail of the offender.'

But if every garment, incensed by that calumnious 'old', is going to rise upon its skirt or basque or waist band to pursue us, waving malignant sleeves—I, for one, will have no friend unless she go naked.

To put a stop to this nonsense, I have just received from 'The Times' this very damnatory review. I am cut down like a poppy that gives only one red squint out of the pod before the mowing

1. Swinburne, *The Garden of Proserpine*, l. 84 [' . . . may be '].
2. Emily Una King (b. 1882), Lawrence's married sister.   3. Not identified.
4. Mrs. Lawrence's sister Lettice, then Mrs. Berry (in Skegness).
5. Horace, *Odes*, III, 2, 31–2.

machine trips him up. It is 'The Times'—and I am low, very low. It is, perhaps, cruel to send you the slip, but here it is.

The other cutting Mac found for me. It is not a severe cutting. It came from the Observer, a paper of some standing, I believe.[1]

I am glad the posts have finished for tonight. They've brought letters—oh dear!—one from a friend of mine, a not very close friend, tis true—in Plymouth—asking me to lend him £5 so that his wife can have an operation to replace the womb. He was married last midsummer, and it appears his wife had been strained in some way before that.—I have n't got five pounds in the world, and am just considering not paying my dentist's bill, borrowing the addition, and sending him the fiver. What do you say?

Don't bother about Aunt Ada. She is vexed with me because I wont answer her last dithyrambs—I mean didactics (what's becoming of my head)—and because Ada[2] wrote her very coolly over a little matter, and we are altogether a thankless lot, ill in grace, and rude to our maternal aunties. I hear a faint resonance

'Dies irae
Dies illa.'

Don't go to Leicester—just send postal order & be sufficiently nice —then leave the dear lady alone.

I'm glad you liked Aunt Let. I have meant to tell you that one of the three snowdrops you sent spread perfectly, and is still blithely flying. It will last tonight out, anyway—so that'll make a week. It's a long time for a snowdrop.

How strange of you to be angry with J.[3] for writing. I believe it was in answer to some question of mine, and it certainly wasnt an amatory epistle. Don't be jealous, will you? On the whole, it is not a nice feeling.

Then—I had forgotten for a moment that I was enumerating tonight's post—there came a letter from America asking me to give an order to the 'Press Cutting's Company'—allowing them to send me the American notices of the book—in return for five dollars. Their letter & pamphlets are just flaming under the grate.

---

1. *The White Peacock* was briefly reviewed in the *Times Literary Supplement*, 26th January 1911. It was praised for its natural descriptions but censured for its lack of 'a well-knit plot', its 'aimlessness', and the banality of much of the conversation. *The Observer*, on 29th January, considered it 'a confusing, strange, disturbing book; but that it has the elements of greatness few will deny'. (For 'Mac' see p. 87 n. 3.)
2. His sister.   3. Jessie Chambers.

Then I had a letter from Grace Crawford[1] in Rome. She complains of having written before: her Mother also wrote me very kindly: so I have answered her at once, being in a quaint humour for a wonder.

The translations don't go well at all—nothing does (Whoa!!)

Don't be mad about The Times diatribe. They are anti-progressive, you see. But I wonder why so vindictive.

Now I am going to close—like a daisy afraid of the night.

Goodbye, my dear DHL

·❬[74]❭·
12 Colworth Road, Addiscombe, Croydon
3rd March 1911

My dear Lou,

I wish you could have come—I do wish you could. Never mind: one learns patience in the long run. It is a hard lesson for me: I am a long time indifferent: I don't bother with much useless vain desire: but once a thing is visible & I want it, & it is feasible, I would go mad to have it immediately. I could wait for ever for a far-off thing: but for the slow coming of the sun out of a cloud I could go mad.

I have promised to go to Hampstead tomorrow: I had promised. So think of me in London.

Tonight, for four hours, I have been drawing the 'Idyll'—you know Maurice Greiffenhagen's thing.[2] It is to be a big picture—as big as ever my board will hold. It is for you. It has taken me four hours, & I have not finished drawing. It will take me to finish 12 or 14 hours in all. Then I will give it you, & voilà, a day of my life.—.

I have learned such patience as almost surprises me: patience in executing a work. By nature I am rapid & facile. But by teaching, & horrid discipline of life, I get very much schooled to accuracy.

Perhaps you will come next week.[3] In five weeks we shall be

1. An American whom Lawrence knew in London; she married the painter Claude Lovat Fraser.
2. Lawrence eventually completed three copies of the *Idyll* by Greiffenhagen (1862–1931): one for Louie; a second (smaller) for his sister Ada (*Collected Letters*, i. 75); and a third as a wedding present for Agnes Holt (see No. 105). The picture is the subject of discussion between George and Lettie in *The White Peacock*, chapt. 3.
3. Louie did spend the following weekend—probably 11th and 12th March—at Croydon. (See 75.)

coming home—no, in six. Six weeks today I shall be with you (DV). I wish it were n't at Eastwood. If it were n't that they insist, I'd rather stop in school than go there: I'd rather have no holiday.

But I want very much to see you. I dream, & dream, & dream, very sweetly, often, about us. But it is inclined to make one bitter after. The reality is so absurdly different, and so unnecessarily insufficient.

I still do not hear from the Publisher—I am not sorry: he will only bother me. Oh, if only I were just a private individual, with not any bartering with the public, how glad I should be. I wish all this toil of writing were put away, & we were perfectly untroubled & unanxious, in a quiet country school. —But who can alter fate, and useless it is to rail against it. When I get sore, I always fly to the Greek tragedies: they make one feel sufficiently fatalistic. Im doing Oedipus Tyrannus just now—Sophocles. I wish with all my heart I read Greek. These Greek tragedies make one quiet and indifferent. They are very grand, even in translation.

Well, if you were coming tomorrow, how nice it would be—I shall do another hour's work, & then go to bed—work is a fine substitute for a wife. I work work—you will marry a very ant. How horrid for you.

But if you were here, I shouldn't need to work. But you are not here, for God knows how long. So it is 'laisser aller'

I kiss you— —I paint love pictures to you. Ah—I kiss you closely next week

Addio DHL

·ᴳ[75]ᴰ·
12 Colworth Road, Addiscombe, Croydon
13th March 1911

My dear Lou,

Are you feeling sad now the week-end has gone?—I am. We could be so happy if we could be together, & alone it is so difficult. However, it is useless to moan.

I have begun Paul Morel[1] again. I am afraid it will be a terrible novel. But, if I can keep it to my idea & feeling, it will be a great one.

I am wondering what you will be saying to me tonight. Are you being serious and telling me your trouble?—I wonder. We cannot

---

1. Re-named *Sons and Lovers*.

83

marry yet awhile for a long time. That, I can see, is your most serious and settled conviction: and to anything you seriously decree, I bow my obedience. But sometimes life pushes very hard, and we have to be careful.

I want you to speak before I say anything. Between life and death and honor, it is a rum pass.

O dear, I am a cursed nuisance. I must pluck the very concentrated heart out of each of my mysteries and desires. I go straight, like a bullet, towards my aim. I cannot loiter by the way. I cannot slowly gather flowers as I saunter. I wish to heaven I could. I cut straight through like a knife to what I want. I cannot, cannot slowly enjoy watching the rose open. I can't help it, Louie, I can't. I am really dangerous in my fixed mad aim. I love my rose, & no other: and when I can have her I shall want no other. But when I have her not, I have nothing. Your pleasure, which you enjoy, in the thought of me, is nothing to me. What I want I want and quarter measures are nothing to me. I am a nuisance & a trouble to everybody. Always I am cursing myself, but it doesn't alter me what I am.

I will borrow a translation of 'Trésor des Humbles'[1] for you, because I want you to understand it thoroughly. It will help you to understand yourself and me.

Life is a strange, inflexible, dreadful thing which turns us slowly in its lathe. The thing is not to resist too strenuously this graving tool.

Oh Lou, how horrid it all sounds. I wish before heaven I was like you. Never mind, things will turn out all right for us, and you shall be happy.

My dear, I feel such a wretch and a nuisance. Gott in Himmel. But what am I going on about—Smoke.

I kiss you, my dear. Court[2] is less worthy of you even than I am —else I'd say have him. But he's got no understanding. But a man who causes sorrow by his deeds & yet has understanding is better than a righteous stiffnecked fool who gives disgust.

Which is vanity on my part.

And after all, I'm not doing anything wrong, so what am I talking about.

You will never let me make you unhappy, will you?

Goodnight, my love D. H. Lawrence

1. Possibly a conflation of the titles of two works by François Coppée (1842–1908): his play *Le Trésor* and poems *Les Humbles*.
2. Cf. p. 67 n. 3.

12 Colworth Road, Addiscombe, Croydon
27th March 1911

My dear Lou,

You may put in my room (imaginary) a scarlet cactus plant in blossom—no more. Now let's quarrel about it, just to enliven this deadly dull day.

The almond blossom is out, full out, mixing in grey miserable rain, poor little devils. There's a lot of almond blossom in Addiscombe, & I like it.[1] The hedges are in rosettes. Hawthorn leaves, opened no further than half blown rosettes, on a wet evening, are the vividest green things I know.

It is a very cold day, after yesterday also cold. I ought to go out to see Humphreys:[2] he's not been to school—more work for us. But it's too cold to visit the ruddy sick.

I've been reading Swinburnes Tristram of Lyonesse. Some parts of it are very fine, parts again are barren to excess, stretches of noisy desert. You mustn't try to put too much thought into verse, as I often try, &—presumptuous contiguity—Meredith does. But to let your metronome go on ticking when the music & meaning is gone is tiresome. Swinburne is shallow. Do you know Merediths poetry— 'Love in [the] Valley'—& 'Woods of Westermain' & 'Modern Love': very fine indeed. 'Love in [the] Valley' is a bag of jewels, rare, precious as can be, & beautiful—but they want a bit of setting.

[*MS torn*] them together some day [   ] you like poetry—I know I've enough long neck and soulful aspect for two—but I'll shorten my gizzard & you can share the soulfulness,—make you look 'intéressante'—then we'll have sweet & ring-dovey times.

I send you a little volume of French kids songs. Learn them & we'll sing them at Easter, for fun. Learn them, & astonish & delight the private parties of Gaddesby: if you don't show 'em the book. It is the dodge of an artist—& most folks are artists where their own ends are concerned. Sneak a thing from a simple obscure source, & then make the catch to shine as a light through a chink, indicating a houseful of bright knowledge—so we attain greatness & distinction. You can make Gaddesby believe that you are intimately acquainted with the French young heart.

---

1. Cf. his poem *Letter from Town: the Almond Tree* in which he chides his 'love' for forgetting to send violets; then—'Here there's an almond-tree—you have never seen/ such a one in the north . . . . '

    2. Ernest Humphreys, a Croydon friend and colleague.

Oh dear, what a lot of rot. You know Lou, you make me ashamed of passion—I've finished the Idyll,[1] by the way—& ashamed of lamenting, & ashamed of complaining, & ashamed even of dreaming —I know I'm given to disgraceful extravaganza—so remains only to be trivial & ironic. I beg your pardon. I am, and always shall be, a bad writer of love letters.

I hope Miss Cox[2] is better—give her my love. I wish it were Easter—will it be a beautiful yellow morning on Good Friday, with all the primroses out in Berkshire—as it has been other years—or will it rain. It is only 17 days after you get this. There is time to forget all separation & fallings short. We'll have a good week. Till then, we rest patient

With love Yours DHL

·⧼[77]⧽·
Davidson Road Boys School, South Norwood SE
29th March 1911

My dear Lou,
I think I will write you from school. Here, before night falls, & I'm at Colworth, I'm more good humoured. Forgive me for being disagreeable. I'll mend—how many times do I say that—but I'll mend, surely.

We have just finished As You Like It. It's very jolly, & the boys enjoy it: only they do want to caper round in a dance while Rosalind delivers the epilogue, & there's not enough room. Poor Orlando forgot to take the duster off, so he was married with his arm in a sling. We act as if the front of the class were a stage: good fun. And they spy so anxiously to see if I laugh: as a rule it's up my sleeve I'm grinning, but they're satisfied.

To tell the truth my cold has not quite gone, & has left me rather low. But I shall be all right in a fortnight.—Humphreys[3] is back at school, thank Goodness.

I'm going to Lil Reynolds[4] to tea this evening. I'll give her your love. Your Idyll looks ever so nice. I began a new sketch, but have

---

1. Cf. p. 82 n. 2.   2. Not identified.   3. Cf. p. 85 n. 2.
4. Miss Reynolds, a friend of Helen Corke, Agnes Mason and Lawrence, was a Croydon teacher. From a remark made later (No. 112), it appears that she probably accommodated Louie for the weekend of 11th–12th March.

spoiled it through not being in the painting humour. Strange, when I can write I can't paint, & vice versa. I'm just amusing myself with a short story.

Austin Harrison[1]—English Review—wants to see some stories. I've got a dozen in rough but none done up. So I'll do one or two. Tomorrow I'm going to call in the evening to see him about the story he's got, which I think he wants altering a bit.—I'll tell you what he's like—though I may not be home in time to write tomorrow evening.

As to the black furniture—do as you like. I've got a bit of verse to you somewhere—a teasing bit, merely—nothing serious

'I will give you all my keys
You shall be my châtelaine
You shall enter as you please
As you please shall go again

When I hear you jingle through
All the chambers of my heart
I shall sit and smile at you
Playing your housekeeper's part.'[2]

etc etc—but this is all of the 'jingle' I can remember. I must must get some composition marked: oh the stack that awaits me. The boys are very funny. I gave them 'a newspaper account of any event.'— One boy took the school concert, & I found this jewel '"A Pot of Broth", an Irish play, was perfectly performed under the direction of Mr MacLeod,[3] before gorgeous scenery, exquisitely painted by Mr Lawrence. The Head master, Mr Smith, was very busy in control, running hither and thither, whilst Mr Aylwin & Mr Byrne attended to the stage carpentry.'

There's nothing so amiable & decent as boys—big boys, when they know you. I'm having VII again next year. Really, while I am at school, I never wish myself elsewhere. I look at the register. Two more weeks to fill in—what a little way! I look back at the term's twelve—I look back at last terms sixteen or seventeen—Heavens— I stick my face hard to the future, I don't want ever to look back. The future will be fine, must be. Oh yes, this day of ours—chrono-

---

1. Cf. p. 49 n. 6.
2. An early version of the much longer poem *Teasing* first published in *Poetry and Drama*, December 1914 (*Complete Poems*, i. 95–6).
3. A. W. McLeod, a friend and fellow-teacher at Lawrence's school.

logically, our lives are about at 11.0 o'clock, aren't they—will brighten up. I know I shall have 'a gorgeous afternoon, exquisitely painted towards evening by x x x'

Au revoir, my dear. I have thousands & thousands of kisses for you, ready to burst onto wing.

I can smell a pink hyacinth in the window, as I write. The boys in the hall are singing a German spring song.

I've wasted (no) all this spare lesson I have for marking composition. No matter. In school, you are nearer than anywhere, being also in school. I feel as if I would like to turn tramp, & wander north to Leicestershire, and wander till I forget the weedy creek of life I've been bred in. I want to get into a nice running fresh current of life, that has no tang and no taint.

Goodbye, my dear. I wish things happened like As You Like It. I reckon you're a lot like Rosalind. I always think of you.

Baisers—baisers. DHL

·◌[78]◌·
12 Colworth Road, Addiscombe, Croydon
1st April 1911

My dear Lou,

It is unusual for you to miss both Friday and Saturday. Are you scolding me?

I went to Cavalleria Rusticana & Pagliacci at Croydon last night —one shilling in the pit. It's an Italian company from Drury Lane —Italians of the common class—opera in Italian. But I loved the little folk. You never saw anything in your life more natural, naïve, inartistic, & refreshing. It was just like our old charades.

I love Italian opera—it's so reckless. Damn Wagner, & his bellowings at Fate & death. Damn Debussy,[1] and his averted face. I like the Italians who run all on impulse, & don't care about their immortal souls, & don't worry about the ultimate. My immortal soul can look after itself—what do I care about it. I don't know the creature, even. It's a relative I only know by hearsay.

Comment, that, on Italian opera!

But if you were here tonight we'd go to Carmen, & hear those delicious little Italians love & weep. I am just as emotional & im-

1. But see 63: 'I love Debussy.'

88

pulsive as they, by nature. It's the damned climate & upbringing & so/on that make me cold-headed as mathematics.

I've done the transcript of the Legend tale.[1] It's jolly good. If Austin Harrison wants it, you can have the proofs.—And soon, in a day or two, I'll send you the Chrysanthemums[2] to copy—shall I.

Ada seems very miserable. She's dipped into disbelief.[3] Tragedy is like strong acid—it dissolves away all but the very gold of truth. Poor Ada—I'm very sorry. I would not, for worlds, have her go through this bloody bludgeonings of unbelief, and the struggle for a new faith. But I suppose it's fate. What life has set in progress, life can't arrest: There is nothing to do but to leave her with her own sorrows, to love to smash up the old Idea which is nothing but an Idol, & to find in the emptiness a new presence.—Rhetoric!— but it'll suit you better than harshness.

Will you, I wonder, get through life without ever seeing through it. I will never, if I can help it, try to disturb any of your faiths. You will secure yourself by praying for my conversion, eh?—There the balance.

Am I ironical again?—It's Ada has upset me. I'd rather a thousand things than that she were in the mill of truth, being milled.

I've got a blue bowl full of daffodils, with green expanded buds of lilac twigs, and two or three small boughs of beautiful almond blossom. I wish you could see it—it's very pretty. I will take a walk into the country & see how the primroses are. Your violets are just dead[4]—still they smell faintly: 'Odours when the violets sicken'[5]

I haven't got any verses; those lately are sad ones. The Egyptians have lost interest for me:[6] you will say 'Fie!' I am sorry. When I am—but I can't write to order. I'm sorry Very soon I shall be meeting you at Loughboro, & we shan't need ink.

Now I'll dust. I got up so late, & larked with the kiddies in my bedroom till after 10.0. So, having made Mrs Jones late, I dust to make up for it. Thank Heavens there's no ornaments.

The weeks will be gone immediately. Mother's constant motto to me 'Blessed is he that expecteth little, for he shall not be disappointed'—makes me laugh now. She lived up to it very well, in latter years: & I begin just to understand it a bit. And as you are

---

1. Cf. p. 6 n. 2. 2. Cf. p. 50 n. 4.
3. A letter (9th April 1911) of consolation and advice to his sister Ada is printed in *Collected Letters*, i. 76.
4. Cf. p. 85 n. 1. 5. Shelley, *To Music* ['. . . when sweet violets . . .'].
6. Cf. p. 57 n. 2.

not inclined to bolt through the hedge of circumstance—why, circumstance, like a hedged lane, will have to lead us where it will. I suppose in the end, since we are each determined to take each turning usward, our separate lanes will debouch to an amiable, grassy camping ground, like a couple of gipsy caravans met. Meanwhile, I can't see over my hedges, nor you yours—so the lanes have it all their own way. They'll come out when they will. 'Ambulo'—I amble.

Goodbye, my dear. I feel like doing a little prance, with the shadow of my own wilfulness for partner.

> And—one-two-three-four
> Off we go
> To peep behind the shut door
> And see the show.

I believe I'm a wicked tease—as Mrs Jones says I am.

Addio—addio DHL

I've had a letter from Agnes Holt.[1] I think she's going to marry in August, & live in Ramsey.—We'll then go & see her. I like her very much—and you will like her too. I want you to know her. Somehow, I always feel sorry for her. She's not strong in health. Poor A!

·◅[79]▻·
12 Colworth Road, Addiscombe, Croydon
2nd April 1911

My dear Lou,

Here are the MSS—it's a really good story.[2] The desideratum is to shorten sufficiently the first part. Of course that part has to reveal the situation. I hope you'll manage to make out all the alterations: it's not particularly plain. Send it me when you've done, will you. You need not hurry. Write small enough, will you—& don't be flourishy, my dear. If I haven't sent enough paper use any sort—exercise or any sort.

---

1. Cf. p. 67 n. 2.
2. Most probably *Odour of Chrysanthemums* the first, heavily corrected proofs of which he sent to Louie. For further details see p. 93 n. 1.

It has been a most horrid day; yellow as a guinea. I have not been out. I must go somewhere tonight—the kids are so obstreperous. We've still got 'Mignonette'—the African lady.[1] But she's cleared off to the Plymouth Rock meeting. You should hear the Jones carry on about her immediately her back is turned. It wearies me very much.

Sunday evening is a damnable time—the fag end of everything, the wretched hesitation between two weeks. I hate it. I'll go & see Aylwin[2] I think—or to a concert: too far to Wallington—I'll decide when I'm shaved.

I wish we were a bit more accessible one to another. Tonight I'd give anything to be able to spend a quiet evening with you. It is this spinning on a loose end which is so risky. I'm always trying to avoid doing things you'd reproach me for. I don't always succeed to my thorough satisfaction: but then, who would.

A fortnight today is Easter Sunday. I hope it's not like today in weather.

It has taken me such a long long time to write those last two pages of the story. You have no idea how much delving it requires to get that deep into cause & effect.

I am reading Meredith's Tragic Comedians, which is wonderfully clever: not a work of art, too turgid.

I went into the country yesterday & found the first primroses. It's very pretty here, between Addington & Farley. I love that part of the country—some time I'll take you.

It's an evening gloomy as hell, outside. How's Miss Cox?[3] My regards to her. Oh for you, a little warmth and cosiness!

Addio—je vous embrasse de tout mon coeur—I really want you very badly indeed.

DHL

·◁[80]▷·

12 Colworth Road, Addiscombe, Croydon
4th April Tuesday 1911

My dear Lou,

Your letter did not come till noon: I wonder why. And then, being new note-paper, & your handwriting so altered, I could hardly

---

1. Mrs. Wilkinson. (Cf. 82.) 2. A fellow teacher (Cf. 77.). 3. Cf. p. 86 n. 2.

recognise it. Did you feel in a wild mood towards the close? Sometimes I get in such an extravagant paddy with things I wish I could pull fortunes or fates toppling on my head like the stones of the Temple on Samson. So long as one says nowt, moods don't much matter.

I wish I could go violetting with you: it sounds so jolly, and so goodly. I wish with all my heart I could be—I was going to say Gaddesby railway porter, but there isn't such a thing. Lord, how we beat ourselves bloody against the face of circumstance.

No matter. I'm sorry I was disagreeable. I know you'd help things only too speedily if you could. Some day the ravel will untwine. Your father is not better then? If I get some money, if we marry, part of the income is yours, and with that part you do as you like. If I had anything, you should have it to do just as you liked with. Then that way you could help your father: I should be glad. But it's easy talking when I've got nowt, & no prospect. I swear I'll be a good husband: it's now, as exile, or separé, that I wouldn't vouch for myself, as an impeccable person. No matter!

Don't sark me[1] by telling me I said I didn't expect much of you. I expect everything—life almost: but not—& I never know whether to say unfortunately or happily—a companion in my philosophy:—happily, for it's a philosophy that, shared, would be aggravated to abstruseness & uselessness. Forgive me when I'm priggish & superior. One part of me is insolent & overbearing to a degree. But you very brutally put your foot through the paper thereof when we're together: to my great ultimate joy.

The wind is in the north again hang it. There are touches of snow now and again, among the almond blossom. The wind is like the edge of a hatchet. Thus spring comes in.

I have just been to the library & got Rouge et Noir.[2] I shall enjoy it. The worst of being a novelist, & having dreams & fancies, is that you know all this is fiction. You know the inanimate dumminess of them—& demand life direct like a blow.

A week or so & we are at home. I am annoyed that I can scarcely look forward, anticipate—even a day. I am peculiarly hour-bound—as regards the future—I can't project myself even into tomorrow: & everything not immediate seems a tale.

---

1. i.e. be sarcastic at my expense.   2. Stendhal's novel (1831).

Oh Lou—I feel like a river out of its banks: a straying Hoang-ho.
And I love you—whatever.

Goodbye, my love DHL

You are quite right—in your way—& I never want you to alter.
My way is a form of abnormality—damn it.

DHL

·◁[81]▷·
Davidson Road Boys School, South Norwood SE
6th April 1911

My dear Lou,

On Thursday afternoon I have the last lesson off to get my
marking done. Behold me, in the boss' room, with a stack of composition books at my elbow untouched.

Isn't it cold. I look down & see the field & everywhere dried pale
drab with cold, the sky leaden grey, & only a handful of steam flying
from a train, sheer white & vivid.

My cold is about better, thanks. I've forgotten all about it by
now. But I hate cold weather: I swear I'll flee to the tropics first
opportunity. You would look well in a scarlet bandanna.

Do you know, I've had your yesterdays & Tuesday's letters both
this morning: how funny! The letter posted on the 4th got here not
till noon: the one posted yesterday, at 8.0 this morning. The
officials of the post office are cracked, I think.

I'm glad you like the story.[1] Mind you leave out all I have crossed
away. All the playing part—most of the kiddies share—goes out, I
think. I intend it to. The story must work quicker to a climax. The
other story[2] wont want copying, I think. I think it'll stand just as it
is. You shall see it in a day or so.

By the way, will you send me—no, bring it to Eastwood—the
book of pictures J.[3] gave you. Tear off the cover & the inscription—
which is an impertinence—and I may get a copy or two out. I've
painted nothing since the Idyll:[4] am busy with these silly short

1. *Odour of Chrysanthemums* (cf. p. 90 n. 2). The proofs sent to Louie show frequent
excisions of childish chatter and actions in the early part; the original prominence of the
children is greatly reduced.
2. Probably *A Fragment of Stained Glass* (mentioned in 78). (An MS of this story is
among the Burrows papers with an earlier title '*The Hole in the Window*' crossed out.)
3. Jessie Chambers. 4. Cf. p. 82 n. 2.

93

stories. Don't worry about my fame: it'll certainly not trouble you too deeply during my life-time, I think.

Men & women are very different in some respects. Man's the animal baby 'who won't be happy till he gets it—whatever he wants' —woman is the queer reluctant thing, who, I verily believe, enjoys much more the dream & anticipation, than the realisation, with its pangs.

This seems a very little letter—but it's nearly 4.20. I think of going to Purley to tea, for a bit of music. Laura MaCartney[1]— remember she's 35 or 36—plays Chopin's nocturnes very well indeed. I do love somebody to play the piano well to me. I wish— that's the one thing I wish you could do—play really well. You are such a scandalous splasher, aren't you. You'll splash away at me, just the same: which makes me chuckle to contemplate.

Don't talk about 'my heights'—they aren't heights. I winna be sarked.

There are three rooks strutting like mad old maids in black, down below in the field. Three for a letter.[2]

A week today, at this minute, we shall be broken up. Oh yes, time limps along famously. We shall be fifty before we know where we are. Imagine *you* fifty—what a joke

There's a patter of a myriad feet, I close. Goodbye—this room's as cold as the grave. I guess you're nice & warm, O mon nid!—I hum a bar of the Tear and the sigh!—Addio—I can hear Sammarco[3] in Traviata 'Addi-i-i-i-o.' It gives my heart a twinge. Addio—if I were but near you, then— —Hélas! Addio.

                                                                    DHL

1. A pianist to whom Helen Corke introduced Lawrence. He went once or twice to musical evenings at Miss MacCartney's house at Purley; one occasion—with a melodramatic ending—is recorded in his story *The Witch à la Mode* (published in *A Modern Lover,* 1934).
2. Cf. *The White Peacock,* chapt. 7: Lettie, seeing a crow, recites the jingle: 'One for sorrow, two for joy,/Three for a letter . . .'
3. Mario Sammarco (1873-1930), famous Italian baritone; he performed regularly at Covent Garden, 1904-14.

12 Colworth Road, Addiscombe, Croydon
7th April 1911

My dear Lou,

It's just striking nine, & here I've been all this time larking with the kiddies. It's their bath night. I really think Mary is the prettiest youngster in England.[1] And she's such a rascal. When she's bathed, her hair comes out in full blossom like a double flower, and her face is like apple blossom buds. She insists on sitting on my head, & kicking her heels against my neck. Then she sneaks off & drinks my beer. You should see her with her mouth in the froth, her eyes glancing askance at me, before I rush for her. She likes beer, wicked little sinner that she is.

Pa is out tonight, & that crumpled petal, Mrs Wilkinson,[2] has betaken herself to a 'Rock' meeting—so Mrs Jones & I are 'en famille'. I believe she enjoys the house best, & I'm sure I do, when we are thus on our own. Pa is really a bit gênant. There are rather rotten rows occasionally. But there, it's not my business to talk.

I meant to write a story—but I'm a bit out of the humour. I feel free and easy. If only you were here, I should be so likeable for you tonight. You wouldn't find any fault with me—because the artist is sunk, & I'm aimiable.

Today, we've had an American chap to lecture us, after school, on handwriting—He was very funny. I will be telling you this time next week. Then this afternoon I've been overhauling & checking the library—162 volumes. I shall be having it changed soon. This is the second year I've been librarian, & it's rather a fag. I'll chuck it up after August.

Where shall we go for Midsummer? Let's go abroad. Let's go to France—Normandy, Brittany, Paris. It wouldn't cost much. We'll persuade Ada[3] to go with us. She is my nearest relative now: do you know, it feels to me as if she were my only relative.

Eh dear—how cold it is. Austin Harrison says he's putting in the English two bits of verse I don't want publishing.[4] Never mind—it'll be a scrap of money, & in the state we are, that's the essential.

1. Cf. p. 24 n. 2. 2. Cf. 79. 3. His sister.
4. Lawrence is referring to a letter (6th April 1911, MS LaB 188) in which Harrison says he is keeping two poems—'which, though I cannot say I like personally, I feel I *ought to* publish'. In fact he published neither. One poem, *Sorrow* (*Complete Poems*, i. 106) first appeared in the volume *Amores*, 1916; the other, then entitled *A Husband Dead*, was published as *A Woman to her Dead Husband* in *Poetry*, January 1914. Later it was renamed *A Man who Died* (*Complete Poems*, i. 55–7).

We'll go into the country at Easter if only it'll be fine. We shall have a good time. Ah, if only we were married and Mary were my own & thine, I think I should be a fine man for you. As it is, a vapourer, unstable.

Vogue la galère.

Give my regards to everybody at Coteshael. I can't, can't screw up my courage to write—to anybody. I can't bring myself to write to Ada[1]—it's such an effort. But next week I come home—next week. And I am in such a perfect open humour—& I've nothing to do but read Rouge et Noir[2]—which—I don't want to, now. Wo bist du?

My dear, goodnight. To be your husband is my supremest wish. And so goodnight.

DHL

·◁[83]▷·
Dimanche—minuit

Merci de ton petit billet—je l'ai recu ce matin. Le train parte de Marylebone à 11.30, Vendredi. Ce doit donc arriver à Loughboro vers deux heures. Oui, il y arrêtera pour te prendre. N'aie pas de peur—je ne me laisserai pas passer de toi.

Je me porte bien et j'attend le Vendredi. Demain je t'écrirai

Vale. DHL

De quelle espèce est le nouveau chapeau?—grand?—bleu?

DHL

Addressed: Gaddesby Near Leicester
Postmarked: Croydon AP 10 11

·◁[84]▷·
12 Colworth Road, Addiscombe, Croydon
10th April 1911

My dear Lou,

Having been larking with the kiddies in the garden I am in a breathless & careless mood. Winnie is behind my chair getting

1. Cf. p. 89 n. 3.   2. Cf. p. 92 n. 2.

96

undressed, peeping over my shoulder, & when I turn round to look at her she croodles down to hide her dishabilly state. She always looks so funny in her combins: like, I say, a puffin or a penguin or a deacon in his shorts. She's very tubby. Mary is anxiously awaiting the finish of this to fly down to post with me. She loves to go out & see the dark & the stars & the moon.

'What are they?', she asks of the stars.

'Little girls going to bed with their candles,' I tell her.

'Where do they go to?'

As I can't answer that—'Look!' I say 'the wind's blowing 'em out' She clings close round my neck, and puts her cheek on mine, looking up in wonder—None of which'll interest you. Now I've got a bracelet of red wool & tape to wear. There's no peace in this life.

I shall look out at Loughboro for you on Friday. That makes me feel quite excited. It's not far off: about 2.0 on Friday afternoon. We'll be very jolly.

There's not an item of news. Oh, do send me the story[1] if it's ready. I want to get them off before the holidays.

Another break—Mary removes my bracelet, wipes my nose, and kisses me thrice. That's one better than your two. Never mind— kisses galore next week—eh?

I'm going to write to Aunt Ada tonight. She's been very poorly, she says. Writes to me quite mildly, half apologetically.

Is your Dad all right? I do wish Eth.[2] had got a dozen distinctions. I *must* send her a card. Four evenings from now—je t' embrasse—je te serre contre le sein: je me colle la bouche sur la tienne—quatre jours!

À bientôt—bientôt DHL

Do you want Zola's 'Débacle' or 'L'Assommoir'. I've got 'em both to give away

·◁[85]▷·

Davidson Road Boys School, South Norwood SE
12th April 1911

My dear Lou,

What a beautiful day. It makes Friday imminent. I suppose you don't break up till Thursday morning, so I'll send this to Gaddesby.

1. Cf. p. 90 n. 2.   2. Louie's sister Ethel (then 20 years old).

97

It's so quiet. We've just finished reading Stanley Weyman's 'Under the Red Robe'.[1] It's not much as literature but it's a good tale—the boys like it. I am afraid I am becoming a down-right romanticist. Of course you'd find me realistic because of subject, but the manner is shockingly romantic.

I've got a pack of books to mark—but I'll write this letter first. I've finished the fourth story—it's the 'White Stocking' written up.[2] Mac[3] says it's fantastic Really, it's not up to a great deal. But I intended to do four, & four are done.[4] I'll send them as soon as I get the Chrysanthemums[5] from you. Then Austin Harrison can see how he likes 'em. Though—unless I get Chrysanthemums in the morning, it'll not be much good sending till after the holiday. I don't care.—I have just done one folio, a dozen MSS pages, of Paul Morel.[6] That great, terrible but unwritten novel, I am afraid it will die a mere conception.

It is such a sunny day, and I feel so easy and indolent. Nothing more strenuous than making love would suit me just now, & that I could do deliciously.

At this time, in two days, we shall be in Nottingham, you & I. I fully expect it to be a beautiful day, as it was last year.

How tiresomely & rebelliously the blood beats in spring. I wish we were only fauns & nymphs. This black suit of convention is most gênant. I feel a very wicked and riotous person got up to look & behave like a curate. And my temper is so sudden & impetuous, I am astonished. Not irritability—inflammability. I should like to suggest all the—you would say wicked—plans in the world. I say, only that is wicked which is a violation of one's feeling & instinct.

The poetry you are curious over is not love poetry—saddish. You shall have out of me what you like if you'll ask for it—in two days time. But remember, I am not a very ready talker, about my own work especially.

Where shall we go on Easter Monday. Let's go to Bakewell or somewhere there. I am very shabby, & have only one suit: I shall be too shabby to go out anywhere on Sunday.

1. An historical novel (1894).   2. Cf. p. 6 n. 2.   3. His colleague, A. W. McLeod. 4. The four stories were: *The White Stocking, Odour of Chrysanthemums, A Fragment of Stained Glass*, and presumably, *Second Best*. Harrison had told Lawrence (6th April 1911, MS LaB 188) that he was looking forward to seeing *Chrysanthemums* and 'the other stories you mentioned'. He did not publish the first named above (which appeared in *The Prussian Officer* volume, 1914); the others came out in the *English Review* in June 1911, September 1911, and February 1912, respectively.
5. Cf. p. 90 n. 2.   6. *Sons and Lovers.*

Let's talk about France, & let's determine to go. Anywhere—I'd give anything to be able to do something rightdown rash.

Goodbye—je te cherche, bouche et gorge, pour t'embrasser

DHL

·❧[86]❧·
12 Colworth Road, Addiscombe, Croydon
24th April 1911

My dear Lou,

Here we are then, back again, & settled as if we had never been away.[1] But all day I have belonged to the yesterdays of last week, so that school has been like a tale one reads without taking in. I swear I've never really seen the boys today. It is lonely, & meaningless, this life. With the meaning gone out of it, it is a dull, sleep-heavy sort of business. And it has been such a sunny sweet day, and I have smelled hyacinths keen in the sunshine several times. It makes me shiver for to have you. It is true, this shallow dim remnant of life which is left when we're apart, is not worth having.

I've been & had my hair cut. The barber is a French & we talked a bit of Fr [*MS torn*] in, a dark and rudd[   ] Never two mortals more alien than at that moment; I indifferent to almost everything, he to nothing; I as quiet as a pebble, he noisier than a paroquet. I wonder what he thought. I still am faintly surprised at the foreignness between us. His bold eyes, like bright brown glass, seem curious to me still.

Coming home, near East Croydon, I saw a pear-tree in full blossom overcast by the lamps behind me to a cream gold in the low twilight; then, right back, the sky was green as verdigris, with a fine evening star.[2]

I am going to write a bit of Paul Morel, if I have any luck with myself.

I have not any news, except the little unpleasantnesses deriving from the cockle-shell cousin.

I think, my dear, it will be best for me to write only twice or three times a week. I have to push myself into correspondence. All that I have to tell you is not for words, much less pen and ink. It's no good talking about [   ]

1. After the Easter holiday.
2. The memory of this scene may have contributed to the poem *Twilight*, published in the *English Review*, February 1914 (*Complete Poems*, ii. 939).

99

12 Colworth Road, Addiscombe, Croydon
28th April 1911

You are really overcast, and by what? No matter, one must know all kinds of weather.

I have just read past the trial and condemnation of Julien in 'Le Rouge et le Noir.'[1] It is a terrible book which almost makes me laugh. Life seems such an escapade. And I feel so much like Julien Sorel—except that, of course, I am English & sentimentalist,—poet to please you—that I marvel at Stendhal's wonderful cleverness—marvellous to me. Yet he misses out the religion, the philosophy, if you like, of life. He is not a bit metaphysical. He doesn't satisfy my sentimentality.

A week has gone by like a mist evaporating. Do you know I simply cannot work. I have done only about five pages of MSS, 'Paul Morel';[2] & that only from sheer pressure of duty. I don't want to work: and I don't care a damn about it. But what William Heinemann Esquire, Great Cham of [*MS torn*] publishers, will say when I fail to p[roduce] a book within the required time, I don't [   ] care.[3] Vogue la galère.

I have not any newses. Unlike you, [   ] have exciting times at school. Everything flows smoothly.

With having read Rouge et Noir for about 4½ hours, I naturally think in French, and have to hold my pen down to English.

Life has a rum fatality about it, and it will go which way it chooses, whatever we say or worry. No matter. The interest is in watching it go. It's like watching a big beetle wander across the table, waiting for the exciting moment when it will go—flop!—over the edge. All of which is Stendhal's influence.

I feel myself a 'Black and Red' myself—black coal bubbling red into fire. Hélas, que vous etes loin d'ici, que votre corps loin du mien.

Vale DHL

---

1. Cf. p. 92 n. 2. Julien is Stendhal's ambitious hero.   2. *Sons and Lovers.*
3. Heinemann rejected *Sons and Lovers* and did not publish any more of Lawrence's work in his lifetime.

12 Colworth Road, Addiscombe, Croydon
29th April 1911

My dear Lou,

So you've been a bit off colour: we'll say it's the weather, which couldn't be more beautiful.

This time next week we shall be going to Eastwood: it will be downright jolly, & I look forward to it very much.

The evenings are so perfect—O my dear God.

I've begun a painting for Aunt Ada tonight—she needs another. It's the first thing I've done since Easter.—It is the most exquisite jewel twilight you ever saw: jacinth, and topaz and amethyst. It's nine oclock. I'm going to do a bit of Paul.[1] I send you this mass. I'm afraid it's heterogeneous; since I have never read it through, very blemishy. Correct it & collect it will you, & tell me what you think. This is a quarter of the book.

Mr Jones[2] has shaved off his moustache, and I dont like him. He's got a small, thin mouth, like a slit in a tight skin. It's quite strange. It shows up a part of his character that I detest: the mean and prudent and nervous. I feel that I really don't like him, and I rather liked him before.

Write to me as often as it doesn't weary you. You don't bore me —why say so. I like to see your letter when I get down in the morning. You know I do.

I'll do a scrap of Paul. What will you think of it, I wonder. I want to take it to Ada[3] at Whitsun.

By Jove—what an empty life!

Au revoir D. H. Lawrence

12 Colworth Road, Addiscombe, Croydon
1st May 1911

My dear Lou,

I suppose you will be writing to me tonight, so that our letters will again cross. I see the new moon is out, with a small star in attendance. I caught sight of it for the first time as I came down the steps

---

1. *Sons and Lovers.* 2. His landlord. 3. His sister.

of the library this evening. 'Bless you, you little devil of a weapon', I said. 'You're supposed to be lucky, but you snip the top of one's hopes off, reminding one.' Such a blue bright night over such ripe still yellow lamps: and at the end of it, pen and ink only. I curse these circumstances in their being and their results—let them be cursed.

At your behest I wrote yesterday fourteen pages of Paul Morel, and I sit with the paper before me to continue when this is done. I should like to be able to execute a will such as this—'I, D.H.L. do hereby bequeath to the devils, daemons, or Gods, all such power or fantasy as makes me a writer. I do divest me of all my extraordinary powers. I do bequeath my body and my life unto Louisa, daughter of — —.' Don't you wish I could do it. I would sell birthrights and deathrights for an embrace of thee, Louisa: toss 'em out of the window, poetic powers, perceptivity, intellect—pouf: for a few kisses and a tight clasp. God help us, what a state.

Well—you see how my letters run riot. Sorry—forgive me.

Thine David Herbert Lawrence

·◁[90]▷·
Davidson Road Boys School, South Norwood SE
4th May 1911

My dear Lou,

How the year slips on: I have only just realised that it is May. Time seems to me to be straying, lost, somewhere near February. I have never known the seasons, the weather, the opening leaves to go round so unnoticed as they do this year: one seems to have lost sight of them.

I am glad you are resolving to practise patience. It is a thing that wears out patience quickest, I reckon. The best way is to drug oneself with work and unhopefulness, then the time drifts like the clouds overhead, without sound of footsteps, no echoes, no impatience.

What the devil am I so high-falutin about this morning. It is a beautiful bright day, with handfuls of white cloud pitched across a very blue sky, & veritable choruses of dandelions shining broad-yellow everywhere.

You asked me if I smoke. I have had, have consumed, nine

cigarettes since the return. Will you allow me so many? Do not be afraid, I am not a child to damage myself for a very little longing.

I have written 90 pages of Paul Morel.[1] I think about 7 of these pages may be called amusing, and 20 perhaps pleasant. The rest are 'navrant.' I wonder how Paul will work out.

I am going to Purley[2] to tea today, that's why I write in school. I'm glad your scare is settled in Gaddesby. That about the holiday is the devil. But you may be at Quorn. At any rate, you won't be booked for all August, will you? At any rate, I will come & stay a bit in Gaddesby, unless it were too shocking. We will see.

Till then, I work. 'Laborare est orare.' Never blame me for irreligiousness at that rate. I admire the Jesuits. Goodbye—Un baiser à la bouche.

D. H. Lawrence

Am just writing to Hilda Shaw.[3] DHL

·◄[91]►·
12 Colworth Road, Addiscombe, Croydon
7th May 1911

My dear Lou,

I have managed my ten pages of Paul: I'm now on with the 112th. I wonder what it'll be like; at present it seems to me very rummy. It is four oclock. I have promised to go to Philip Smith's,[4] but I won't go to tea because Ive no clothes to go in. The only black suit I've got is the one I wear in school. I can't afford to buy another, for God knows when. I am too shabby to go through the town, where folk know me, in daylight, on Sunday. I daren't go out of black yet awhile. So I'm not going to Philip's till this evening. Then he'll be mad. But I don't care in the least whether he is.

I went yesterday a very beautiful walk into the country, over Westerham way, about twelve miles out, in Kent. At Limpsfield the hills are covered with primroses, and the bluebells are just coming out. I got heaps of flowers. I was alone all day long—got home about nine o'clock.

1. *Sons and Lovers.*   2. Cf. p. 94 n. 5.
3. Cf. p. 29 n. 3. Doubtless Louie had told Lawrence that Hilda Shaw feared the onset of tuberculosis; in fact she was in the Ransom Sanatorium, Mansfield, by this date (MSS LaB 195-6).
4. Cf. 21 and p. 21 n. 2.

Will you send me the Corot,[1] by the way? The beech-trees are very beautiful, as if afire with the vividest green.

I don't think the last chapter of Paul has action enough, moves sufficiently. It is the bane of my life, to get the action of a novel hurried along.

What about your coming down before Whitsun? It's a month today. Are we going to Eastwood for the first? I don't like to impose too much upon Emily.[2] Then to yours for a day or two? Then Auntie[3] wants me a bit at Leicester. It will need arranging. I must begin to think about it.

What about your coming down for the week end? It would be nice. Can you afford it. I suppose I can squeeze that out all right. It is very beautiful weather.

I must be getting shaven. I think I am stupid this afternoon, and fear this is a stupid letter. Never mind. I wish you could come down here for good. We will talk about midsummer at Whitsun. Oh, work!

Addio—it will be a fine evening, if only you were here.

Addio D. H. Lawrence

·◅[92]▻·
12 Colworth Road, Addiscombe, Croydon
9th May 1911

My dear Lou,

Sorry I worried you about this cursed suit. It troubles me at no time except just when I want to change & get into something decent. I wrote immediately before getting ready to go to Wallington. Today I don't care a damn.

Will you really only come for the day on Saturday? It is such a rush! But half a loaf's better than no bread. We can hardly go into the country: we can go to the Zoo, where I never have been; and I'll take you to the Tate—though there is no 'New Tate'—only a new room. There is a pretty little garden by the Houses of Parliament where we can sit and look at the River & talk. Let me know

1. Perhaps a reproduction of this artist's work which Lawrence wanted to copy; two months later he speaks of having begun 'a nice big Corot' (105). See also his poem *Corot*, first published in *Love Poems and Others*, 1913; and for details of his interest in the artist see *Complete Poems*, ii. 976–7.
2. His sister. 3. Ada Krenkow.

what time you get in, & what time you go again. Then I can think what we shall do.

The 112 pages of Paul[1] are pages such as this on which I write. Am I a newspaper printing machine to turn out a hundred sheets in half an hour?

This weather is wonderfully fine—one can scarcely think of work.

Oh—as for Whitsun—we shall have to give them a few days at home—say till Wednesday: then till Friday at Quorn—then just Saturday at Leicester. You know I don't in the least mind Billy and Nora's[2] racket: but one has to hold oneself to an attitude, I don't quite know how, when one is with one's opposites. I think you understand.

I had a letter from Hilda Shaw this morning. I think she will get well again.[3] She writes me very nicely—her letters are worth reading. I must answer her soon.

Well—I must close. Saturday is very near. These evenings are so beautiful, it is cruel to waste them writing. I wish you were here, so we could walk together. It is the knowledge that the holiday is so brief which makes it pass so strangely when we are together.

I kiss you bon soir—

D. H. Lawrence

·◦[93]◦·
12 Colworth Road, Addiscombe, Croydon
11th May 1911

My dear Lou,

Having got a vilainous headache owing to the thunder, I'm only going to write half a line. You get in at 10.40, don't you?[4] That's the time I shall be at Mary le Bone unless you contradict. And I'm sure, with a day ticket, you can go back by a later, an express train. I am sure, because Auntie does. Bring a bill.[5] I look forward to Sat —or I should if I weren't squint-blind just now. A day, no more. Did you write to Ada?[6] Will you send or bring Corot.[7] Un jour seul

Addio—je t'aime D. H. Lawrence

1. *Sons and Lovers.*
2. Louie's youngest brother and sister, then aged six and four respectively.
3. Cf. p. 103 n. 3.
4. Louie was to spend Saturday, 13th May, with Lawrence in London.
5. Probably a handbill giving details of excursion trains.   6. His sister.
7. Cf. p. 104 n. 1.

12 Colworth Road, Addiscombe, Croydon
14th May 1911

My dear Lou,

We were bound to forget something—here is your scarf.

Doesn't yesterday seem as if it belonged to another existence?[1] I have been in bed all day, that's the reason. I'm afraid I wasn't as jolly yesterday as I should have been: but I was feeling queer, having been rocky since Wednesday. I don't know what it is— nothing—the weather, I suppose. I've been in bed today, following your sage advice: and as soon as the bed's made, I'm going back. One must occasionally sing soft. I wouldn't be ill in digs, not for any money. I shall be all right for school in the morning.

You look also a bit queer. It's love & the weather, like me, eh? But we're neither of us die-ers, & there's no need to worry. I intend to have a good time somewhere in the future—I don't hanker for Orcus.[2] We won't let the filching rascally Fates pick the future from our pockets, will we.

Sursum corda & vogue la galère which is, translated 'Lift up your hearts, however the dam boat cockles.'—if only it didn't make one sea sick.

And now 'To bed, to bed, to bed.'

Embrasse D. H. Lawrence

Sympathetic to Miss Cox[3]—fellow feeling.

Davidson Road Boys School, South Norwood SE
16th May 1911

My dear Lou,

How strange!—it makes me laugh. You imagine I imagine you are mean—how mean of me! I could never mean that you are mean or even slightly mercenary, for I know,—need I tell you so, that you're generous more than ordinary. How could you think that I should sink to such a depth of base suggestion?—it makes me blush and crimson flush to be the object of such a question.

1. Cf. p. 105 n. 4.   2. The nether world.   3. Cf. p. 86 n 2

The idea is, my dear, just mad enough to send me dotty:—whoa!

But what ever made you think such things? I never for a moment doubt your splendid generosity—nor doubt you in any way except to wonder whether I shall ever get you: which is, of course, only the doubt of the baby in the Pear's Soap bath.[1] You are very fantastical, my dear, in your imaginings: they really amuse me, like Alice in Wonderland.

> 'Twas brillig, and the slithy toves
> Did gyre & gimble in the wabe'

No, but I am so Hamletty—I am so confoundedly & absurdly Hamletty, it's enough to make you sick. When I begin to rant in the 'To be or not to be' style, you should say 'Hello, he's off again', and wait for the rhyme which rings conclusion if not reason. Sithee? And if I say about seeing me with J,[2] why I only mean for half an hour: and doubtless, soon or late, you will see me with J for half an hour: and doubtless you won't mind a scrap.

Do lay this to your gentle feminine soul: that, in the opinion of the lady in the Chapter House,[3] I am surely mad. Say to yourself, on lots of occasions that will arrive: 'Well, the lady in the Chapter House says he's mad . . . . . .'. You can fill in the dots.

If you can cook you will be perfect: two cakes! I shall keep henceforth a list to appraise and condemn you by. 'My wife can cook thirty seven puddings and fifteen different cakes: all plain roasts, all haricot stews, curries etc etc etc—.' Kindly keep me informed, so that I can compare you with other men's wives, to my renown.

I, for my part, am going to struggle like the devil to establish my health. A thin blade stands best, goes deepest, and cuts nearest: but if you get too thin in the blade you double up. I proceed to substantiate. Either I shall become a 'garçon solide', or else a mere blessed wraith.

I didn't write any Paul last night—went to bed quite good & early.

It's a very close day today.

I don't feel like undertaking Ordeals, do you?

I'm supposed to be teaching Composition at this minute. I'll now recite the 'Ode to Duty', to get my muscle up, & then I'll fall to.

Addio—I wish it were holidays.

Addio, carissima D. H. Lawrence

1. A currently famous advertisement. 2. Jessie Chambers.
3. An allusion to some incident in, possibly, Westminster Abbey, during their day together on 13th May.

12 Colworth Road, Addiscombe, Croydon
23rd May 1911

My dear Lou,

Have you yet recovered from your indisposition? Dont let it trouble you long.

About Whitsun—they are raising such an outcry at home, because I say I will come late to Eastwood. Ada[1] seems quite upset at the thought. I must not stay at Quorn long: not longer, probably, than the Monday evening. Shall we go home to Eastwood on Monday evening? Your people wouldn't mind, would they? Ada will be very disappointed even then that we are so late in coming: I would not delay further. Shall I write to your mother to thank her for the invitation and to say the time of my departure?—our departure, I mean, of course. I hope to goodness you haven't let me spoil your Grandpa's visit: I wouldn't have that for anything.

And will you, this week-end, make enquiry if there is the Saturday half day trip to London on Whit-Saturday? I'm afraid lest it should be knocked off. If it's not I'll come by the return half. The ordinary fare would beggar me to pay. What a damnation to be so penurious! Never mind, we might be much worse.

It is only a very short time to Whit now.

Everybody here seems a bit off colour and cranky. It's tiresome to live with people who jangle.

I can only work a very little, which annoys me.

Why do you dream such unfinished dreams?—You never did ride, you see. It makes me think of Browning's 'Last Ride Together' not coming-off.

You'll get Quorn I suppose.[2] When shall you go, in that event? Before August?—No.

We'll discuss Coronation[3] at Whit.

Your folk are getting quite tolerant of you.

---

1. His sister
2. Louie had obviously applied for the post (which she obtained) of headmistress at the Quorn Church of England Junior School; her appointment at Gaddesby ceased on 31st July; that at Quorn began on 1st September.
3. George V's coronation was due to take place on 22nd June 1911; schools would be given a holiday.

Have you ever read Hewlett's[1] 'Spanish Jade'? I'll give it Ada at Whit, unless you'd care for it. I don't value it myself, much.

I hope you'll be sound & well at Whit.

Addio. D. H. Lawrence.

12 Colworth Road, Addiscombe, Croydon
26th Ap May 1911

My dear Lou,

You see I was writing 26 April—I am wool-witted. Today has been sultry, full of black vapour, with brownish fiery lightning, and thunder like enormous cats bounding on a sound-board ceiling.— Very fine that!

I remark that you have broken up, and felicitate you on the point. It will be very nice to lie low awhile. I wish we had broken up. The fever has not been your enemy. Was it scarlet, or typhoid, or typhus, or malaria, or which, by the way? I imagine a lurid, malignant disease rampant in your little school room, but know not how to name the brute.

I am quite sure that your father and I will get on heavenlily before long, being, as we are both, 'bons garçons, bons enfants'. Forgive me if I'm impertinent. The weather gets in my head.

Again, I have not answered the question concerning the verses. If you will allow me, I will not give them to you. They are all very well dancing up and down the pages of my little note book, shut safely in the cupboard—but wandering, even as speech from me to you, as yet, 'no', permit me to say. —My style is certainly 'fetching'. —But at Whit. I will show you the first two hundred pages of 'Paul,' that book of books.[2]

My health is so-so: I do not grumble. In truth, or rather in act, I am as good as an angel. I am sure I do nothing to the detriment of my physical well-being: I go to bed pretty early, I eschew pleasures of all kinds, I keep a cheerful frame of mind; I do nothing in excess, nor work, nor read, nor think, nor drink, nor eat, nor smoke. Docile, I am, and good as an angel. I offer myself to your commendation: and

---

1. Maurice Hewlett (1861–1923).   2. *Sons and Lovers.*

109

I never even fib to you. I *am* very tolerably well, I thank you. I *will be* better.

Dreams! I could cap you there. My sleep, in the morning, is a passionate second-life of dreams. This mornings was you: yesterday mother's: so that my dreams seem by far the realest part of my life at present. The day is only a drift, a sort of sleepwalk—oh quite amiable. I dare scarcely tell you this mornings dream. I dreamed we were bien mariés, et que tu étais accouchée de notre premier enfant. Tu souffrais beaucoup; tu gémissais de douleur, et moi, en entendant, je sentis les entrailles me fondent. Et puis, je m'éloignais un peu, et tout était sombre. Revenant ensuite, tu te guérissait, tu sourissait, et on m'a montré l'enfant: garçon très joli et doux, avec les yeux bleu foncés. Quand je l'avais vu, c'étais moi qui devait disparaître de la scène, et il y avait une ombre noire à ma place.—Je puis encore ressentir les entrailles se fondre dans mon corps au son de les gémissements, et je puis encore ressentir le coeur me bondir de joie et de grâce en voyant l'enfant.

—Et après, c'était ma soeur Emilie, et ce n'était pas toi: tout était confus

Mon rêve sans doute te fait rougir—j'en demande pardon.

In a week I shall be coming north—I wish it were tomorrow.

I salute you. My regards to all of your family.

Your D. H. Lawrence

They say it's a very bad dream in our family to dream of a new-born baby.

·◅[98]▻·
Croydon—Tuesday

J'ai été tellement occupé ce soir, ayant commencé un autre tableau pour ma tante: la femme d'un pêcheur, tenant son enfant, et regardant loin sur la mêr. En souvenez vous? Je crois qu'il viendra bien, mon tableau, et je veux qu'il était pour vous. Chaque fois que j'arrive à une bonne effet, je me dis 'Cela devrait être pour Louie'.

Avez vous reçu Paul?—et a-t-on vous fait payer une surcharge sur le paquet.[1] Je n'avais que trois timbres-postes, et il fallait quatre. M'en pardonnerez vous?

1. Presumably some (or all) of the 200 pages mentioned in 97.

Et, si vous aller à Leicester cette semaine, vous me ferez un bonté si vous m'apportez le tableau que j'ai donné à ma tante aux Pâques, et auquel il faut faire une réparation; il y a un morceau de papier à colle s'attache au visage de la femme, et on veut que je le peigne de nouveau, ce morceau. Je peux le faire à Quorn, car je ne veux pas aller à Leicester.

Il ne reste que quatre jours. Dieu, comme je m'impatiente! Je vous embrasse, amante.

Beaucoup de choses de ma part à votre famille.

D. H. Lawrence

Addressed: 'Coteshael' Cheveney Lane Quorn Loughboro
Postmarked: Croydon MY 30 11

·৪[99]৯·
12 Colworth Road, Addiscombe, Croydon
1st June 1911

My dear Lou,

Thanks for fetching the picture from Leicester.[1] I have got on pretty well with the other—I shall finish it tomorrow. It doesn't look bad, so far. I get quite a dab hand at manipulating water color. If I had time I would do original stuff—but it is impossible.

Re—the holidays: I'm very glad you will be restored to us for August; and I guess that, in the end, we shall go to the Lakes: I am always a devil for complaisance. It is true, I was rather keen on France: and it would cost no more than England. Lodging is *so* dear in this country, that folk after folk say to me: 'I can't take a holiday in England, it's so dear. I go on the Continent.' However—heaven is on the side of the big battallion—which word I can't spell —tell me, when you write how to.

I'm glad you like Paul, but doubt whether you tell me 'the truth, the whole truth, and nothing but the truth—so help me God.'

I've painted till nightfall—& talked to the neighbours over the fence till dark—and written to Kit Holderness[2]—it's *such* a long

1. As requested in 98.
2. One of the Eastwood 'Pagans', daughter of George Holderness, headmaster of the British School where Lawrence was a pupil teacher in 1902.

time since I heard from her—& now I write to you. It is quarter to ten: shall I do a few pages of Paul?—or is it too late. Too late, I think. I will vegetate, as Kit says.

Yesterday we had such a storm: the lightning beat about in the sky like a frightened bird (is that over poetic for you? Sorry!)—And I had a 'Nuit blanche' And this morning I would have given anything to be near you, near enough to rest. And tonight I bristle with activity & irony. I shall never rest in this life—not long. I think I shall go out now for a while—from 10.0 till 11.0. There is a young moon.

Auntie[1] was quite concerned on a postcard this morning, about my health. How funny things are!

Why were n't you going boating with Tom Smith[2]—he's no lady-killer, for sure—& lonely, poor devil. Oh, will you write & tell Ada what time we shall get in Newthorpe on Monday night. Do please. I shall come to Quorn by the 6.25 from M. le Bone.[3]

I shan't do any Paul tonight—I'll go out [a]while

You are too far away—it is abominable. Tonight is tonight—& where is Sunday? I kiss you!

D. H. Lawrence

·◦[100]◦·
12 Colworth Road, Addiscombe, Croydon
14th June 1911

My dear Lou,

Let me write in pencil again.

Isn't it damnably cold? I hope the weather'll warm up for next week.

This week has got the lid-on—I merely exist in a box of days, until Saturday. So I'm not going to write much of a letter.

I've heard from Secker[4] & from Hueffer[5]—both very nice. The book of short stories is practically promised for the spring: agreeable all round.

I've worked quite hard: begun a picture, long promised, for

---

1. Ada Krenkow.   2. Cf. p. 45 n. 3.   3. Marylebone Station.
4. Martin Secker who, from 1921, to the end of Lawrence's life, was his regular publisher. Secker had offered to bring out a volume of his short stories (*Collected Letters*, i. 78); in fact it was Duckworth who published *The Prussian Officer* collection in 1914.
5. Cf. p. 46 n. 3.

Mac.,[1] and written a short story, 32 pages long, in two nights.[2] Smart work, eh?

Don't worry, I shall be lively enough next week. But the nights are cold as the icy tomb.

I don't believe there's an item of news. Oh, by the way, would you like to come down to the Suffragette procession on Saturday?[3] I enclose bills. It will, I think, be very nice—& we could return 6.25, or 7.30, or midnight as you please. Puccini's new opera is on in the evening:[4] but alas—my debts are very deep already—oh dear! Please yourself about coming—but tell me.

I don't want to work—I don't want a bit to work—Oh damn Gut Nacht, meine lieben Schatz. (Brahms)[5]

D. H. Lawrence

By the way, I've got a 'Swan'[6] number of the 'Studio'. Shall I bring it? Rather a nice tiger

·◦⟦ 101 ⟧◦·
11 Queen's Square, Eastwood, Notts
23rd June 1911

My dear Lou,

I had a very exciting time yesterday.[7] George[8] had been waiting at the station for me, & then missed me. There was no news of Ada. We went to the Castle 'en famille'—& by the way, the local artists are very good indeed—Tom Gillott has got the Second prize of the year.[9] When we were coming down Friar Lane, there was Sam[10]

---

1. Cf. p. 87 n. 3.
2. Possibly *The Soiled Rose* (published in *Forum*, March 1913) which became *The Shades of Spring* when it was collected in *The Prussian Officer* volume.
3. The suffragist demonstration on 17th June was larger than any before; the *Times* reported a five mile procession of 40,000 people.
4. *La Fanciulla del West* was performed at Covent Garden on 17th June.
5. Op. 14, no. 7 ('. . . liebester . . .').
6. In 1901 *Studio* (xxii. 74–86, 150–61) published two articles—illustrated by pictures of tigers—on the animal painter John Macallan Swan (1847–1910).
7. Lawrence was home for a brief holiday on the occasion of George V's coronation on 22nd June.
8. His brother.
9. Thomas Gillot entered two works in the annual Local Artists' Exhibition held in Nottingham's Castle Art Gallery; one of them 'A Country Fair'—probably the prize-winner referred to—was acquired for the Gallery.
10. Samuel King, husband of Lawrence's sister Emily.

bolting by for dear life. And then Ada, Frances, Gertie Floss Eddie, Emily[1] & Baby discovered feeding at Lyons: ices all round, & up to Forest.[2] Such a crowd you never saw: Nottm teemed & spewed with people. The fireworks very pretty—reminded me of Cowes, with mother, two years back.[3]

Sam had driven the party in a wagonette—behold us sailing home towards midnight, singing, & roaring to everybody we passed—most common, but extremely jolly. I sat in front, arm round Floss, because she found it rummy to be so perched. I wished indeed you were there. The subcurrent of passion, oh Lord, makes you shudder.

Perhaps you'll come to Croydon soon. Gott!

Bring me Howard's End[4] on Sunday, if you can.

Love to all
                    Baiser
                                        D. H. Lawrence

·◁[102]▷·
Purley, Surrey
27th June 1911

My dear Lou,

I'm having to scribble a quick note here, because I've not had a glimpse of time at home. Ma Jones & the family went out for the day, so I had Mac[5] to dine with me, & had to be host, hostess & maid in one. But it was jolly.

Then I got a card from Miss Macartney[6] asking me to tea & a musical evening. So far I've been mowing the grass—such a stretch —with old Macartney, who is grumbling because his gardening man hasn't turned up this week. It's a nice garden—big walnut tree in the centre, and long regiments of great delphiniums blue as strips of heaven—& pink roses, heavy & full.

I thank you for your belated advice—won't work too hard I promise. Damn Paul![7] Why mustn't I write Old Adams?—& New Eves[8] are much wickeder I assure you.

1. Respectively: Ada Lawrence, Frances and Gertrude Cooper (cf. p. 5 n. 2), Alvina ('Floss') Lawrence, William Edward Clarke (Ada's fiancé), and Emily King.
    2. A large open recreation area in Nottingham. 3. Cf. 39.
    4. E. M. Forster's novel (1910). 5. Cf. p. 87 n. 3.
    6. The letter was written at her house. Cf. p. 94 n. 1. 7. *Sons and Lovers.*
8. Presumably a jocular reference to his short story written at this period, *New Eve and Old Adam* (published in *A Modern Lover*, 1934).

I think the holiday has been very good for me—too short—damn it. As for midsummer, I'm sure it'll all turn out A1.—only let it be quick. I was rather looking forward to your coming to Croydon soon. But we'll take what comes, for the best. Now for a Beethoven Sonata

Love DHL

·◁[103]▷·
Davidson Road Boys School, South Norwood SE
30th June 1911
My dear Lou,
 You write also very hastily: I suppose there is no news: except the important point about Gaddesby.[1] This time next week, and you will be spending your last session with the Gaddesby kiddies. You will find a big change at Quorn—no more 'en famille' at school: no more the patriarchal—or matriarchal system. You won't like the other so well, but it will be a change for you, & you'll soon get used to it: and, heaven knows, it will be easy enough, even at Quorn. You'll like it all right.
 I'm very glad that you will go to Wales with me. France seems off, because of money chiefly. I have written to Auntie for the addresses of the cottages at Pwllelli—or Pwllelhi, however they spell it—and will try & arrange for the first three weeks of August, if not for the month. Do you know, the Hall's want to go with us, as of yore. So that would mean Coopers.[2] I should like it all right, if you would. You see, it would mean that Ada[3] would have more pals—and it is very jolly. Then, if we kept the cottage for the month—if we could —we might have Emily or Ethel or even Tom Smith[4]—if he'd come —for a week or so. We must see. Don't say anything about it yet, except just that we propose to go to Wales.
 I had a letter from Ethel[5] this morning: they are moving today to

1. Cf. p. 108 n. 2.
2. Lawrence was assuming almost the same party as shared the holiday at Shanklin in 1909. Alice Hall was one of the 'Pagans' but she is unlikely to be in question here: her husband, only in February 1911, had threatened a lawsuit over the presentation of Alice as Alice Gall in *The White Peacock*. Some other members of the Hall family must be intended. For the Coopers see p. 5 n. 2.
3. His sister.
4. Respectively: his sister Emily (King); Louie's sister, Ethelreda; and their College friend (cf. p. 45 n. 3).
5. Lawrence's cousin, daughter of Aunt Nelly. She was married to Max Hunger (listed in the Jurors' Book for 1914–15 as 'an importer of gloves').

115

St Margarets' on Thames, wherever that may be: somewhere near London. 'Oak Lodge'—sounds rather nice. I am going for the week-end in a fortnight.

And in a month today we shall have broken up—thank the Lord. I feel less and less like work. Certainly I shall have to turn gentle-man, and do nowt. I wish we could be married: it is such an effort to carry all things on, sans aide ni appui. Well—in a month we shall have a month to ourselves—which is more than everybody can look forward to.

I[t] is rather cold & dreary here today: I wish I were at Coteshael:[1] I think that is more like home to me than Queens Square.[2] Don't tell Ada I said that—but it's true. Regards to everybody.

With love to you. DHL

·⊲[104]⊳·
12 Colworth Road, Addiscombe, Croydon
4th July 1911

My dear Lou,

So your managers are being fussy?[3]—damn them. Say now—are you *sure* you won't go back on the eighth? Of course, in the safety of July youll protest your will, but when August creeps on us —what then. O damn the fools, why can't they be sensible.

The Hall's,[4] also, fatheads, want to go to Barmouth. I've partly arranged the Pwllheli digs—sounds ever so nice. We might have a sweet bungalow cottage for £2··10 a week. I have sent the letter to Eastwood for them to consider & decide. They'll let us know. But do try to wring from the necks of your managers some words of certitude.

Don't talk about honey-moons—the atmosphere's too inflam-mable. It's only 3 weeks to breaking up.

Do you know I went to the Opera on Sat. & heard Bohème.[5] Melba took leading part: very good, but a bit tense, strenuous as a singer. Twas nice—wished you were there. Was there anything I

1. Louie's home.
2. Ada Lawrence and her father had given up the house in Lynn Croft, in March; they now lived at 13 Queen's Square, Eastwood.
3. Presumably the managers of the Gaddesby school had not been able to replace Louie; they were now obstructing her move to Quorn. (Cf. p. 108 n. 2.)
4. Cf. p. 115 n. 2.
5. Puccini's opera *La Bohème* (1896) was performed at Covent Garden on 1st July.

had to answer you?—I forget. Yes, I'm very well—and you? I've done a fair amount of Paul[1]—theres no more news.

We break up in three weeks—how I harp on it. It won't be long going. I wish something nice would happen.

You will be enjoying yourself tea-ing with so many folk. I'm glad you're going out a bit. Don't get thin—I like you to be fat—dont get any thinner. I am a Turk—like my houre plump. Sounds bestial —it's only brevity.

The English hasn't paid me yet:[2] Devils!

I've insured father for £9··12: he wasn't insured.

Here's my mouth

D. H. Lawrence

·◁[105]▷·

12 Colworth Road, Addiscombe, Croydon
7th July 1911

My dear Lou,

I hardly know how your calendar goes from now. Have you done at Gaddesby?—unless you are constrained to start again in August? Do you put in your first day at Quorn on Monday?[3] I suppose you will be very excited and turmoilsome this week-end: and then the heat. For the Lord's sake, don't go & knock yourself up. I often wonder, as I walk along in the still, intense heat, going to school, whether you are flagging like a broken holly hock. It doesn't ill-suit me, this weather.

Ada has applied for the bungalow[4]—for the first two weeks of August, I believe. If we get it, how jolly! I sincerely hope that the Halls[5] won't go, then we shall be a jolly little party. I believe its a very nice place—I dreamed of it the other day. At any rate we shall see the sun set over the west sea.

Nothing happens here—the days go slowly by, like barges. I began a nice big Corot,[6] half did it, spoiled it, & tore it in thirty pieces. Shame! Now I've begun a little Idyll for Agnes Holt.[7] She marries in early August, & has asked me for this picture. I must race & get her a couple done.

---

1. *Sons and Lovers.* 2. For *Odour of Chrysanthemums* published in June.
3. Her appointment began on 1st September.
4. Cf. 104. 5. Cf. p. 115 n. 2. 6. Cf. p. 104 n. 1.
7. Cf. p. 82 n. 2. Lawrence presented two pictures to Agnes Holt (cf. Introduction, p. xvi, and p. 67 n. 2)—the *Idyll* and *Wind on the Wold*. Both are now owned by the University of Nottingham.

I think we are going to live in Clyde Rd. near here in September.[1] The house is a nicer one than this, pleasantly situated. They are negotiating terms. I had thought that when the lease of this house expired I should be far away—but things turn out differently. I may be here a long time. Even we make between us little arrangements for the school year that follows next—that goes on into 1913. Shall I be here then—& still with the Joneses? Gott in Himmel!!

We break up on Thursday 26th. I shall come up on that day—to Quorn for the night at least, eh?—for the two days, eh? I hope holidays turn up trumps.

I wish you were here. This sultry weather makes one burn like a fire that wants feeding. I wish you were nearer. It's no good saying I kiss you, because I can't. Ah well—in three weeks.

Love. D. H. Lawrence

·⬥[106]⬥·
12 Colworth Road, Addiscombe, Croydon
11th July 1911

My dear Lou,

I hear from Ada today that the bungalow in Nevin is taken—that they're getting a girl at ten bob a week to do the work—& I think everything will go like a coon song, now you are safe & sure. Halls are going, worse luck: & Frances & Gertie—not Neville,[2] because he's not breaking up till the 4th.

Ada complains you haven't written her.[3] Georgie, by the way, is playing the goat: hasn't answered Floss' letter for three weeks.[4] I've done with him—he's a fool.

Now for the holidays, which will be here in a fortnight. We break up Thursday 27th, as I told you. Shall I try & get off by the morning trip—I will. If I can't manage it, Ill come by return half. I really ought to go to Eastwood, because of dragging all my luggage to Wales. What shall I do?—Shall I stay with you & we'll join the party together in Nottm on the Sat. morning, or shall I go on to Eastwood on Friday? We must decide.

1. The Jones moved to 16 Colworth Road. Cf. 125.
2. Cf. p. 11 n. 4. For the others named see 103.
3. Ada had sent a postcard to Louie on 29th June (MS LaB 199).
4. The reference is to Lawrence's brother George and his cousin Alvina (cf. p. 114 n. 1).

Oh, and I'll tell you now so you won't revile me when I come: We've promised a few days to Kit Holderness[1] from the 3rd week, Ada & I—& I'm booked to Lincoln a few days for the 4th week.[2] Now *don't* say I haven't told you.

The English have paid me at last,[3] & more than I expected, so that I shall be able to pay off all my encumbrances, get some boots & shirts & a suit, & have just a bit left. I want, when I come up, to bring Mrs Burrows something really nice. Will you tell me what. If you don't tell me something worth getting, I'll spend a quid on table-cloths for her—for *her*, not for you, mind you.

And if still there remains anything—I have such elastic ideas of £10—then you and I we will not pinch a bit in the holiday, eh?— I've had to send a tidy bit to Eastwood, to settle matters there.

Tomorrow we've got a holiday for the sports. I am glad, for I am as tired as a dog. I think I shall go to St Margarets—which is just over Richmond Bridge—& see how Max & Ethel have settled down.[4] It will be a relief, this hot weather, to get into Richmond Park.

How are you: you sounded very sweaty & enervated in your last. But the Welsh sea will pull you together, I am sure.

I shall miss your wretched Quorn post, which goes so early. Tell me how you have gone on: I've been wondering every morning & afternoon. Tell me how you are. Your letters are scroddier[5] even than mine.

Give the girls a kiss round from me (I shall ask them if you did it). I look forward to getting to Quorn again.

And by the briny in a three week's time, we will be veritable Tristan & Isolde. what!

Now I'll rush to post. I kiss you, you flagging hollyhock. Tell the Time to shuffle along.

Goodbye—goodnight—au revoir—

x Baisers x x x D. H. Lawrence

---

1. Cf. p. 111 n. 2.   2. Cf. 116, 119.   3. Cf. p. 117 n. 2.   4. Cf. p. 115 n. 5.
5. i.e. scrappier.

12 Colworth Road, Addiscombe, Croydon
13th July 1911

My dear Lou,

I am afraid you are falling out with me for not attempting to save. And does 10 quid seem much to you. Pah—it is nothing. Shall I make you out a bill of how I spend it? Shall I say how much goes to Eastwood, what I give Agnes Holt for a wedding present,[1] et cetera. No, my dear—we won't quibble about the money for Chrysanthemums.[2] Remember, my shirts are patched, my boots are—well, not presentable. Hueffer asks me to the Reform Club—I can't go because I've not got a decent suit. Well well—and what is left out of ten mere quid. You haven't told me what to get for your mother, so I am left to my own devices.—I don't chuck money about—ten quid doesn't seem to me a lot of money—but a scroddy bit.—I went to Dover yesterday alone—trainfare 2/6—tea 1/—oddments, 1/-. I suppose it *was* extravagant. No matter, it's done.

But listen;—if I don't make money in a fairly large sum, I can never save: I have too many calls. So beware—chuck me if you're going to be sick of my failures: but they may be successes.

I can see you're offended.

I'll come up Thursday—today fortnight. We'll meet 'tothers at Nottm. I have promised Kit[3] the Monday Tuesday Wed of our return. They *wont* let me leave Eastwood the moment I get back. I can't help it—I am not able to do just simply what I prefer. There are many ties, many influences.

When I feel you are a bit offended, I'm no good at a letter.

Shall I send you Olive Schreiner's 'Woman and Labour'?[4]—the library copy. Say yes at once if you'd care for it, so that you can send it back before the holiday.

It is only a fortnight: such beautiful hot weather—such heavy thick blood! A fortnight seems a lifetime. But it'll come—Addio

D. H. Lawrence

---

1. Cf. p. 117 n. 7.   2. Cf. p. 117 n. 2.   3. Cf. p. 111 n. 2.
4. This sociological work appeared in 1911.

12 Colworth Road
Saturday [15th July 1911]

My dear Lou,

How horrid of me!—I'm awfully sorry. And the tone of your letter in answer was really beautiful, and I love you for it. My dear, it was the answer of a gentlewoman, I fairly rejoice over it. The artist in me rejoices in sympathy with the man. I love you profoundly at this minute.—The profundity of love is a thing that varies, eh?

Oh, I've been writing all day long, 38 pages of a long short story.[1] I've written all day long & all night. And now its ten oclock, I'm going out. I wish you were here—there's nowhere to go.

Nevin[2] is off—can't arrange about the house. Halls[3] are not going. I want to go to France. Write to Ada; let's go abroad. We shall go somewhere, at any rate. I'm glad Halls aren't going. I wish it were here, the holiday. Don't have headaches. I kiss you most sweetly, my dear.

Your lover DHL

12 Colworth Road, Addiscombe, Croydon
Sunday evening [16th July 1911]

My dear Lou

Well, I've finished the short story—called 'Two Marriages'[4]—& you can see it as soon as you come to Croydon: it's not worth sending by post.

I send you Woman & Labor.[5] Parasitism is not bad—nor Woman & War. Myself I skip the rhetoric. But read the book, will you. I think it's worth it. You'll see, it's short.

I wonder what we shall do about the holidays. What fun if we really go abroad after all. What ever we do we'll make a good time out of it. Only a fortnight now—it seems very near, thank goodness.

---

1. Cf. n. 4 below. 2. Cf. 106. 3. Cf. p. 115 n. 2.
4. Later entitled *Daughters of the Vicar*; published in *The Prussian Officer* volume, 1914.
5. Cf. p. 120 n. 4. 'Parasitism' and 'Woman and War' are titles of chapters in Schreiner's book.

Excuse me if this is a tiny note—it's late. I hope your headaches are better, & that you've forgiven me my nastiness of the last letter but one: I repent me still: which is a long time for me.

> We shall know each other better
> When the mists have rolled
> away
> When the mii-i-ists etc!

Lord, that hymn.[1] No, Ive not been to church. Write to Ada, do. Love to everybody. With my love to you

DHL

12 Colworth Road, Addiscombe, Croydon
17th July 1911

My dear Lou,

I am a failure at everything tonight—writing, verse, painting, reading, everything. It is one of the times when one feels as if one were in a 'cachot' or in an 'oubliette.' There's nothing to do but sit & pant—but it's near enough to bed-time. I don't know what's the matter with me this week-end—I am quite well. But I feel as if I'd got a bandage over my eyes and mouth ugh! I've tried to do a lot of things, & in the end I can only sit still & wait to go to sleep. If you were here! This is one of the times when you are indispensable: this, now, is much less aimiable than death, I swear.

No, I've not done any Paul[2] lately. I've only done a short story.

You got a letter from me this morning, surely. You don't say that you did. And I've sent the book.[3] They will shortly be teasing you with your number of epistles received.

This evening, & last evening it's been ghastly. —But what's the use of talking.

I think it will turn out that we go to France 'en quatre'. You, me, Ada, Neville.[4]—and the second week: that is, sail August 3rd. Will you like it? It is not far off, by calendar.

---

1. From Moody and Sankey's famous hymnal; by Annie Herbert.
2. *Sons and Lovers.*   3. Cf. p. 120 n. 4.
4. His sister and George Neville (cf. p. 11 n. 4).

I am going to bed. You shouldn't make me tell you how dreadful today is, and yesterday.

If I had my way, of course I should have come long ago: or rather, you would be here living with me. But I have no way, at present—and there is no way, at present. But August is very near. It is foolish of me to get like this.

I hope Ethel[1] will have a suave & romantic time.

Goodnight, my love D. H. Lawrence

·◅[111]▻·
Le Train 5.15 [*19th July 1911*]

Ma chère Lou,

Me voici en train pour Londres. C'est aujourd'hui le jour de naissance de ma mère,[2] et je veux l'oublier.

J'ai été un peu frappé de votre lettre. Cependant, je suis nullement mis en courroux. Ada s'est decidé d'aller à Prestatyn, en N. Wales, pour le premier quinze jours. Il y aura Ada, moi, et vous. Cela, est il assez pour votre vertu ou doit on avoir une vieille tigre de femme de plus. N'importe quoi qu'on dit, nous irons, moi, et vous, et Ada, à Prestatyn, le 29 de ce mois. Qu'est ce qu'on veut, donc? Dis nettement à ta mère notre dessein, et ne permets pas de questions. Mon dieu—sommes nous des enfants. Il est possible que Neville[3] vienne à Prestatyn pour la seconde semaine. Il a été blessé par un bal de criquet: en ai-je vous parlé? La blessure a été telle qu'on ne la peut pas nommer. Cependant, il se guérit, et probablement il viendra chez nous en villégiature. Si cela va compliquer la question, en tais toi. Que de sottises! Je n'ai pas compris très exactement ta lettre (Je le trouve difficile à te tutoyer). Est ce que vous voulez dire que votre famille ne croit guère dans mon amour pour vous? Mais pourquoi? Peutêtre je me trompe: votre style n'est pas précis.

Nous passons tout près de Crystal Palais. Ce pays ne cesse pas d'être étranger.

En huit jours je vais venir chez vous. Il me parait impossible. Et en dix jours, nous voilà en route pour Wales. Assurément on trouvera Ada assez de chaperon. Ah, quelle sottise!

1. Louie's sister. 2. 19th July 1852. 3. Cf. p. 112 n. 4.

Comment allez vous—mieux? Je l'espère. Je ne peux pas travailler cette semaine. J'erre par ici, par là, comme un papillon de nuit. Tu devrais aimer un autre que moi, garçon plus solide, plus stupide, plus convenable. Je ne te donnerai que des chagrins.

Il fait très chaud. Nous sommes à New Cross.

Adieu. D. H. Lawrence

12 Colworth Road, Addiscombe, Croydon
21st July 1911

My dear Lou,

So things do not go so well with you at Coteshael.[1] It is there, if anywhere, that the rub of the change will be felt. But that is not for me to say.

I find I should really have to leave too early to come by the morning excursion on Thursday, so if you will be good enough to send me the excursion ticket I will come in the evening as I have done before. You will not forget the ticket, will you?

I have been thinking that it would be better for me to buy your mother her table cloths in Leicester, while you are there. That would save my carting them from London: and I shall have a month's luggage,—though I'm not bringing many clothes—and also it would prevent my buying the wrong size. So that this day week we will have a days shopping in Leicester: or at least, half an hour's shopping. On Saturday morning we shall be en route for Wales. That will leave us assez peu de temps à Coteshael: qui est ce que nous voulons. I think I would tell them exactly how we are going to Wales: they are sure to ask me, and I shall not trouble to equivocate. But please yourself, only tell me if there is anything I must reserve. Il est tout très stupide.

You will be pleased to hear that Miss Reynolds has got a school in Redhill—about eight miles south of Croydon, in the Reigate district: the average attendance is 150—salary £110: which is for her a fall of £10, but that is not serious. She commences duties on Sept 4th I think: at any rate, finishes here on Sept 2nd. So you will

---

1. See the suggestions in the preceding letter about the hostility of Louie's family.

124

never stay at Kenella again, I am afraid.[1] Never mind: Mrs Humphreys[2] would always put you up.

I send you the MSS of the story that is to appear in the September English.[3] I have corrected and returned the proofs. Hope you will like the tale.

It is exceedingly hot here. Coteshael will not be a particularly restful place this weather. I commiserate. Are you flagging again?— is it your 'malaise' which makes votre monde a little bit displeased with you: or have you been venting advanced opinions?[4] You really shouldn't.

Ah well—in a week's time today we shall have done our shopping in Leicester. It seems impossible. We'll laugh at every thing in seven days' time—will we not?

Good night—love D. H. Lawrence

◦◖ 113 ◗◦

St Margarets on Thames

Am down here for the week end. Max[5] has got a delightful house, just a meadow down from Richmond. We have been on Exotic Island,—open air restaurant, river crowded with boats, & just beginning to twinkle with lights—everybody at the tables & on the terraces, dressed in white—très gai, très charmant. I wish you had been there—but we'll go one day.

DHL

Addressed: Coteshael Cheveney Lane Quorn Leicester
Postmarked: JY 23 11

---

1. Cf. p. 86 n. 4.   2. Wife of Ernest Humphreys, one of Lawrence's colleagues.
3. *A Fragment of Stained Glass.* Cf. p. 6 n. 2; p. 93 n. 2.
4. Perhaps arising from her strong sympathies with the suffragettes.
5. Cf. p. 115 n. 5.

12 Colworth Road, Addiscombe, Croydon
24th July 1911

My dear Lou,

That's all right then, if things square themselves out pleasantly for you at Coteshael. I was afraid there was a certain—increasing—amount of incompatibility between you and the rest. I am glad if it is not so. As for your flinging yourself at me—I like you for this frankness—I only wish you flung yourself a bit farther. I wish we were married, could be married. God alone knows when it will be possible. Honestly, my dear, when I think how I may keep you dragging on, I am in a temper, and feel like telling you to give me up. I have not any great hopes of material success. Which doesn't mean that I'm wallowing in melancholy: simply, I cannot see success on the horizon, gaze as I may. By success I mean an assured income of £150, and a hundred quid to marry on: oh, that ancient problem, how to arrive at this much! However, tonight I care less than usual whether it's success or just Mean Street which leads down into my future: and by success I mean merely enough to marry on. I *do* want to get married. But damn it all, what's the good of worrying. If you can't eat, why, curse it, starve and have done with it. That's what Neville[1] heroically writes me.

Which ends my tirade for tonight

Ada wants to know about the railway tickets. I shall write & say to her she is to book us both from Kimberley along with her own ticket, and that we will go to Eastwood on Friday. Do you hear—it will be much more convenient for us to go to Eastwood on Friday afternoon. I shall write & tell Ada we will come then. Do you decide on the train, & inform her of that.

You *do* misuse the English language. How can you write to me '*Won't* you come by the early train.' I *will*. I will come tonight, now, I will hurry off to East Croydon. But I *may* not. We break up on Thursday morning at 12.0. The excursion leaves London at 12.15, Midland. I could not get to St Pancras till 1.15. We are a teacher short: I *cannot* ask for time off. I cannot, cannot come by the early train. Please send me my ticket, and expect me by the 6.25.

Thank you for your eulogium on the 'Stained Glass' story.[2] It is a bit of tour de force, which I don't care for.—the tale I mean.

---

1. George Neville. Cf. p. 11 n. 4.
2. p. 125 n. 3.

I had a pleasant time at St Margarets[1] during the week end. The new house I find very charming. We must go there some time.

I shall be quite willing to discuss Olive Schreiner with you. Do not worry, pray, about Parasitism in your own case.[2] If you married me I'm afraid you'd find plenty to do. You'd have to be

'O I am the cook an' the captain bold
And mate of the 'Nancy' Brig.
An' bosun' tight, and the midship-mite
And the crew of the captain's gig'[3]

No—I'd be the 'captain bold'—and you could be all the rest. I fancy you reciting, in rhetoric vein
'O Captain, my Captain, our fearful trip is done.'[4]
But it ain't begun yet.

It's actually raining, and the very rain smells musty. If I were capable of an effort, I could write well tonight. But I loathe the thought of effort—I shall read a bit then go to bed.

I wish we were at Prestatyn. Ah well—we groan so often, I wonder 'Time' doesn't refuse to budge. I often remind myself of a half drunk ill-tempered driver bullying the meagre beasts of my own little applecart: but they jog on unheeding, & at last I hear myself, & laugh. Gott—Gott—

Addio, my dear. Ton amant D. H. Lawrence

Ethel[5] sent her love to you—much good may it do you.

·◅[115]▻·

Arrived here about two after a sweltering ride & a flood of cider.[6] It's such a quaint place, Eakring[7]—a bit Ratcliffey, but pretty: red houses among trees like apples in foliage. The school house is

1. 113. 2. p. 121 n. 5.
3. Sir W. S. Gilbert, 'The Yarn of the Nancy Bell' in *The Bab Ballads* (1869).
4. Walt Whitman, *O Captain, My Captain*. 5. Cf. p. 115 n. 5.
6. Louie, Lawrence and his sister Ada probably returned from Prestatyn on 12th August after a two-week holiday beginning on 29th July (see 111). Louie had then returned to Quorn; Lawrence was carrying out the programme of visits mentioned in 107.
7. Presumably the home of Kit Holderness where he had promised to spend three days, 14th-16th August (cf. 107).

attached to the school, which is about twice as big as yours at Ratcliffe. I drink a brew of fermented honey & eat apples. I'm changing my name to Corydon or Damon & think of adopting a leopard skin. Southwell is just the same. Love to all

D. H. Lawrence

Addressed: 'Coteshael' Cheveney Lane Quorn Leicestershire
Postmarked: Eakring 14 AUG 11

·◁[116]▷·
Eastwood—Thursday night

I have written to T.A.S.[1] to ask him to let me off from my visit to Lincoln—if he will, I will come to Quorn on Tuesday at the latest: & not before Monday, for Shirebrook[2] is a clinched thing. I'll let you know as soon as Tom writes: I don't want to go to Lincoln now —I don't. Ada is at Leicester—Auntie is not seriously ill. I would liefest of all come to Quorn on Monday. I hope I may.

Love DHL

Addressed: 5 Kingston St. Derby
Postmarked: Eastwood AU 18 11

·◁[117]▷·

Biked here—a Hell of a place—Mr & Mrs Dax[3] very well. I got your card—you are in a high feather of adventure. Don't get damaged in the riots.[4] I shall get to Quorn on Tuesday if I can.

Love D. H. Lawrence

Addressed: 5 Kingston St Derby
Postmarked: Shirebrook Mansfield AU 20 11

1. Tom Smith (cf. p. 45 n. 3). The visit to Lincoln is mentioned in 106.
2. Cf. 117.
3. Henry Richard Dax, pharmacist, and his wife Alice whose personality contributed to the portrait of Clara Dawes in *Sons and Lovers*. (Shirebrook is a village 4 miles north of Mansfield; Henry Dax lived at 29 Station Road.)
4. A national railway strike caused rioting in many places including Derby where Louie was staying with her uncle, George Campbell Burrows.

·◄[118]►·
Eastwood—Tuesday

T.A.S.[1] is rather cross, & won't let me off since this strike is settled.[2] I am sorry, but shall have to go to Lincoln: I had promised so definitely, you see. I will leave on Thursday though. Perhaps I may have to run straight into Leicester from Lincoln—but I'll let you know that later. Do not be cross, I beg you: I can't help it. Go & see Ada—Auntie is rather seriously ill.[3] What a business altogether!

Love to everybody D. H. Lawrence

Addressed: 'Coteshael' Cheveney Lane Quorn Loughboro.
Postmarked: Eastwood AU 22 11

·◄[119]►·
3 Colegrave Street, Lincoln

I will come tomorrow[4] by the first train after 6.15 from Arkwright St. I get in the Midland at Nottm at 6.15 p.m. I can't see what train is forward to Quorn. They are fearfully cross with me here for departing so soon. I am in hot water in every direction. T.A.S. is going to slay you when he sees you, & I tell him you are going to slay him: funerals! My love to everybody—Your renegade

D. H. Lawrence

Addressed: 'Coteshael' Cheveney Lane Quorn. Loughboro.
Postmarked: Lincoln AU 23 11

---

1. Tom Smith.
2. There had been rioting in Lincoln; indeed Lawrence saw 'riot and a fire' there (*Collected Letters*, i. 79).
3. Cf. 116.
4. Confirmation that he did go to Quorn is provided by the existence of a letter written from there on 25th August (*Collected Letters*, i. 79).

12 Colworth Road, Addiscombe, Croydon
29th August 1911

My dear Lou,

Two days of school over—& I must say they have been pretty rotten. My new kids—well, they are not my old ones: & I have 50 —and, at the bottom, I don't like teaching—it wearies me to death. Amen.

How have you gone on with your fleas, all slippers & tongues, is it?

I find Colworth queer after a month of absence Mr & Mrs Jones are very quiet—not on the very best of terms Mary is the wildest & rampagest kid on the face of the earth. I have just sported with her for an hour: she's a real brick. I popped her in the back yard at tea time, and she howled till Addiscombe re-echoes. But all the neighbourhood knows Marys howl by now: if not, it ought. I've been reading William Morris' 'Defence of Guinevere etc.' Do you know, I am rather fond of Morris. That should please you. And then Mrs Jones has been telling me things—very un-Morris-like: marital & faintly horrifying.

I had back the play that Hueffer had sent to Granville Barker[1]— with a 'read it with much interest but afraid I don't want it' note. Hueffer has gone again to Germany. I hope you haven't expected the Lincoln bit[2] in the Daily News: it won't come now: that, however, I dont mind, myself.

I am just going to do another story for Austin Harrison.[3] I did one last night—I will send him a couple. Then some for Edward Garnett.[4]

I feel very unsettled. I should like to lift up my feet & depart again from here—to Hades or elsewhere, I don't mind. Really, I think I shall have to turn that proverbial tramp.

It is not that it seems a long time since Sunday, but that everything further than an hour back seems fictional—all a mere drift of a tale. I really must begin to suck permanency out of something. I

1. The play sent to the dramatist and critic Harley Granville-Barker (1877–1946) was probably an early version of *The Widowing of Mrs. Holroyd*, itself an expansion of Lawrence's story *Odour of Chrysanthemums*. (It was published in 1914.)
2. Lawrence had probably offered to the *Daily News* an account of his experiences in Lincoln. Cf. p. 129 n. 2.
3. Cf. p. 49 n. 6.
4. Garnett (1868–1937), an editor for the publishing house of Duckworth, had invited Lawrence to submit stories for publication in the American journal *Century*. (Cf. 121.)

suppose it'll have to be work: so I'll begin. Prosper with your wood carving—be busy, it'll keep you happy.[1]

Goodbye—love D. H. Lawrence

·◦[121]◦·

12 Colworth Road, Addiscombe, Croydon
1st September 1911

My dear Lou,

I'm glad your school is going to turn out another Gaddesby[2]—let me write in pencil, will you, I want to write on my knee.—My kids aren't horrid—only different & rather stupid & I hate being back in school because of the confinement—nothing else. And it's not so bad at all these later days.

I am interested to hear of the wood-carving. I know how those gouges do score out lumps. Sometimes when the boys are doing wood carving in the workroom I have a go myself, if the kid's a raw one. But it's a thing, so it seems to me, in which one can acquire a fine nicety of touch. I will paint you a Fisherwoman when I get a bit of time. I did not mean I had written a new story on Monday, but I've done one up. I sent two, yesterday evening, to Austin Harrison.[3] I was advised to send something to Edward Garnett for his approval for the Century, an American mag. Tonight & tomorrow I am going to spend doing up a couple for him.[4] I will let you know if anything comes of it. I am glad you feel sure of soon prosperity: my prophetic instinct isn't working just at present. I am using my vol of Morris in school just now—Mac[5] gave it me—but I will send it you later on. You will like it, I think.

It is most exquisite weather here—most beautiful. It would be rich if you were here. But then we should only be falling into a conflict of unaccomplished passion, so perhaps it's as well. I'm wondering about your coming down to London this term. I must get somebody here to take you in—Mrs Humphreys[6] or somebody. I'm

---

1. An interest learned from Louie's father (see Introduction, p. x).
2. Cf. p. 108 n. 2.   3. Cf. 120.
4. Cf. p. 130 n. 4. One of the stories was called 'Intimacy' (*Collected Letters*, i. 80). None of Lawrence's works appeared in the *Century*.
5. A. W. McLeod.   6. Cf. p. 125 n. 2.

not keen for you to come to Colworth, & I don't like fragments of days ripped off. However, it's full early to bother—we're only a week back.

If you happen to be in Leicester & to pass that bookshop, will you look if there still remains that volume of verse by Jean Moreas,[1] which I hesitated over & didn't buy—to my eternal regret. A volume of verse has the value of several days' life: and this is only 6d.

I've got to work when I don't want. I'm simply topsy turvy with lovingness—every woman I meet I think looks sweet & kissable—not that I want to kiss her—but—& here I am—nothing but ink.

Jones is playing Miserere Domine, & singing it falsetto. He'll borrow a dollar from me in half an hour. Good night—je t'embrasse

D. H. Lawrence

·ᴕ[122]ᴅ·
Davidson Road Boys School, South Norwood SE
7th September 1911

My dear Lou,

I have just finished marking my science books. Oh Lord, what a fag! These close afternoons, it is enough to keep oneself alive, without bothering correcting books & kids. But the class is in quite comfortable order again—settling down. Oh, we're all serene.

Today I've got 14 boys away. The Cherry Blossom Boot Polish people are giving a free day at the Palace,[2] so half Croydon has trooped off. You can get in with a tin lid, or something like that. Mrs Jones has gone with the kids, so I shall have a quiet night of work. I have had two off nights—one at a party of one of the teachers—Tuesday—& I was out to tea down Kenley last night. I really must get a bit of writing done, though I don't feel much like it. I feel like wandering & dodging about.

On Saturday Laura Macartney is giving one of her famous music parties[3] It will be jolly, but I'd rather go as I did last week right down into the country and pick blackberries. It was really fine down at Leith Hill.

I haven't got a bit of literary news—I've not written anything: Hueffer has gone to Germany: Harrison has gone to Paris, but will be back sometime next week. I have not had a letter for two days, which is a miracle for me.

1. Jean P. Moréas (1856–1910), a French poet.   2. Crystal Palace.   3. Cf. p. 94 n. 1.

How funny that the folk in Hilda's[1] sanatorium should be so poor. I thought surely she would be among the swells there. I am sorry she's got no pals. Yes, I will certainly write her. It makes me sorry I dropped my N.U.T. subscription—I did it all unknowing when I was at Eastwood last fall—when I hear how good they have been to her.[2] I am glad to hear of it. What's Nell Slater[3] like—just the same? Is there no news of the Coll folk to be told?

It is very hot down here. I think of you & wonder if Quorn is the same. Everybody flags, even I, in the afternoon. It is a weariness of the flesh to teach & make efforts in the heat.—What a joke you have got a sudden desire for dress. Well—I can make myself fairly smart just now, to keep you company. Addio—je vous embrasse

D. H. Lawrence

·◁[123]▷·
12 Colworth Road, Addiscombe, Croydon
11th September 1911

My dear Lou,

How funny, I bungled at the date![4] I got your parcel at breakfast this morning. The clock made me laugh. Why a clock, O impulsive! But it is very pretty: it will adorn your bedroom sweetly. I should always call the rooms yours. It seems to me inconceivable that I should own property: a house. It will have to be yours. The serviette ring is just as I like it—nice and severe in cut. It will accompany me through the ages, I hope: and you will be so used to setting it by my plate. How strange it all seems, stranger than the stories I write, by far. And the strangeness is fascinating too. I wonder, when will it be that you will take my serviette out of our sideboard, and lay it beside my plate for dinner. I cannot believe it—but I wish it were here. I wish we had a home in the country, away from school. The boys are all right, only issued from God a good deal below sterling intelligence: but they are nice enough. Only school trammels me and makes me feel as if I can't breathe.

1. Cf. p. 103 n. 3.
2. As a teacher, Hilda Shaw would probably benefit from the National Union of Teachers' Benevolent Fund.
3. Possibly Mary E. Slater, a contemporary at University College, Nottingham.
4. Lawrence's birthday.

Emily sent me some handkerchiefs, and Mrs Jones gave me some. Ada[1] is going to send me a dressing gown. She insists.

I sent last night two stories to Edward Garnett. I wonder, will he accept. The Century would pay well.[2] But the stories are not of the length he wished. That I cannot help. I am going to write another short story tonight, or part of one.

I hope Loughboro fair won't come too near to Goose Fair. You know my brother George is coming down here then. You must find out, and tell me, and we will have a wild time.

Do not think Laura Macartneys[3] music is wonderful: it is not. She only plays well. We had a jolly time at the party. This week, no parties. I think I shall manage to work a good bit.

Mrs Jones' mother has come. She is old, over seventy. It is a great age to be coming sight seeing. And this week, I think, while she is here, we are going to move to No. 16 Colworth.

There, the light is nearly gone. I wish, in some little country house of our own, you were lighting the lamp for me. Mein Gott! I kiss you

D. H. Lawrence

·◁[124]▷·
Davidson Road Boys School, South Norwood SE
15th September 1911

My dear Lou,

You will not mind if I write to you from school. Somehow, I feel more like writing you from Davidson than from Colworth.

We have had a fine old rousing week: four inspectors in for two days.[4] Of course they're all all right: in fact they are rather flattering —and very considerate indeed. But it mucks up the work so. As a matter of fact, I am rather tired of school. There are so many things I want to do, and can't. I can't settle down of an evening nowadays. This week I haven't written a scrap. Should you be cross if I were to—& I don't say I shall—try to get hold of enough literary work, journalism or what not, to keep me going without school. Of course, it's a bit risky, but for myself I don't mind risk—like it. And then,

1. Respectively his older sister Emily King; his landlady; his younger sister.
2. Cf. p. 130 n. 4, p. 131 n. 4.   3. Cf. 122.
4. For one account of an inspector's experience with Lawrence see E. Nehls, *D. H. Lawrence*, i. 86.

134

if I get on with literature, I can increase my income, which is a process so slow at [*MS torn*] to be discreditable. I may try: I'll tell you when [I] do: I am really rather,—very—sick of teaching when I want to do something else.

But don't think of this seriously. It is only a small idea.

I was pleased to get Ethel's[1] card. Neither of you tells me when Loughboro wakes comes. I think it's the Goose Fair in a three week (is it?). I haven't written to George.[2] I must do so.

After all we shall not get the removal over this week, owing, I think, to the plumbers. It is very stupid. The new house is painted, & looks very nice. It is almost exactly the same as No. 12. We shall go in some time next week.

Last night I was at Humphreys[3] to tea. They have staying with them a young French girl of about 15, who would serve me in good stead for practice of my French, but she is very stupid and wordless. We went to the Picture Palace in the evening, & I was nearly killed with laughing. Really, they are very daft, these pictures. But as they get more melodrama & intensity into the gestures, they get the humanity out. It is a pity. Now, it is often rather like pictures of wonderful marionettes—the individuality is gone.—It is a day, sunny & cloudy & fresh, rather like March. When *is* Loughboro wakes?[4]

Je vous embrasse,

·◁[125]▷·
12 Colworth Road, Addiscombe, Croydon
21st September 1911

My dear Lou,

I shall have to snatch this dinner hour for a letter or else goodness knows when you'll hear from me. We're in the last anguish of removal. I sit in a stark room, bare floor, bare walls, and the poor little isolation of a dinner table with its chairs creeping under it, all forlorn. I've just got ten minutes to write you. Tonight Mrs Humphreys is giving a little party, & I've promised to go. I was out

---

1. Louie's sister. 2. His brother. 3. Cf. p. 85 n. 2.
4. A three-day local festivity beginning on the Thursday nearest to 11th November.

Tuesday & last night. I feel quite a gad-about. Tonight the last goods are going to No 16, all but the beds. Tomorrow night I shall work at house arrangements like the deuce. I shall have all pictures to hang and books to arrange & so on & so on. By Jove, what a life

Edward Garnett sent me back the Century Stories because they aren't suitable to the stupid American taste.[1] I am to write something more objective, more ordinary. I shall when I do—when I have time.

Last night I dined with Austin Harrison at the Pall Mall Restaurant—quite swelly. After dinner we went to the Haymarket. Harrison had got seats. 'Bunty Pulls the Strings' is the play,[2] a delightful comedy on Scotch manners of 1845 (circa). The play amused me very much. Harrison is very friendly. He suggests that I do a bit of reviewing for the English. I think I shall. He bids me select from the forthcoming books one I should like to review. What shall it be?

Garnett—who is a very well known littérateur, editor of big things like the World's Famous Literature, wants me to go & see him and take lunch with him some Wednesday or Tuesday. Unfortunately the day is wrong for me. I will try to go some time or other.

I think this is all the news—except Harrison says he'll make me an appointment to meet Frank Har[r]is[3] at dinner next week. But I'm not keen a bit on being a swell—I'd rather not bother to go.

I'm sorry the bookbinding has gone pop. But there 'the best laid schemes' etc etc. Mine all go up the flue. I shall be jolly glad when we're settled in peace again. George hasn't written me yet to say he'll come at the Fair.[4] He's very dilatory. I hope Is'll have some money for Loughboro Wakes—I must mind my p's & q's. What a penniless set we are. Oh, that house in the country! Where on the map of Fate is it? I *must* answer Eth's card—my love to her. I'm sorry to scramble the letter so—

Love D. H. Lawrence

I'll send you this month's English[5] when we get settled

Addressed: 'Coteshael' Cheveney Lane Quorn Loughboro
Postmarked: Croydon SP 21 11

1. Cf. p. 130 n. 4.   2. By Graham Moffat (1911).
3. Editor, journalist, and author (1856–1931).
4. His brother visited London at the time of Goose Fair, 7th–8th October (cf. 128).
5. The September issue of the *English Review* contained *A Fragment of Stained Glass* (cf. p. 6 n. 2).

Davidson Road Boys School, South Norwood SE
25th September 1911

My dear Lou,

You sound désesperé—what's up? Is it the remoteness of Loughboro fair. We'll stalk it, & wing it yet.

We're safe in 16—it'll be comfy by & by. Why should Garnett see us flitting, by the way?—and he's not great, & I should certainly tell him myself that he'd have to invite me other days than Tuesdays or Wednesdays, if I were mad on seeing him. But I'll contrive to get an hour off some Wednesday—& I'll try to send him something American (God help me)—what have I got to say to Harrison?—at any rate I'll say it. I am sure I listen to you—but what do you want me specially to heed.

I've got a cold like hell—that's flitting—feel as if my long pipe were a stove chimney got red hot. Dear o me, what a state! And now you'll have more injunctions to give me. But the cold'll be better by your next letter.

I'm not going to frivol this week. If Harrison doesn't want me to dinner on Tuesday, I'm going to hear Moody-Manners folk murder Samson & Dalila in Croydon.[1] That's all Im going out—unless I go to Scott's to hear him brilliantly render Grieg on the piano. He's only a young chap of 18, swotting BA—a good, individual pianist, though.[2] Perhaps he'll make a mark. I'm not keen on Grieg, though.

I don't know whether George is coming at Goose Fair—he won't answer yes or no. But he'll come.[3] After that, perhaps you'll come, if you have any cash. I shall have some when I'm paid for the next story.[4] I think Ada intends a visit this autumn. She sent me her photo—the Leicester one. It is jolly good, but she looks older. Will you have your photo taken, a decent sized one, not midget.

It is rather a bother to get translation work. The only thing for Miss Rutter[5] to do would be to translate part of some work she admires—or a short story—& send it to a publisher, with stamps for return, as a specimen of her cleverness in rendering French style into English. If she wants to do fiction, she'd better try Wm Heinemann or Methuen—or if it's anything racy, John Long; if it's

---

1. Saint-Saens' opera was performed by the Moody-Manners company at the Grand Theatre, Croydon, on 26th September.
2. Not identified.   3. Cf. p. 136 n. 4.
4. The next to appear was *Second Best*, in the *English Review*, February 1912.
5. Not identified.

137

essays, Duckworth or Martin Secker or Dent; if its Drama—well, drama's a bit risky; if its philosophy—a complete Montaigne, for instance—then 'The Open Court'—or Macmillan. You see, there's the French Copyright to arrange, then the English publisher, then the translator's fee. It's a bit of a toil but with patience, and an admirable specimen, she might do all right. But literature is a toil and a snare, a curse that bites deep, & Miss Rutter is wise to avoid it.

Having a bit of a cold, & being a bit tired, makes one a bad, distant letter writer. But count your damson stones—this year, next year, sometime, never—mine usually come this year. You like tokens. I would be glad if this fulfilled itself—I would be glad enough for the house in the country—God knows. Be happy—I kiss you with all my heart. I will get some work done—that is the only way

Love D. H. Lawrence

·◦[127]◦·
16 Colworth Road, Addiscombe, Croydon
2nd October 1911

My dear Lou,

I was glad to hear you restored to exuberance again in your last letter. Certainly it is good luck to have got the school: if it's not too much work. I think night schools are a frightful fag. But you are taking it very nicely—I congratulate you. I hope it will again be like a family—or friendly—gathering. I will send you some drawings later on—when you've started. But my things as you know are very rough and, I am afraid, hardly good models to set before meticulous village girls. However, you'll have your way.

I've been bowing my head & been quite subservient—sent Garnett a long 3-part story which he thinks the Century may accept when I've had it typed out, & I've promised to go & lunch with him on Wednesday.[1] Now do not be excited, nothing tremendous will happen. He is merely curious to see what sort of animal I am—& I'm willing to be seen. Nothing more. But he's very nice.

Yesterday I had a ripping time—went to Peckham to tea & for the evening to Miss Herbert's—German lady, 45 (circa), quite ordinary. She lives with her brother-in-law Franklin an elderly but brisk

1. He had sent the story *Two Marriages* (cf. p. 121 n. 4) to Garnett on 25th September; Garnett had returned it with comments; and now Lawrence ('subservient') is revising it. *Century* apparently did not accept it. (Cf. *Collected Letters*, i. 80–81.)

138

German, a bit of a bounder, speaks 7 languages, travelled God knows where. There was there a Portuguese lady from Brazil—with her husband. She spoke hardly any English, so we chattered in French. She is the most exquisite woman pianist I have ever heard. She played me Chopin's Nocturnes—which I love exceedingly 'Quelque chose de triste et un peu ironique pour vous', as she said, smiling. She was very good looking, and 'vive'—about 26. She is giving a recital in the Bechstein Hall on Thursday.[1] I shall go if I can. But probably George is coming—I think he will. He is a model of indecision. If I don't have to meet him at the wrong hour, I shall go to the Bechstein, to hear Mrs Miller.

It is very wintry, & cold now. You will be glad. Do you keep pretty well?—you have not told me. I am all right—there's no news.

I should like you to hear Antonietta Miller play Debussy's 'Jardin sous la Pluie.' I am so busy revising 'Two Marriages' for the type-writer. What a rush this life is. Goodbye—je t'embrasse, ma chère

D. H. Lawrence

·◅[128]▻·
16 Colworth Road, Addiscombe, Croydon
10th October 1911

My dear Lou,
You've waited a long while for my letter. George's visit[2] fagged me frightfully—chasing round.

I saw Garnett on Wednesday. He's quite sweet. I am going to stay with him this week-end at Edenbridge, Kent.[3] He's going to try & get me published a vol of verse, for Spring—and would also get the three plays placed, for publishing—only two of them are missing.[4] I sent them to Hueffer, as you know, before the holiday. And last night I had a letter from Hueffer to say he'd never had them and that he didn't know anything about them—and he's married Violet Hunt.[5] However, no doubt the plays will turn up.

---

1. The *Times* reported the 'reappearance of the Brazilian pianist, Mme Antionietta Rudge Miller' at the Bechstein Hall on 5th October.
    2. Cf. p. 136 n. 4.   3. At Garnett's cottage, 'The Cearne' (cf. 129).
4. Lawrence's first volume of verse, *Love Poems and Others*, was published by Duckworth in 1913. The plays referred to were probably *The Widowing of Mrs Holroyd* (cf. p. 130 n. 1), *The Merry-Go-Round*, and *A Collier's Friday Night*.
    5. Cf. p. 46 n. 4. (Hueffer's 'divorce' and re-marriage proved invalid.)

139

While Garnett & I were having lunch who should come in the place but Atkinson, Heinemanns man.[1] Garnett doesn't like Heinemann's people, so he was beastly sarky with him. I hate Atkinson—I don't go to Heinemanns because I don't like the sneering, affected little fellow. But he made me promise to call there. I did last Thursday. It appears my contract with Heinemann was for yearly payment—so the Peacock money[2] is not justly due till February. They owe me £40—and Atkinson said they'd send me on a cheque. It's not come yet. I shall put it all away if I can. I shall probably lend it Auntie, to make up her partnership share.[3] I am afraid I have offended Heinemann's people mortally. I haven't done a stroke of Paul[4] for months—don't want to touch it. They are mad, and they are sneery. I don't like them.

George & I had a very hustling time if nothing else. We went to Sumurun, the wordless play at the Savoy, on Saturday evening.[5] I liked it very much. On Sunday we were at St Paul's for part of the afternoon Service, at the City Temple, hearing R J Campbell in the evening.[6] I liked him all right, but I could preach as well myself. But it was as good a sermon as you'd hear in England—on the positivity of death. George didn't care for it.

I am very busy now getting verse ready to take to Garnett on Friday. Life is such a rush with me. I haven't time to think of anything but the things that are pressing close around.

I should think that this Spring will give me a bit of a reputation. I hope the dramas will turn up.[7] I should be angry were they lost. It is just like Hueffer

For half an hour, I've got the house to myself. I am fagged after the weariness of George's visit. I must get some of that stuff done. I am in quite good health—how is your cold?—better, I hope. Don't talk about cossetting. I feel as if I should never know a bit of

1. F. N. Atkinson, Heinemann's reader (succeeded in that capacity by Walter de la Mare); highly regarded by his employer and himself an accomplished translator.
2. Royalties on *The White Peacock*.
3. The aunt was probably Ada Krenkow. She and her husband were associated with a hosiery company in Leicester.
4. *Sons and Lovers*.
5. The musical, wordless play *Sumurum* was presented by Max Reinhardt and the company from the Deutsches Theater, Berlin.
6. Lawrence may have heard of Campbell through the minister of High Pavement Unitarian Chapel, Nottingham—Lloyd Thomas—to whom Campbell was well known. (Information from Jessie Chambers's letter to Helen Corke, 18th December 1910. MS LaM 3.)
7. He received them from Hueffer on 5th April 1912 (*Collected Letters*, i. 107).

quiet, neglectful cossetty life again. I am swallowed up in worrying through my affairs—not worrying *about* them, I don't do that.

When is Loughboro wakes? I am in debt. I hope the English or Heinemann will send me a cheque soon.

You shall see the Christmas shops—bien! These pressures of one thing and another make me feel very affairé. I cannot imagine myself looking at Christmas shops.

But that'll come like everything else. Ah well—goodbye—It is goodness knows how far to Quorn.

Addio D. H. Lawrence

Addressed: 'Coteshael' Cheveney Lane Quorn Leicestershire
Postmarked: Croydon OC 10 11

⋅◅[129]▻⋅
16 Colworth Road, Addiscombe, Croydon
16th October 1911

My dear Lou,

At last I can sit down to this letter which I want to write to you. I have been to tea to Ansell's—at the Actors' Home.[1] It is rather nice. They have two great houses in Morland Road, which they have turned into a home. Mr Ansell takes beautiful photographs; he is a genuine artist. There are goodness knows how many daughters of the house, such rum girls. It is very funny to go there. They keep great dogs, danes, enormous creatures, which bound about you.

I had a fine time at Edward Garnetts. He has got one of these new, ancient cottages; called the Cearne. It is a house thirteen years old, but exactly, exactly like the 15th century: brick floored hall, bare wood staircase, deep ingle nook with a great log fire, and two tiny windows one on either side of the chimney: and beautiful old furniture—all in perfect taste. You would be moved to artistic rhapsodies, I think. The house stands on the last drop of the north downs, sheer overlooking the weald of Kent. The wood in which the cottage is lost ends with the scarp slope. It was very fine. Garnett was alone. He is about 42. He and his wife consent to live together or apart as it pleases them. At present Mrs Garnett[2] with their son

---

1. 'Lawrence was greatly interested in a section of boys who attended the school from the English Actors' Home.' H. T. Moore, *The Intelligent Heart* (1955), p. 79.
2. Constance Garnett (1862–1946).

141

is living in their Hampstead flat. She comes down to the Cearne for week ends sometimes. Garnett generally stays one, or perhaps two days in the week, in London. But he prefers to live alone at the Cearne. But he is very fond of his wife also—only they are content to be a good deal apart.

We discussed books most furiously, sitting drinking wine in the ingle nook, cosy & snug in the big, long room. We had a fine time, only he & I. He thinks my work is quite extra. So do I, of course. But Garnett rather flatters me. He praises me for my sensuous feeling in my writing.

The country looks very charming on the north downs—all the trees are quite fluffy and thick with yellow, like fires among them.

We have got a new little dog called Fritz—that the Ansells gave me. He is such a jolly little chap, black, with white paws, & very frisky. I like him very much. He is weeping on the hall-mat because Mrs Jones has gone out.

Did I tell you Ford Madox Hueffer had married Violet Hunt.[1] I think it is scarcely legal in England, as the divorce—so Garnett says —was never really accomplished. They were married in Germany. I heard again from Violet Hunt from Brussels. She is coming home on Saturday. I shall go & see her in South Lodge in a little while. She wants me to.

Garnett is going to introduce me to quite a lot of people. I am not keen on it, but he says my business is to get known.

Heinemann & I have been squaring up our accounts. Really, my agreement is a yearly one: i.e., I should be paid for the Peacock next February. I have asked him to leave it like that, then I can draw the whole cheque at once, since that is the legal arrangement. I have promised to go to Lunch with Wm Heinemann on Friday. He wants to make some or other terms with me. Damn him—but I shall have to go.

I am very busy indeed with one thing and another—so busy, that I have only time to think about work & the things I've got to do tomorrow. I have no leisure for thinking or worrying. It is very funny to live so. Things I've got to do, things I've got to do—there seems nothing else in the world but that.

When is it I come to Quorn?—is it a fortnight on Friday? I want to arrange my week ends. I have promised Miss Reynolds[2] a week end, and I must fix the date. I will come on Friday evening.

1. Cf. 128. 2. Cf. 112.

142

It is queer to think of Quorn just now. It seems out of the atmosphere of all this. It would be nice if there were not so many folk. It will be, after all, only a change from one form of rush to another. But after all, I suppose that is what suits me.

Now I must get to work—my dear, I canna write a love letter—there are too many things in my head. When I come you shall have the love. I put it aside nowadays, & work instead. I kiss you (what a farce to write it)

Goodbye—I dreamed of you last night—you looked sad.

Goodbye D. H. Lawrence

Addressed: 'Coteshael' Cheveney Lane Quorn. Leicestershire
Postmarked: Croydon OC 16 11

·◦[130]◦·
Davidson   23rd October 1911

My dear Lou,

Scuse me if it's a scrap I write. Shall I come to Quorn this week-end—I think I will. I've got a central timetable & I cant get an excursion on Friday night—I want a week-end—I can come first thing Sat. morning. I will, however, try Midland to Quorn, & let you know. Ada[1] wants to see me in Nottm. on the Sat. I come up—& Gert Cooper[2] is in hospital again—not very serious—so I must go & see her.

Heinemann was very sweet—no news to speak of. He's mad with me for promising the stories & verses. I've had to withdraw the offer of the verse from Duckworth, & give Heinemann the promise of the things.[3] I shall send in the MS in a week or so, & they'll be out in Jan. or February. Then I've promised to withhold the stories from Secker, & to let Heinemann have the MS of a novel—probably Paul Morel—in March. You can see I am going to be kept most damnably up to the neck.

I was down the Chipstead Valley—down in Surrey—on Sat. The country is very beautiful—very much like John Linnell.[4] Tonight

1. His sister.   2. Cf. p. 5 n. 2.
3. But it was Duckworth who published *Love Poems and Others* and *Sons and Lovers* in 1913. Cf. p. 112 n. 4.
4. Landscape painter (1792–1882).

143

I'm promised to tea with Humphreys[1]—they've got a Frenchman I'm to entertain—but he speaks most awful glutinous French—it is such a struggle. I wish I hadn't promised. I *must* get these damned verses shipshape.

I hope I shall be able to come on Friday night—I'll let you know directly. Do you write & tell me at once whether you want me to come. I hope your cold is better, & that Mrs Adams[2] has subsided for good. I laugh to think of you being so sweet, over & above your wrath.

Friday or Saturday then—here is Philip[3]—I fly—tis 12.30

Goodbye—love D. H. Lawrence

Addressed: Coteshael Cheveney Lane Quorn Leicestershire
Postmarked: Croydon OC 23 11

·◌[131]◌·
16 Colworth Road, Addiscombe, Croydon
26th October 1911

My dear Lou,

I will come tomorrow—Friday—evening, by the 6.20 out of Marylebone, which gets in Leicester at 8.14. There I shall have to change & come on by the 8.34, or something like that. At any rate, you'll know the train

There was no excursion, so I shall have to come up ordinary. But for the return I have got a half day excursion from Nottingham, so that I can go back with the return half, by the train leaving Victoria at 7.30 on Sunday night, getting in Kings Cross 10.40. That was the only excursion available.

In that case, you see, I think it will be much better for us to stay Saturday night in Eastwood. Therefore, when we meet Ada in Nottingham on Saturday morning, we will have a jig round the town, & then return to my home. It will be best, all ways round, for they were rather cross with me the other way.

It will not be long at Quorn, will it—but, as I say, it's the best I can do. I wish I had a holiday tomorrow.

1. Cf. p. 85 n 2. 2. Mrs. A. E. Adams (b. 1883), a teacher at Quorn from 1902.
3. Philip Smith, the headmaster.

144

I am very glad I am coming. I think of it in school, and when the rain comes sweeping, I wonder how it will look over the Midlands. You will be better, you say? That is right. I myself am very well.

If you are in Leicester tomorrow, stay for me. In 24 hours I shall be 'en train'. Goodnight then—tomorrow I will say it in person.

Je t'embrasse D. H. Lawrence

Addressed: '*Coteshael*' *Cheveney Lane Quorn Leicestershire*
Postmarked: Croydon OC 26 11

·❄[132]❄·
16 Colworth Road, Addiscombe, Croydon
30th October 1911

My dear Lou,

I got home by midnight, quite sober, and quite sound. I have not got a cold, my insurance policy has not increased in value by one denarius. Voilà.

But it is very damnable. Today it has rained like Hell. 'It rains outside, and it rains in my heart' as I've read somewhere or other (very toshy). But the long slow drag of hours is very trying. I've now got to digest a great lot of dissatisfied love in my veins. It is very damnable, to have slowly to drink back again into oneself all the lava & fire of a passionate eruption. I have to say to myself all day—'Don't natter the kids—it's your own fault—don't growl—it's your own fault—don't scowl—why inflict it on anybody else—go on, make another effort'—& so one goads oneself through a live-long day. It is just the same with you I guess—perhaps worse: but it can't be worse, or you wouldn't keep your presence of mind.

How did you find Ilkeston, & your Aunt Nell?[1] Very well, I hope. But oh damn, I can't get through the platitudes.

I wish the next four or five days would get over. I feel as if I'd got lead in my veins—it's quite a business to drag about. Damn it. It's the digesting of one's spleen with a vengeance.

'What is love?' said jesting Pilate.

1. Helen Burrows, a teacher in Ilkeston.

145

The most of the things, that just heave red hot to be said, I shove back. And that leaves nothing to be said. All this, you see, is very indelicate & immodest & all that . . and I always want to subscribe to your code of manners, towards you—I know I fail sadly.

Goodbye—just imagine all the things I don't say—they're there

Goodbye D. H. Lawrence

Addressed: 'Coteshael' Cheveney Lane Quorn Leicestershire
Postmarked: Croydon OC 30 11

·❧[133]❧·

16 Colworth Road, Addiscombe, Croydon
3rd November 1911

My dear Lou,

I am very sorry about that train[1]—it must, you see, have been the fault of the time-table, which was 3 months old: I think I looked out the right thing.

I think I have finished the verses. I must send them off at once. You see Heinemann will be waiting for them.[2] When they come back from him, I will send you the proofs. Patience, nice child. I wish the typewriter would send me back Two Marriages for the Century.[3] Damn him, he is devilish dilatory.

Tonight I am going to begin Paul Morel[4] again, for the third & last time. I shall need all your prayers if I'm to get it done. It is a book the thought of which weighs heavily upon me. Say a Misericordia.

Tomorrow I am going to Miss Reynolds.[5] I have been buying a couple of dishes for Mrs Reynolds. I wonder when I shall buy things for ourselves. One of the bowls was so pretty—a French theme in violets & grey leaves, on pure china. It is a nice shop for pots—Birds, in Croydon—one of the nicest I've ever seen. And Mrs Bird, I like her.

I have been to a Promenade concert in our Public Hall this week.[6]

1. Perhaps Louie was to visit London the next day, Saturday.
2. Cf. 130. 3. Cf. p. 138 n. 1. 4. *Sons and Lovers.* 5. Cf. 112.
6. Given by the Croydon Symphony Orchestra on 1st November.

146

They did Schubert's 'Unfinished' Symphony, which I like very much. Alice Esty was singing. She sang the Miserere scene from Trovatore, which made me laugh very much. She's not bad,—just a trifle meaty & common.

I read Lerozs[1] letter with—I must confess—only rather faint interest. I could show you a hundred times more interesting page in Baedeker. Leroz is too impersonal to be interesting.

I really dread setting the pen to paper, to write the first word of Paul—which I'm going to do when I've written the last word of this.

I should be thankful for a cottage with one room up & one down. This eternal cultivation of the habit of going without what one wants —needs—is very damnable.

I kiss you goodnight

D. H. Lawrence

Addressed: 'Coteshael' Cheveney Lane Quorn Leicestershire
Postmarked: Croydon NO 3 11

·◁[134]▷·
16 Colworth Road, Addiscombe, Croydon
10th November 1911

My dear Lou,

Your bundle of news makes me feel impoverished: I have nothing to send you in that line.

You know, by the way, that I must be at home for Christmas itself. I think I told you—I know I told Mrs Burrows. I shall have to spend at least the first week in Eastwood—otherwise the whole world of mine would be set by the ears. You will have to come over after the party, since you are bound. And when *is* Maggie's wedding by the way?[2] I will contrive to give you half a quid to her wedding present. Really, you know, I have a lot of claims. To a good many people, I am well off, and they are poor—et voilà.

The verses aren't at Heinemanns yet—they have gone via Garnett —who had done me a good turn in putting me in the Nation.[3] Then,

1. Not traced.
2. Louie's favourite cousin, Marguerite, daughter of Campbell Burrows; she married Mr. Percy Burgess on 26th December 1911.
    3. Two poems *Lightning* and *Violets* appeared in *Nation* on 4th November.

147

when that supreme publisher[1] has gone through them, & selected them, I shall still have a bit more revising—so I don't expect the proofs'll be here till directly after Christmas. I'm in no hurry—but I'm sorry if you are disappointed. Perhaps you'll like the plays Garnett gave me.[2] *Don't* show them to your people: it will be enough for them that 'The Breaking Point' is censored, to make them look at me very much askance. And I really hesitate to send the Belgian Poetry[3] into Coteshael—although none of your family are great poetasters.

Next week I am probably going again to Garnetts for the week-end—to meet Scott-James, editor of the Daily News. I rather want to get him on my side.[4]

I am really very tired of school—I can*not* get on with Paul. I am afraid I shall have to leave—and I am afraid you will be cross with me—and I loathe to plead my cause.

I am glad your father is better: I have most terrible visions of Mrs Burrows as a widow.

It is so—I am on the brink of a complaint—I'll right about.

When I come down Everton Road, and see the man and the woman laughing in the firelight, which picks out the silver of the teatable in red. (oh Lord, how long winded!)—I do, my dear good God I do wish we also had a hearth. It is very dreary here. I am ashamed, however, to wish for a home, because I seem to get no nearer. Think—it is a year.

The alternative is—don't think.

I don't care for Garnetts plays—they are not alive. A Little Dream is rather good—a bit mechanical.[5] But you'll like it. Mac[6] gave it me on my birthday. I kiss you—I mean I wish I could—

Goodbye D. H. Lawrence

---

1. William Heinemann, 'the Great Cham of Publishers' (*Collected Letters*, i. 85).
2. These plays by Edward Garnett were *The Breaking Point* (1907) and a 'Norse play', *The Feud* (1909) (cf. *Collected Letters*, i. 83).
　　3. Probably *Contemporary Belgian Poetry*, ed. Jethro Bithell (1911).
4. Anxious to abandon teaching, Lawrence hoped for work in journalism (cf. *Collected Letters*, i. 85).
　　5. No play is known by Garnett with this title.　6. A. W. McLeod.

16 Colworth Road, Addiscombe, Croydon
15th November 1911

My dear Lou,

It is very swanky to write you in type. Mr Jones brought home an office typewriter the other day,[1] and already I am quite proficient. I shall soon take to writing novels on a machine.

I am frightfully busy this week. On Monday I was up at Covent Garden to hear Siegfried—Wagner—one of the Ring cycle that I had not heard. It was good, but it did not make any terrific impression on me. And now George[2] has asked me to take a friend of his—a Nottingham chap—to the theatre tomorrow evening—in London. The man is quite a stranger in London. Then on Friday I have promised the boss[3] I will go to a glee-singing party Mrs Smith is giving. And on Saturday I am going again to Edenbridge to stay the weekend with Edward Garnett, who has asked Scott-James—editor of the Daily News to be there. So you see I am rushed. Poor Paul,[4] I don't know when he will be done.

You always tell me such a lot of news, I forget it. What shall we do about Christmas? Will you come to Eastwood on the Thursday, and I will return with you to Quorn on the following Monday or so. Let us not this time muddle—always either your mother does not know what we're doing, or Ada[5] doesn't, or somebody. Let us be pretty definite. Of course I know it depends also on Maggie's wedding.[6]

It is only five weeks to Christmas—how time flies. And I have done so little work this term. I dont know when I shall have time to get finished. It is Aunt Ada's birthday on Sunday, and I dont know what on earth to get her. I shall have to cudgel my brains.

I will let you know what sort of folk I meet at Garnett's. Meantime I feel so squashed with work, I can't write a letter fit to read. It will not be long to Christmas—it will not be long till 1961—tempus fugit.

Now I will to Paul. I need not say to you cheer up, because by this time you will be quite gay and frisky. These black and starry evenings, I should like to go a walk. I echo you, 'why cant we live our own lives'. Ah well.

---

1. Lawrence's landlord was a school attendance officer.   2. His brother.
3. Philip Smith, Headmaster.   4. *Sons and Lovers.*   5. His sister.   6. Cf. p. 147 n. 2.

Good-bye, I wish you were here. My mouth seems to be lifted blindly for something, and waiting, puzzled. It is shocking how I curse within myself.

Good-bye D. H. Lawrence

⊲[136]⊳
16 Colworth Road, Addiscombe, Croydon
2nd December 1911

My dear Lou,

The roses are very sweet smelling, & the yellow jasmine I am fond of.[1]

I look forward to seeing you next week

Love D. H. Lawrence

⊲[137]⊳
[c. 4th December 1911]

Dear Louie,

Bert reads his own letters now. When you come you can sleep with me. I shall be so glad to see you—let me know when you will arrive.

I'm hoping by Saturday Bert may be able to sit up in bed, but of course we mustnt be too venturesome seeing he has not yet moved off his back. On Wednesday Mr Garnett is coming to see him.[2] For his dinner today he's going to have an egg & toast—doesn't that sound alright?

Love Ada.

He's always talking about you coming.

[contd]

---

1. He had become ill with pneumonia in the third week of November; the 'crisis' in the illness came about 29th November (according to letters to Louie from Ada Lawrence who was nursing her brother—MSS LaB 203–4).
2. Garnett was due on 6 December (Collected Letters, i. 86); hence the conjectural dating of this letter.

My dear Lou

I am going on still very well. I wish I could sit up. It is very wearisome, always on one's back

The roses are still living, and I can smell them in the room

I look forward to seeing you on Saturday

It is very nice of Billy & Alf[1]

Love D. H. Lawrence

·◁[138]▷·

7th December 1911

My dear Lou

Were you very much disappointed when you got Ada's letter? I am very sorry—but the doctor is emphatic.[2] When will you come? Will you come at Christmas, when I am up. When I am in bed, I am no good to visit.

I think the doctor will let me go to Bournemouth, or somewhere, for the New Year. Will you come too for the week? What shall we do?

I mayn't sit up in bed yet. That is very wearisome. But one must be patient.

Your little clock still gains an hour in the night, silly little thing.[3] I can't read very much today—only a very short time. Then I have to give up, & be still. And I mustn't have anybody to see me. It is very stupid to be ill.

In a fortnight it is Christmas. You must come then and stay with me.

You are a great one for a romance. I hope Ethel's[4] will flourish

I won't write any more—Goodbye

I give you my love D. H. Lawrence

---

1. Louie's brothers.
2. Either that Louie could not visit him, or that Lawrence had to abandon teaching.
3. Cf. 123.   4. Louie's sister.

16 Colworth Road, Addiscombe, Croydon
9th December 1911

My dear Lou,

I am propped up in bed—it is the doctor's order. He wants to get me up & get me away. It makes me feel a bit queer, and soon tires me.

It is great news, is it not, that we may go straight to Bournemouth in a fortnight. I am glad. I want to leave Colworth now. I want to leave Mrs Jones, and Mr Jones, and the children. It is queer, how I have turned, since I have been ill. But I do not want to be here for Christmas. What will you do—find an excursion & go straight to Bournemouth on the Friday, if we can go then—or the Saturday, as best suits? Will the journey scare you?

Do not tell me so often to be patient. Do I complain so much? I think I do not. I accept the inevitable, & say nothing. And I take very little nursing—Ada crochets and reads for hours, without paying me any attention, except to give me my medicine, or milk. Do you imagine I fret & chafe?—I know too well it's no good. I am progressing very well—I have [*MS torn*] passive. But I must read. My mind is so active, [   ] it some stuff to work on, it would grind itself away. Rem[   ] are different natures: I am intense & concentrative, you [   ] a muser. I cannot muse—do not prescribe it me.

[   ] jasmine you sent is very charming. [   ] me of primroses, and of spring. It is delightf[   ] it opens and opens afresh. I like it better than flowers which cost more.

It will be delightful, a fortnight hence. It will make up for everything, to be in a warm place at the seaside. And it will soon be here. I make wonderful progress, the doctor says. Let that be a proof to you that I handle myself wisely.

Nurse says a knitted waistcoat would be a fine thing for me. But, my dear, it would take you ages to get it done. You choose the color, so long as it is nothing startling, it will suit me.

We will let the next week-end go, then, & you will come straight to Bournemouth with us. That will be fine. There are pine trees at Bournemouth, pine woods, and a warm sea. And it is only a fortnight

I must lie down now—Goodbye, my dear—I kiss you

D. H. Lawrence

152

16 Colworth Road, Addiscombe, Croydon
11th December 1911

My dear Lou,

I am glad you went to see Auntie,[1] & that you cheered each other up. Tell her I am sorry she has been poorly again.

The doctor is not so sure, now, when we can go away. He says the Wednesday after Christmas. But I do not want to be here for Christmas, if it can be helped. We must see.

I can sit up in bed quite a long time now—propped up with the pillows, of course. And I have done such a feat today—I have shaved off my red beard. Nurse clipped it short, & lathered me, then she held the glass while I shaved. It was a good, clean shave too, I can tell you. My nerves are wonderfully steady. It is a thing I rather pride myself on, my control.

Nurse bids me say, I am very patient & cheerful, I bear everything with becoming fortitude, I swallow everything that is given me, I leave nothing to be desired as a patient.—This I have written at her dictation—'tis none of my own saying. She laughs so much when I tell her you are counselling me once more to be patient. She is very jolly.

A fortnight today is Christmas day: a week today, the doctor says, I *may* go downstairs. It seems to come quite suddenly, this change. Perhaps he will let me get out of bed on Thursday. Somehow, I am not very anxious, now, to get up.

Eddie[2] has sent two fowls today. I do hope you get this in time to reprieve your wicked young cockerel, to spare his life for a week or so. I will pray the sentence may not have been executed before morning, that his neck be not yet wrung.

There, I am tired, I have had a big morning, what with shaving & writing letters to Emily[3] & you & Agnes Holt.[4] She wants me to go to Ramsey. I say, later.

Christmas will soon be here—& I shall be getting up. The yellow jasmine is so bonny.

I kiss you with love D. H. Lawrence

---

1. **Ada Krenkow.**   2. Ada Lawrence's fiancé.   3. His older sister.   4. Cf. p. 67 n. 2.

16 Colworth Road, Addiscombe, Croydon
13th December 1911

My dear Lou,

Why do you regret my red beard? I hated it. Oh, no more of it for me. I shaved again today. Nurse lathers me like a barber's assistant. She laughs so much when the soap goes in my mouth. I row her like fury for doing me wrong, but she doesn't mind.

I was to sit up a bit today, but my pulse & temperature haven't been behaving quite as they should, so it's a bit doubtful. I am not anxious to get up. The thought of sitting bundled in a dressing gown in a chair makes me feel queer.

Ada is sending the waistcoat. It is one I shall want to wear, so let me have it back as soon as you can. Ada will write another time, she says.

I have done the reviews and sent them off.[1] They were only trifles.

The waistcoat is very exciting.[2] Don't go pedgilling[3] at it & wearying yourself out. I had rather not have it than that.

It is probable Eddie will be down here for Christmas. I am trying to arrange little outings for us. We do not want always to be in number 16.

Hueffer wants to come & see me, but I am not anxious that he should.

It really seems now as if I should soon be going into the world again. It is so queer—& strangely enough, I am half reluctant to get up & start again. But next week I shall be keen enough.

Already this week has nearly gone. Before we know where we are, you will be here. Things seem to whirl round so strangely of their own accord, one ceases to wonder or to bother.

I am sorry about that bird—truly. What a nuisance your mother must think us. Give my love to all at Coteshael. I kiss you goodbye

D. H. Lawrence

---

1. He had received for review 'a book of German poetry and a book of Minnesinger translations' (*Collected Letters*, i. 87). The *English Review*, January 1912 (pp. 373–6), contained unsigned reviews of *The Oxford Book of German Verse*, ed. H. G. Fiedler, and *The Minnesingers*, ed. by Jethro Bithell. (Both reviews are reprinted in *Phoenix II*, ed. W. Roberts & H. T. Moore, 1968, pp. 269–71.)
    2. Cf. 139.   3. i.e. struggling hard.

Addiscombe   Friday

My dear Lou,

I have sat up for half an hour today. It is a weird experience. Tomorrow I shall sit up longer. Emily is coming.

We shall get away on the 27th almost for sure. Ada is going to write for rooms. I do not know what they will be—not much, be easy.

I am very well. This time next week we shall be thinking of your coming. That is very jolly. We wondered not to have heard from you at all today. I hope you have not knocked yourself up—it is what I expect. Do not be queer for next week.

Addio—Love to all D. H. Lawrence

*Addressed: 'Coteshael' Cheveney Lane Quorn Leicestershire
Postmarked: Croydon DE 16 11*

*16 Colworth Road, Addiscombe, Croydon
17th December 1911*

My dear Lou,

Am I becoming again a bad correspondent? I have off days.

Emily came yesterday. Ada went up to meet her, & they did the London shops. They enjoyed it very much. Wouldn't you like to do the same next week? It will be your only opportunity, & I think you'd enjoy it. You'll see enough of me afterwards. Miss Mason[1] stayed with me till three oclock, while Ada was away. She is very nice. Shall you mind sleeping at her house.

I sat up for about an hour at tea yesterday. It did not tire me so very much. But I can't stand on my legs for my life. That disgusts me very much. When shall I be able to get downstairs—heaven knows. I doubt whether we shall get to Bournemouth on the 27th— the 29th perhaps. Ada does not very much want to go, because of the expense. Already she has had to pay out some £15, & it scares her: for not half the bills are paid, she says. That of course is not true. Most of the bills are paid. Nurse has gone today. I shall miss her

---

1. Agnes Mason, fellow teacher and close friend.

very much. Ada is glad, because of the expense. But do not think we are short of money—we are not.

I think Ada would rather like to go home at the New Year, & send us to Richmond for the week, & then I should go alone to Bournemouth. I do not know what we shall do, & don't care much. It depends on when I can walk.

I am tired of being invalid, & I won't be so much longer.

Do not imagine you will get much *rest* in this house. You forget the family. At least I cannot rest here—not much.

In a very short time Saturday will be here. I shall very likely be able to go out on Sunday. We must get on.

I wait for next week.

A bientôt D. H. Lawrence

Of course I will come to Quorn later—when the flowers begin to come—I shall love it.

·⟨[144]⟩·
Addiscombe   Monday

My dear Lou,

How wonderfully you have got on with mon gilet. I shall henceforward believe you capable of anything.

I am very well. If the temperature is high Ada doesn't register it. We wait awhile, then I drink cold water, then lo, it is normal—a huge joke—the doctor gets so jumpy if I'm high. But I am very well, really; distressed only by my legs, which *won't* hold me up. I feel like the poor man sick of the palsy.

Emily came Saturday—it was jolly to have her, but her stay was so short. What a blessing yours won't be a week-end. Eddie[1] comes Saturday midnight—St Pancras at 3.25 in the morning. Heaven knows when he'll be down here.

Bring the bird on Saturday, & we'll have him for dinner on Sunday—the four of us. Won't it be jolly. I can eat anything now—in reason, and in small quantities. I am to be fed, the doctor repeats eternally.

---

1. Cf. p. 153 n. 2.

You make me laugh, talking about rest. I shan't be able to walk half a mile, so I can't rush you about much.

My love to all at Coteshael.

Yrs D. H. Lawrence

Addressed : 'Coteshael' Cheveney Lane Quorn Leicestershire
Postmarked : Croydon DE 18 11

ᴅ·[145]ᴅ·

16 Colworth Road, Addiscombe, Croydon
20 December 1911

My dear Lou,

Don't, don't, don't alarm yourself. I can drink as much cold water as I like (doctor's permission), & I only take it to make my mouth cold to reduce the thermometer. I drink cold water at all hours of the day & night. The doctor has just been in & has the impudence to say I shall do well if I am down by Christmas day. He is a fibber—I shall go down on Sunday.[1] This morning I strolled into the bathroom, prancing like the horses of the Walküre, on nimble air. I am enlarging my Voyage autour de ma Chambre.

You will not get to Bournemouth—your visions of the racing Channel go pop. I should be mad if—if things really bothered me. I am awfully wild when I find a chocolate liqueur—a Kirsch—in bed with me. But it scarcely bothers me at all, what the Fates & Furies may roll out of their laps.

You will be very late coming on Sunday.[2] Even Eddie will be here to Sunday breakfast. Tot[3] is looking forward to meeting you—do not deprive her of the pleasure.

I am waxy about going downstairs—I *hate* entertaining in the bedroom. Garnett is coming today, & Lil Reynolds[4] will be here to tea tomorrow. I have had several folk to tea, & it is great excitement, I can tell you, in this little bedroom.

---

1. 24th December.
2. Ada conveyed her own and Lawrence's disappointment at Louie's late arrival, by separate letter (MS LaB 205).
3. Cf. p. 155 n. 1. 4. Cf. p. 86 n. 4.

My damned pulse is the bother—fancy having a heart that ticks like a lady's watch! There's no room for endearments—à dimanche —con amore

D. H. Lawrence

So sorry Mr Burrows is ill. Condole with him from me   DHL

Addiscombe   Friday

My dear Lou,
     We shall expect you then on Sunday at about 4.45.[1] You'll just be in time for tea.
     The doctor says I shall be lucky if I am downstairs on Christmas day. But I shall be down to take tea with you on Sunday.
     Miss Mason will meet you, & you'll be all serene. I hope you will be feeling more fit.
     My love & Christmas greetings to everybody at Coteshael.

A bientôt D. H. Lawrence

P.S. Mrs Barker, the char-woman, has given us the sack—great indignation on Ada's part

DHL

*Addressed: 'Coteshael' Cheveney Lane Quorn Leicestershire
Postmarked: Croydon DE 22 11*

*Compton House, St. Peter's Road, Bournemouth
8th January 1912*

My dear Lou,
     It is the end of the second day—we've just finished coffee, after dinner. It's a jolly place—you would like it. I wish always you had

1. Louie would arrive on 24th December; she remained until at least 30th December (*Collected Letters*, i. 90).

come. There are 45 people in, all sorts. One gets up at 8.30, & breakfasts at nine—very prolific breakfasts—bacon & kidney & ham & eggs—what you like. I chatter in the smoke room till about 10.30 —then work in my room (where I have had a fire made—until 1.30, when we have lunch—which is a bigger meal, or as big as our usual dinners. In the afternoon I go out, or if its wet, like today, I just stop in the recreation room & we play cards & games. After tea I went out with a man[1] for a stroll, then a gin & bitters, then dinner. When I've done this letter I'm going up to the rec. again for games. It is really rather jolly. You must come some time.

I get such a lot better—the air suits me. The weather is wet, but it's not cold

The town is very pretty. When you look back at it, it's quite dark green with trees. There is a great bay, & long, smashing waves, always close to the prom., because there are four tides a day. At night, with the full moon along the surf, & the foam smashing up, it is lovely. Then I go out alone, & I wish, I can tell you, that you were here. We would have some lovely times now I am getting well & shall be able to walk nice long ways.

I do not flirt with the girls—there are some very pretty—only with the old, old maids.

I am going out to tea tomorrow at Mrs Steel's. She is a friend of Miss MacNairs,[2] & has a house in Lansdowne Rd.

I do about 2 hrs work a day, & get on. When it is finer I shall go out more. I will be very good, & get very fat, & come home 'like a giant refreshed,' to use your language.

I hope school has gone down well, and that Mrs A.[3] is inclined to be sweeter.

They make such a row here, in the billiard room, this is sure to be a scrappy letter.

It would be so fine if you were here. But I shall soon come home. Give my love to all at Coteshael. I shall expect your letter tomorrow

Addio—love D. H. Lawrence

Addressed: 'Coteshael' Cheveney Lane Quorn Leicestershire
Postmarked: Bournemouth JA 8 12

---

1. Probably Mr. Scheinen, 'the little fellow from Finland' (cf. 152).
2. Possibly the proprietress of the Guest-house.
3. Mrs. Adams (cf. p. 144 n. 2).

I have been here today by car—it is a wonderfully fine church, and a queer situation, between two rivers, now in flood.[1]

I am very well—can walk 1½ miles like a bird. The weather has been fine today & yesterday—and so warm. I am glad to miss the snow up in the midlands. One has scarcely a minute here—all full up.

Love to all—Love D. H. Lawrence

Addressed: 'Coteshael' Cheveney Lane Quorn Leicestershire
Postmarked: Bournemouth JA 11 12

Compton House, St. Peter's Road, Bournemouth
12th January 1912

My dear Lou,

Did you get my Christchurch card on Thursday? I believe I posted it in the house, after the box was cleared. I am sorry.

Today there is a big fog. When I was on the West Cliff yesterday afternoon, I saw it coming in from over the sea. It is a peculiar colour, this sea—either milk white, or a very pale, pure stone colour, or a dove grey: so pale and ghostly, with opalescent tints. I admire it very much.

We have real good times. I have a fire in my room & write when I may.[2] If it's fine we go out in the morning. Always, we have games in the recreation room. It is a big, cosy room, with a turkey carpet & deep chairs. There are some ripping chairs here, and some delightful folk, men and women. The Miss Brintons have just had their billiard lesson from the little Finnish fellow.[3] He makes such a row: you would die to hear him. There is a little Russian girl named Stein who has him on an awful string.

I went to see Trubeen's friend, Mrs Steel,[4] on Wednesday—was there for tea. It is a nice house, & they are exceedingly pleasant. But

1. Christchurch, Hants., at the junction of the rivers Stour and Avon; noted for the priory church of Holy Trinity.
2. Lawrence was revising his second novel *The Trespasser*, to be published in May 1912 (*Collected Letters*, i. 93).
3. Cf. p. 159 n. 1.   4. Cf. 147.

they don't love Trubeen, notwithstanding they send their 'best love'.

We usually tea out. It is the fashion here. The house tea is a bit dreary, & there are some lovely restaurants. Tea should be a cosy meal.

We seem to feed so much. There is always such heaps of butter & toast & biscuits about—then four meals a day—& three of them *big* meals. I tell you, I am coming on fast. I eat as much as I can, decently. Already my legs are about as big as before I was ill.

Have you heard from Auntie that Hannah Krenkow[1] wants me to go to Germany, to Waldbrol near Cologne, in Spring. And I want to go in April or May. Won't it be just all right. If I get a living knowledge of German & French,[2] then any time, if necessary, I can go into Secondary teaching.

I always wish you could be down here, it is so nice. But in summer the house is crowded—70 to 80 folk. That is too much.

I don't think I have any more news. Keep well, and be happy.

My love to everybody at Coteshael.

Love D. H. Lawrence

Addressed: 'Coteshael' Cheveney Lane Quorn Leicestershire
Postmarked: Bournemouth JA 12 12

·◁[150]▷·
Compton House, St. Peter's Road, Bournemouth
17th January 1912

My dear Lou,

It's raining here like the devil—it rained ditto yesterday, clearing up for an hour or two about noon. But it was a beautiful rough sea. I have moved downstairs on to the first floor, where I have a bigger room—a large armchair, a broad fire place with a quite impressive mantel of white marble. I have a fire and am cosy as can be, when I want to retire from the madding crowd. But they won't leave me much alone.

1. Ada Krenkow's sister-in-law; Lawrence describes her as his 'cousin' (*Collected Letters*, i. 125).
2. To achieve this Lawrence explored the possibility of becoming a *Lektor* in a German University; in early April he consulted Professor Ernest Weekley, head of the Modern Languages department, University College, Nottingham; and on that occasion met Frieda Weekley with whom he eloped in May.

My rash is better—I am very well—by the time I come home I shall be quite solid. I've had a cold but I think it's better. I drink hot milk morning & night, like a good un. We have some real fun. Now, I have got quite fond of the semi public sort of life: always plenty of folk, plenty to do, no chance to be dull, & yet, if you like, real privacy, such as domestic life never gives. It is not bad. I believe, do you know, you'd like it. You'd be rid of the nuisance of house-keeping. If one were well enough off, would you like to live in an hôtel, do you think.

This is the MS of a story that is to appear in next month's English.[1] I don't care much for it.

I think, like you, I have no news. I am glad you are scoring off Mrs A.[2] so well

Damn the dirty morning—I wanted to go out, & Is'll have to play games instead.

Goodbye—keep well—give my love to everybody—snowdrops are out here—spring's near, all right.

Vale, my dear

D. H. Lawrence

Addressed: 'Coteshael' Cheveney Lane Quorn Leicestershire
Postmarked: Bournemouth JA 17 12

P.S. Don't fret, I dont work much.

◦◦[151]◦◦

Another view of Christchurch[3]—you must go there sometime. Yesterday I was out at Poole Harbour—drove there with the Jenkinsons[4]—it was delightful, such a swell day, & all so pretty. I am really very well—be at your ease.

Yours sincerely D. H. Lawrence

Addressed: 'Coteshael' Cheveney Lane Quorn Leicestershire
Postmarked: Bournemouth JA 20 12

1. *Second Best.* 2. Cf. p. 144 n. 2. 3. Cf. 148.
4. Fellow guests; Mrs. Jenkinson was 'young & pretty', and her husband a wealthy Yorkshireman. Lawrence did not tell Louie that, on their return from Poole, he had a 'fiendish time' controlling Jenkinson 'on the razzle' (*Collected Letters*, i. 96).

Compton House, St. Peter's Road, Bournemouth
23rd January 1912

My dear Lou,

Your pippiness in the last letter is very quaint and unusual for you. It accords with the 'disgusting dreary desert' state I often suffer from. It is no use talking about Ethel[1]—what she will do, she will do, & will only be thought the better of, in the end. Folk who have their own way in spite of everybody's wishes, seem, miraculously, to win the esteem & affection of the same everybody.

I am very well again, after my cold. It is poor sort of weather. Saturday was lovely: we were up on the hills in the pine woods; & had dough cakes & milk in a very charming cottage. Sunday was blank fog—I never stirred out. Yesterday was dullish, but fine: sea an 'eau de Nil' colour. I am beginning to suffer from 'wanderlust' again. I want to go over sea. When the Jenkinson's[2] went up to London yesterday, I would have given anything to go too. Yet, here is as nice as any place could be. But I would willingly move.

I have promised to go to Garnetts on Feb. 3rd. The Haleys[3] want me to stay on till the 5th, when they are going up to London. I may do so. If the weather is decent I shall probably come up to Eastwood on Feb. 9th. It is Margarets[4] birthday then, & Emily wants to give a party in honor thereof, & of my homecoming. We'll see how it comes off.

Today is a bit misty but quite decent. I should rather like to go to Poole—I must see.

Tomorrow it is the 21st birthday of Mr Scheinen—the little fellow from Finland. The girls are getting up a sort of bun fight down in the recreation room, to celebrate the event. Scheinen has promised to drive us out in the big motor car belonging to the establishment. We'll see how that also comes off. There are rather fewer people in the house, but as my table party remains—save the Jenkinsons, who went yesterday, to my sorrow—I am not very much affected.

When is your birthday, by the way?[5] I have forgotten again. Dont let me neglect it—you know what I am.

By this time you will have bucked up & will be quite gay again, I hope.

This, with my love D. H. Lawrence

1. Louie's sister. (Cf. 138.)   2. Cf. p. 162 n. 4.   3. Not identified.
4. Lawrence's niece (b. 1908), daughter of Emily King.   5. 13th February.

Compton House, St. Peter's Road, Bournemouth
Sunday

My dear Lou,

I don't in the least know when I last wrote you, but I suppose it's my turn.

Your questions trouble me considerably I do *not* want to go with a bushel of maidens to the castle. I shall be delighted to accompany you to Bingham,[1] but don't fix the date yet. What else? Oh, I will remember the 13th[2]—what an unlucky date. Was that all I had to answer? My memory's really gone to pot since I've been crocky.

It's such a ripping day. We've been along the sands to Branksome Chine—2 or 3 miles—where we had hot milk & chocs. It is very beautiful here when the weather's decent. Now, & yesterday & Friday have been sunny as you like. On Friday we went to Poole, & then to Wimburne—some 10 or 11 miles. Poole is very pretty—a round harbour, with islands and swans & gulls mixed. Wimburne has an old minster—Saxon & Norman—very fine: ancient oak, old tombs of the Somersets, a chained library, & the lord knows what. It's really very interesting We had lunch in the Kings Head & then walked back to Poole—six miles—*now* am I not a garçon solide. But sometimes I lapse. However I shall not shortly.

Well really—I am invited to Scrivens room to coffee. He often collects the decent folk on Sunday afternoon—& if Im not off I shall find the lot of the beverage swallowed by—goodness knows whom.

We tea'd yesterday at the Haven—on the verandah. Red sunset in S.W.—very rough sea coming over the bar on the left—still harbour right—very nice—refer to map.[3]

The folk here admire my writing so much.

I nearly won the whist drive prize on Friday—a bottle of scotch. I hope Scriven's got some in.

I shall be seeing you directly

Love & kisses D. H. Lawrence

Addressed: 'Coteshael' Cheveney Lane Quorn Leicestershire
Postmarked: Bournemouth JA 28 12

1. A village near Nottingham.
2. Louie's birthday.
3. Lawrence drew a rough map showing the Haven in relation to Poole.

The Cearne, Nr. Edenbridge[1]
4th February 1912

My dear Lou,

You will be wondering why I am so long in writing. I have been thinking what the doctor at Croydon & the doctor at Bournemouth both urged on me: that I ought not to marry, at least for a long time, if ever. And I feel myself my health is so precarious, I would n't undertake the responsibility. Then, seeing I mustn't teach, I shall have a struggle to keep myself. I will not drag on an engagement— so I ask you to dismiss me. I am afraid we are not well suited.

My illness has changed me a good deal, has broken a good many of the old bonds that held me. I can't help it. It is no good to go on. I asked Ada, and she thought it would be better if the engagement were broken off; because it is not fair to you.[2]

It's a miserable business, and the fault is all mine.

D. H. Lawrence

The Cearne, Nr. Edenbridge
7th February 1912

My dear Lou,

I'm sorry I could not wire back as you wished.[3] But I do really feel it would be better to break the engagement. I dont think now I have the proper love to marry on. Have you not felt it so?

But I will see you next week—I will think out a time and a place.

Yours D. H. Lawrence

Addressed: 'Coteshael' Cheveney Lane Quorn. Leicestershire
Postmarked: The Chart FE 7 12

1. Lawrence was staying with Edward Garnett (cf. 129).
2. Ada wrote to Louie on 16th February 1912: '... I think its kinder to you to break off now than to drag on an engagement which would I'm certain end in nothing' (MS LaB 206).
3. Presumably, on receiving 154, Louie had pleaded for a decision on their engagement to be deferred, and had asked for a reply by telegram.

Queen's Square, Eastwood, Notts
10th February 1912

My dear Lou,

I came on here yesterday, & am very well. Shall I meet you in Nottingham on Tuesday?[1] By a cursed irony, that is your birthday. Mrs Dax[2] has asked me to be in town to meet her on Wednesday.

Shall I see you on Tuesday at 2.30 at the Victoria Station? All send regards

D. H. Lawrence

Addressed: 'Coteshael' Cheveney Lane Quorn Loughboro.
Postmarked: Eastwood FE 10 12

Queen's Square, Eastwood, Notts
15th February 1912

My dear Lou,

I was glad to get your letter, & to know you would rather be friends. That is as I wish it. By all means keep the brooch: it's little enough I've ever given you—and it seems so vulgar, sending back the small things that were given in such good spirit. So, I don't think I shall send you the ring or the waistcoat—it's not nice. Keep what of my books you will.

I wanted to get you something for this birthday, then I dared not, under the circumstances

I hope Ethel & the rest are better.

Vale D. H. Lawrence

Addressed: 'Coteshael' Cheveney Lane Quorn Leicestershire
Postmarked: Eastwood FE 15 12

---

1. Lawrence described to Edward Garnett his meeting with Louie in Nottingham on 11th (not 13th) February. Louie was 'aggressively superior. . . . If she'd been wistful, tender & passionate, I should have been a goner' (*Collected Letters*, i. 100).
2. Cf. p. 128 n. 3.

·◁[158]▷·

Queen's Square, Eastwood, Notts
28th February 1912

My dear Lou,

I am very glad things are looking up at your house: it is unusual for Coteshael to be afflicted with maladies.

I am keeping awfully well, really, & not working much. Don't you believe TAS.[1] I went to see him in Coll. last Thursday, & he told me he had met you.

This Saturday I have promised to go to Shirebrook[2]—and am going on thence to Eakring.[3] The weather is so nice I may as well move about a bit. But we'll have a jig when I come back.

Today I have sent in my resignation to Croydon.[4] I don't want that to be dragging on any longer.

The men are out today[5]—& I believe, most of 'em highly rejoiced. I hope they'll soon go back, that I do.

Keep well Yours D. H. Lawrence

·◁[159]▷·

Queen's Square, Eastwood, Notts
2nd April 1912

My dear Lou,

I am sorry I have neglected to write to you. But I have been away a good deal. Last week I was in North Staffordshire with Neville.[6] He is married—did you know?—last November, on the q—t. His baby was born in January. He had to leave Amblecoats. They gave him a tiny temporary place in the country near Leek, where I stayed with him. His wife is with her parents in Stourbridge, some 50 miles away. He lives 'en bachelier'. Which is quite a story![7]

I have got a bit of a cold, with the harsh winds, but otherwise am all right. Occasionally I hear of you from Tom Smith.[8]

---

1. Their college friend, Tom Smith. 2. Cf. p. 128 n. 3. 3. Cf. p. 127 n. 7.
4. It took effect on 9th March (cf. E. Nehls, *D. H. Lawrence*, i. 549 n. 7).
5. Lawrence's letter coincided with the beginning of a national coal strike.
6. He stayed with George Neville (cf. p. 11 n. 4) at Bradnop, near Leek.
7. Lawrence told it more fully to Garnett (*Collected Letters*, i. 103).
8. Cf. 158.

167

They are all pretty well here—we shall be glad when the strikers go in. Father, of course, enjoys it.[1]

Ada says she will write to you directly. The holiday will do you good, no doubt.

Yours D. H. Lawrence

·ᴳ[160]ᴰ·

Am in London on business[2] till Monday—then going home. I was in Leicester only one clear day. It is lovely to be down here again

DHL

Addressed: 'Coteshael' Cheveney Lane Quorn Leicester
Postmarked: Brentford AP 26 12

·ᴳ[161]ᴰ·
Hotel Rheinischer Hof—Trier

I have come on here from Metz.[3] Trier is a delicious place—a crazy old cathedral, fearfully Roman Catholic—sleepy town, river, hills like Matlock with vineyards and woods—the Lord knows what. I don't love the Germans, but this country is awfully pretty. I think on Monday I go on to Waldbröl[4]—about 200 miles up the Rhine. You'll soon be having Whitsuntide.

Yrs D. H. Lawrence

Addressed: 'Coteshael' Quorn Leicestershire England
Postmarked: Trier 9 5 12

1. Arthur Lawrence had voted for the strike in a national ballot (cf. *Collected Letters*, i. 105); work was resumed on 11th April.
2. To see Walter de la Mare, Austin Harrison, and Edward Garnett. He had also arranged to take Frieda Weekley to see Garnett at the Cearne on the following day (*Collected Letters*, i. 109).
3. Lawrence and Frieda Weekley left London on 3rd May; they crossed the Channel to Ostend en route for the von Richthofen home at Metz. Lawrence was seized as a British spy, released by the intervention of Frieda's father, and proceeded to Trier 50 miles away.
4. Cf. 149.

Thanks for your letter—what a great shame about your cast! You don't say how long you are staying in Castle Donington.[1] I have been down here in the Isar Valley for some time now—near Munich —20 miles south. It is very lovely, near the Alps. But next week I think I am going on a walking tour through the Austrian Tyrol, probably down into Verona, over Innsbrück, so I can't give you an address just now—I will when I get somewhere. I am awfully well. It is warm here, and lovely. I hope you'll have a good time on the holiday. I can't say when I return to England.

Yrs D. H. Lawrence

Addressed: '*Coteshael*' *Quorn Leicestershire England*
Postmarked: [*Icking*] *bei M*[*ünchen*] *13 JUL 12*

Villa Leonardi,
Riva, viale Giovanni—Prati No 8, Lago di Garda, Austria
Sunday [? September 1912]

My dear Lou,
Thanks for your letter & birthday greetings. After all, it was too late to get me at Bozen, so it came along to me here.[2] I heard from Agnes Mason,[3] & she said she had had a jolly letter from you. You had a good time in Whitby.

I have been walking through the Tirol down here. It was very nice—& sounds swanky, but isn't. Riva is fearfully nice—at the head of Lake Garda. It is quite Italian—so is Trient, for that matter—only the Austrians have collared them & stocked them with Chocolate Soldiers. The folk are Italian, speak only Italian, even use a lot of Italian money. But the border is only about 3 miles down the

---

1. Near Loughborough.
2. Louie had obtained Lawrence's address at Bozen-in-Tirol from Ada, on 5th September (MS LaB 208). He had arrived in Riva a few days before his birthday on 11th September (cf. *Collected Letters*, i. 142).
3. Cf. p. 155 n. 1.

lake. At night, the search lights amuse me tripping & dodging about to catch the poor bits of smugglers. The lake is dark blue, a beautiful colour, and so sunny. Here we have had only one shower in a fortnight. It is beautiful weather, & warm. Figs are just ripe—2d a lb—and grapes—miles & miles of vineyards—& peaches. They are also just getting the maize. It's fearfully nice.

I think I shall spend the winter in Gargnano—about 20 miles down the lake, in Italy. I don't know any Italian, but it doesn't matter. Gargnano is a funny place, rather decayed, like Italy—fearfully pretty, backed with olive woods & lemon gardens & vineyards. I think I shall be happy there, & do some good work.

Ada, as you know, intends to be married in May or June,[1] & insists on my being in England then. I wonder if I shall be. Out here seems so much freer than England.

Did you know Jessie had got her Frenchman over[2]—he is staying in Tim's[3] house. What'll happen there?—I haven't heard from her for months.

Thanks for all your news. You'll have a lively winter, in that evening dress

Yours D. H. Lawrence

*Addressed : 'Coteshael' Cheveney Lane <u>Quorn</u> Leicester Inghilterra
Postmark torn off*

·ɢ[164]ᴅ·

*'Villa Igea', Villa di Gargnano, (Brescia), Lago di Garda, Italy
19th November 1912*

My dear Louie,

Your letter & the little photo did wander here after me all right. The photo is so like you—it seems queer.

I want to say that it grieves me that I was such a rotter to you. You always treated me really well—and I—well, I only knew

---

1. Ada married W. E. Clarke in August 1913.
2. Marc Boutrit with whom Jessie had corresponded; she had stayed with him in France and he was returning the visit.
3. Cf. p. 13 n. 1.

towards the end we couldn't make a good thing of it. But the wrong was all on my side. I think of you with respect and gratitude, for you were good to me—and I think of myself in the matter with no pleasure, I can tell you. And now all I can do is just to say this.

I am living here with a lady whom I love, and whom I shall marry when I come to England, if it is possible.[1] We have been together as man and wife for six months, nearly, now, and I hope we shall always remain man and wife.

I feel a beast writing this. But I do it because I think it is only fair to you. I never deceived you, whatever—or did I deceive you? I may have done even that.—I have nothing to be proud of.—

I shall only get into a bigger mess if I go on writing. Don't say anything about me and this to anybody, will you? I shall be able to be married and make everything public in the spring, I hope.—if the divorce comes off.

I am ever so well in health—poor in pocket—but happy enough. I wish I could make up for what I did to you. But if we go on writing, I feel I am only doing you more wrong, & it would be easier to stop altogether now—wiser perhaps.

The best thing you can do is to hate me.

I loathe signing my name to this

D. H. Lawrence

Addressed : 'Coteshael' Cheveney Lane <u>Quorn</u> Leicestershire
Inghilterra
Postmarked : Bogliaco 22 11 12

·◁[165]▷·

Votre lettre est venue ce matin. Faites certainement ce que vous voulez des morceaux de vers dont vous parlez. Mais je crains qu'ils ne soient trop rudes pour la musique.

Vous auriez reçu à cette heure mon autre billet. Faîtes-moi en grâce.

1. Frieda Weekley's divorce *nisi* was declared in May 1914; she and Lawrence were married on 13th July.

Oui, l'Italie est fort belle—je m'porte bien. Et je suis content de vos nouvelles de Hilda Shaw,[1] et de vos occupations. Il fait un merveilleusement beau temps ici.

D. H. Lawrence[2]

Addressed: 'Coteshael' Cheveney Lane Quorn Leicestershire
Inghilterra
Postmarked: Bogliaco 25 11 12

1. p. 103 n. 3.
2. Ada Lawrence gave Louie her brother's address on 7th February 1913 (MS LaB 210); if Louie then wrote and received a reply it has not survived.

Appendix

·❬[166]❭·
Lynn Croft, Eastwood, Notts
6th July 1905

Dear Miss Burrows,[1]

I return to you your album, little improved I fear. Yet I have found much pleasure in trying to embellish it, hoping that I might give you a moment's gratification.

This is an opportune time for the expression of my gratitude for the help you gave me at Centre; I trust I was not too troublesome a pupil, I can avouch for the patience of the mistress. Centre days are happy days, I wish they could be repeated.

If at any time it were possible for me to be of assistance to you, I shall be most delighted to do what is in my power;

I am Yours Sincerely D. H. Lawrence.

Addressed: Miss Burrows Ilkeston
Postmark: None (letter sent by hand)

·❬[167]❭·
[Friday ? 17th April 1908]

J'ai trouvé fort bonne votre lettre et je savoure la fable.[1] Elle est

1. Although Louie placed this among the letters written to her by Lawrence, the tone and content suggest that she was not the addressee. The letter was probably intended for her aunt, Miss Constance Burrows, who was a teacher at the Pupil-Teacher Centre, Ilkeston.
2. Written in Lawrence's hand, this is presumed to be part of a letter drafted for Louie to send to her French 'pen-friend'. Cf. p. 16 n. 2.

exquise, si nette, si fine mais triste, n'est-ce pas, sceptique comme le
XVIII me Siècle.

Vous vous jouiriez de notre vie de collège j'en suis sûre. Nous
avons en effet une assez bonne liberté, mais dans les Collèges
Normales[1] où on demeure en residence il y a tant de régulations, et,
dans les Collèges pour les filles, ces régulations sont aussi rigoureux
que les vôtres. Mais dans cette Université nous ne sommes tous des
'Normaliens'—on vient ici pour toutes les études de Science et de
technique. Ainsi on ne peut pas nous contraindre trop, et ici il y a
peu de sottises, de galenterie, de folle amour. Une fille peut etre la
'bonne camarade' d'un homme—quelquefois. Nos danses et nos
sociales sont tout simples et naturels—n'y

Tous les Samedis nous avons des assemblées du 'Students
Associations'. Nous nous rencontrons à sept heures du soir dans le
Collège pour un discourse, un concert, ou un petit drama. Demain,
il y a un 'Lecture on Prehistoric Man' par Dr. Swinnerton[2]—la
semaine prochaine 'Concert—By the Men'—après cela 'L'Art
d'Euripide' par Dr. Granger[3] et suivant—'La Médée de Euripide'[4]
—donnée par nous-mêmes. J'aime beaucoup nos Soirs de Samedi.
Quelquefois, aussi, nous avons un thé dans le corridor. C'est une
fonction charmante—nous, filles, nous donnons le thé aux hommes et
nous nous amusons beaucoup. Notre vie de Collège est assez
agréable.

La semaine passée je suis allée au théâtre pour entendre 'Les
Gondoliers'—opèra de Sullivan. J'ai beaucoup ri—et j'ai admiré
sûrtout le magnifique mélange de couleur. Aimez vous le théâtre.
Après le thé, mon ami nous a conduisis au château pour voir les
aquarelles—croquets de Turner, Peter de Wint—David Cox.[5] Oh,
comme elles étaient belles! C'est un galérie splendide.

Aimez vous la poèsie. Voici je vous envoie un morceau de

1. Colleges for training teachers.
2. Henry H. Swinnerton, Lecturer (later Professor) in Geology, University College.
3. Head of the Classics Department, University College.
4. Among the Burrows papers (LaB 225) is a programme of a production of the *Medea*
by students of University College, on 9th May 1908.
5. The *Nottinghamshire Guardian* (18th April 1908) included an account of an exhibition
in the Castle Art Gallery containing 'a collection of fine mezzotint engravings from
Turner's "Liber Studiorum", . . . drawings by Copley, Fielding, D. Cox etc'. (Cf. *The
White Peacock*, chapt. 3: George Saxton 'liked Copley, Fielding, Cattermole and
Birket Foster' but 'could see nothing whatsoever in Girtin or David Cox'.)

[*August 1908*]

J'ai gr[1]
rochers avec M
l'écume m'a mouille
et le gros vent m'a battue
C'était bon.
Quand recommencez vo
vos devoirs. Je veux que mes vacances ne
finissent jamais. Cependant, mon petit frère
a un petit mal, et il est enfant
terrible, ainsi j'echapperai a lui
en revenant
à l'école
me
les
lus. J'n'ai pu
revue qui contient les
mpique, car on les a vendus
tôt qu'ils étaient issus. Cependant
en commanderai un pour vous. Il
me faut dire encore 'peccavi', car je ne
vous ai pas envoyé vos erreurs anglais. Je
suis vraiment parasseuse.

Nous sommes au bord de la mer Scarborough, vous connaissez,
est 'The Queen of Watering Places'. Il y a là deux baies magnifiques
qui sont séparées par un grand pic couronné d'un vieux château.
Là je vais regarder la mer, qui est bien orageuse, et je parle aux
vieux pêcheurs. Hier matin un de ces vieillards delicieux m'a dit que
j'etais la jeune fille la plus belle (the finest girl) qu'il n'eût jamais
vue.[2] Mon père a eu le mauvais goût à dire qu'il n'était qu'a ce
moment revenu de la pêche.
Aujourd'hui j'ai passé un jour splendide a Filey,

1. This fragment, written in Lawrence's hand on a torn envelope, is thought to have
been designed for the same purpose as the preceding letter. (The envelope, postmarked
12th August 1908, is addressed to Jessie Chambers at 10 High Street, Flamborough.)
2. Cf. Introduction, p. xiv.

Selective Index

Roman numerals refer to the Introduction,
arabic figures to the Letter numbers.

Composed in 11-point Ehrhardt 1-point leaded
and printed on Abbey Mills Process Cartridge

Made and printed in Great Britain by
William Clowes and Sons, Limited
London and Beccles

DESIGN BY M. CANE